The Invention of the "Underclass"

At century's close, American social scientists, policy analysts, philanthropies and politicians became obsessed with a fearsome and mysterious new group said to be ravaging the ghetto: the urban "underclass." Soon the scarecrow category and its demonic imagery were exported to the United Kingdom and continental Europe and agitated the international study of exclusion in the postindustrial metropolis.

In this punchy book mating intellectual history, participant observation, and conceptual analysis, Wacquant retraces the invention and metamorphoses of this racialized folk devil, from the structural conception of Swedish economist Gunnar Myrdal to the behavioral notion of Washington think-tank experts to the neo-ecological formulation of sociologist William Julius Wilson. He uncovers the springs of the sudden irruption, accelerated circulation, and abrupt evaporation of the "underclass" from public debate, and reflects on their implications for the social epistemology of urban marginality.

What accounts for the "lemming effect" that drew a generation of scholars of race and poverty over a scientific cliff? What are the conditions for the formation and bursting of "conceptual speculative bubbles"? What is the role of think tanks, journalism, and politics in imposing "turnkey problematics" upon social researchers? What are the special quandaries posed by the naming of dispossessed and dishonored populations in scientific discourse and how can we reformulate the explosive question of "race" to avoid these troubles? Answering these questions constitutes an exacting exercise in epistemic reflexivity in the tradition of Bachelard, Canguilhem and Bourdieu. And it leads to sounding a clarion call for social scientists to forge their own concepts and to defend their intellectual autonomy against the encroachments of outside powers, be they state officials, the media, think tanks, or philanthropies.

Loïc Wacquant is Professor of Sociology at the University of California, Berkeley, and Researcher at the Centre de sociologie européenne, Paris. His books are translated in two dozen languages and include *Urban Outcasts: A Comparative Sociology of Advanced Marginality* (2008), *Punishing the Poor: The Neoliberal Government of Social Insecurity* (2009), and *Body and Soul: Notebooks of an Apprentice Boxer* (expanded anniversary edition, 2022).

The Invention of the "Underclass"

A Study in the Politics of Knowledge

Loïc Wacquant

polity

Copyright © Loïc Wacquant 2022

The right of Loïc Wacquant to be identified as Author of this Work has been asserted in accordance with the UK Copyright, Designs and Patents Act 1988.

First published in 2022 by Polity Press

Polity Press
65 Bridge Street
Cambridge CB2 1UR, UK

Polity Press
101 Station Landing
Suite 300
Medford, MA 02155, USA

All rights reserved. Except for the quotation of short passages for the purpose of criticism and review, no part of this publication may be reproduced, stored in a retrieval system or transmitted, in any form or by any means, electronic, mechanical, photocopying, recording or otherwise, without the prior permission of the publisher.

ISBN-13: 978-1-5095-5217-7
ISBN-13: 978-1-5095-5218-4 (pb)

A catalogue record for this book is available from the British Library.

Library of Congress Control Number: 2021946573

Typeset in 10.5pt on 12pt Sabon LT Pro
by Cheshire Typesetting Ltd, Cuddington, Cheshire

The publisher has used its best endeavours to ensure that the URLs for external websites referred to in this book are correct and active at the time of going to press. However, the publisher has no responsibility for the websites and can make no guarantee that a site will remain live or that the content is or will remain appropriate.

Every effort has been made to trace all copyright holders, but if any have been overlooked the publisher will be pleased to include any necessary credits in any subsequent reprint or edition.

For further information on Polity, visit our website: politybooks.com

To Bill Wilson, role model extraordinaire
of intellectual courage

Contents

~

Figures   ix

Prologue   1
Concepts matter   2
Chasing after an urban chimera   9
Anti-urbanism and the fear of the (black) city
   underbelly   15

PART ONE: THE TALE OF THE "UNDERCLASS"
Entry   29
1. Between concept and myth: genealogy of a shifty
   category   33
2. "The tragedy of the underclass": Policy theater and
   scholarship   53
3. Anatomy: The three faces of the "underclass"   66
4. The strange career of a racialized folk devil   106
5. Implications for the social epistemology of urban
   marginality   122
Exit   133

PART TWO: LESSONS FROM THE TALE
Quandaries and consequences of naming   143
Forging robust concepts   150

viii   Contents

Epistemic opportunity costs	168
Bandwagons, speculation, and turnkeys	172
Coda: Resolving the trouble with "race" in the twenty-first century	179
Appendix: The nine lives of the "underclass"	189
Acknowledgments	195
References	197
Index	227

Figures

~

Figure 1. Cover of *Time Magazine* in the wake of the
"Harlem blackout riot" of August 1977   30

Figure 2. The causal chain articulated in Wilson's
The Truly Disadvantaged (1987)   99

Figure 3. The rise and fall of the "underclass" in
public debate, 1960–2017   107

Figure 4. The peregrinations of the "underclass"
across the academic, policy-political-
philanthropic, and journalistic fields
(1963–1996)   115

Figure 5. Mentions of "underclass" in the Social
Science Citation Index, 1970–2020   190

Figure 6. Publications on "underclass" in the Social
Science Citation Index, 1970–2020   191

Figure 7. Mentions of "underclass" in major national
newspapers, 1970–2020   192

"The history of the social sciences is and remains a continuous process passing from the attempt to order reality analytically through the construction of concepts – the dissolution of the analytical constructs so constructed through the expansion and shift of the scientific horizon – and the reformulation anew of concepts on the foundations thus transformed. It is not the error of the attempt to construct conceptual systems *in general* which is shown by this process – every science, even simple descriptive history, operates with the conceptual stock-in-trade of its time. Rather, this process shows that in the cultural sciences concept-construction depends on the setting of the problem, and the latter varies with the content of culture itself. . . . The greatest advances in the sphere of the social sciences are substantively tied up with the shift in practical cultural problems and take the guise of a critique of concept-construction."

Max Weber, "'Objectivity' in Social Science and Social Policy," 1904

Prologue

~

> The sociologist may find a special instrument of epistemological vigilance in the sociology of knowledge, as the means of enhancing and clarifying the knowledge of error and of the conditions that make error possible and sometimes inevitable.
> Pierre Bourdieu et al., *Le Métier de sociologue* (1968)

The Invention of the "Underclass" is an ethnographically grounded case study in the sociology and politics of knowledge. It draws on the conceptual history of Reinhart Koselleck and on the theory of symbolic power and fields of cultural production of Pierre Bourdieu to chart the stunning rise, multi-sited flourishing, and sudden demise of the urban "folk devil" of the closing decades of the twentieth century known as the *underclass*.[1]

Fusing the trope of disorganization with the drive to exoticism, cycling in and out of the social sciences, journalism, and the political-policy-philanthropic field, this woolly and

---

[1] "In the gallery of types that society erects to show its members which roles should be avoided and which should be emulated, these groups have occupied a constant position as folk devils: visible reminders of what we should not be." Stanley Cohen, *Folk Devils and Moral Panics: The Creation of the Mods and Rockers* (1972, 3rd ed. 1987), p. 10.

2 Prologue

inchoate notion dominated the academic and public debate on race and poverty in the American metropolis roughly from 1977 to 1997. Its advocates, conservatives and liberals alike, claimed that the novel term was needed to capture an unprecedented development: the insidious incubation and cancerous growth of a subpopulation of the black poor, distinct from the traditional lower class, characterized by self-destructive behaviors, social isolation, and cultural deviancy, and responsible for the ravaging of the inner city. During this same period, the category and its demonic imagery were exported to the United Kingdom and continental Europe to agitate the international study of exclusion in the postindustrial metropolis.

Concepts matter

It turns out, upon close scrutiny, that this "terministic screen" was not a *reflection* of reality so much as a *deflection* from reality.[2] The "underclass" started out as a proto-concept à la Robert K. Merton, that is, "an early, rudimentary particularized, and largely unexplicated idea,"[3] but quickly morphed into an instrument of public accusation and symbolic disciplining of the threatening black precariat in the hyperghetto – the novel sociospatial constellation that emerged from the rubble of the communal ghetto of the Fordist era.[4] It follows that the notion enters into the sociology of urban marginality, not as *tool*, but as *object* of analysis, and an object whose study has much to teach us about the political epistemology of dispossession and dishonor in the city as well as about the craft of concept-making more generally.

---

[2] "Even if any given terminology is a *reflection* of reality, by its very nature it must be a *selection* of reality; and to this extent it must function as a *deflection* of reality." Kenneth Burke, "Terministic Screens," in *Language as Symbolic Action* (1966), p. 45.

[3] Robert K. Merton, "Socio-Economic Duration: A Case Study of Concept Formation in Sociology" (1984), p. 267.

[4] Loïc Wacquant, *Urban Outcasts: A Comparative Sociology of Advanced Marginality* (2008), chs. 2–4.

Prologue 3

Inspired by the *Begriffsgeschichte* of Reinhart Koselleck and the reflexive sociology of Pierre Bourdieu,[5] the present book offers a kind of "microhistory" of the "underclass," centered on the period of its hegemony. I pay close attention to the circumstances of the invention, the timing of the diffusion, and the variegated meanings of the term as well as to the institutional positions of those who pushed for and (more rarely) against its deployment. I draw up a genealogy of the notion by tracking its peregrinations across the boundaries of the scientific, journalistic and political fields from the heady days of the progressive 1960s to the somber years of the neoconservative 1980s and the late boom of the neoliberal 1990s.

Turning to anatomy, I distinguish three faces of the "underclass": the *structural* conception coined by the Swedish economist Gunnar Myrdal to forewarn about the dire consequences of postindustrialism for working-class formation; the *behavioral* view favored by policy researchers and think-tank experts, which quickly diffused to achieve hegemonic status; and the *neo-ecological* approach developed by the sociologist William Julius Wilson to highlight the role of the neighborhood as multiplier of marginality. Together, these form what I call the "Bermuda triangle of the underclass," in which the historical nexus of caste, class and state in the metropolis effectively vanishes from sight.[6]

Conceptual history meets reflexive sociology

Two strands of social inquiry provide resources for probing the fabrication and fate of a concept: the *Begriffsgeschichte* of the German historian Reinhart Koselleck and the reflexive sociology of Pierre Bourdieu, grounded in the applied rationalism of Gaston Bachelard and Georges Canguilhem.

---

[5] Reinhart Koselleck, *The Practice of Conceptual History: Timing History, Spacing Concepts* (2002), and Pierre Bourdieu, *Science de la science et réflexivité* (2001).

[6] Loïc Wacquant, "Marginality, Ethnicity and Penality in the Neoliberal City: An Analytic Cartography" (2014), which stresses the role of the state as a *producer* of racialized dispossession in the city, as distinct from its mission of control and succor of the same.

Drawing on historical philology and the hermeneutics of his teacher Hans-Georg Gadamer, Koselleck's "conceptual history" is exegetical; it focuses meticulously on texts to trace the changing semantic charge of "fundamental concepts" (*Grundbegriff*) and "keywords" (*Stichwort*) as "indicators" of evolving historical constellations across conjunctures and epochs. It stipulates that language is not "an epiphenomenon of so-called reality" but "a methodologically irreducible guiding authority, without which experiences could not be had, and without which neither the natural nor the social sciences could exist." It enjoins us to capture "historical arrangements of concepts" synchronically in their "concrete contexts" as well as diachronically as part of the "linguistic arsenal of the entire political and social space of experience" (1); to link them to the political conflicts of the period of their circulation; and to critically evaluate these concepts for their use in social analysis. A study of the "underclass" informed by Koselleck must thus excavate the layers of meaning of the term, check its sources, probe its dissemination, and establish its relation to current sociopolitical issues.

Koselleck relies on the political theory of Carl Schmitt, for whom politics is fundamentally about the opposition between "friend and enemy," to develop the notion of *asymmetrical counter-concept*, by which he designates pairs of opposite notions (hellenes/barbarians, Christians/heathens, *Übermensch/Untermensch*) that serve at once to build self-identity and to effect the exclusion of others by denying them mutual recognition and social reciprocity: "Asymmetrical counter-concepts have a lot to do with the art of silencing. They are means of attributing things to other people, to those who do not belong to our group, through a binary conceptualization that reduces them to a purely negative semantic field" (2). Koselleck then urges us to ask: who benefits from the use (and abuse) of such pairs? In the case of the "underclass," what is the "we-group" that forms the tacit component of this *asymmetrisch Gegenbegriff* (3)?

Reflexivity in social science comes in three varieties (4). *Egological reflexivity* involves a sociological return onto the person of the researcher in an effort to control how her social position and trajectory (gender, class, ethnicity, age, etc.) affect her intellectual output. *Textual reflexivity* concerns

Prologue

itself with the ways in which the rhetorical forms employed by the researcher (voice, trope, metaphors, style, etc.) shape her object. *Epistemic reflexivity*, as advocated by Pierre Bourdieu, aims to control the "scholastic bias" introduced by the categories, techniques, and theories the sociologist uses as well as by the "scientific attitude" itself, which differs fundamentally from the "natural attitude" of everyday life dear to phenomenologists. Accordingly, Bourdieu deploys the "science of science" as vehicle for a reflexivity aiming to increase our collective capacity to design, engage and master properly scientific problematics (5).

In this regard, the French sociologist extends to social science the principles of *historical epistemology*, the discontinuist philosophy of science developed by his teachers Bachelard and Canguilhem, according to which science advances through rupture and reconstruction, thanks to an endless work of "rectification of knowledge" already there, and by overcoming "epistemological obstacles," among them the contamination of scientific thought by ordinary constructs and turns of thought (6). Canguilhem urges us to ground the history of science in the genealogy of "conceptual filiations" to detect how these shape and displace problems over time. The present book is an application, to the thematics of the "underclass," of the tenets of historical epistemology – a practical exercise in epistemic reflexivity.

Bourdieu takes us beyond historical epistemology with his theory of *symbolic power and fields of cultural production*, which serves to map the nexus of institutional positions and symbolic position-takings adopted by cultural producers such as artists, journalists, knowledge experts, state officials, and scientists (7). Thus, the *scientific field* is a space of forces that orient the strategies of scholars (their choice of objects, methods, theories, publishing outlets, etc.) and a space of struggles for the monopoly over the definition of scientific competency. The scientific cosmos itself is embedded within the *field of power*, where holders of rival forms of capital – artistic, scientific, religious, journalistic, juridical, bureaucratic, and economic – vie for establishing their supremacy and their particular interest as universal (8). It follows that to decipher a body of texts, such as competing discourses on the "underclass," one must link the position of their producers and consumers, not in society at large, but in the relevant microcosms – in this case, the social scientific, journalistic, and political-policy-philanthropic fields – to the particular stance they take on the existence, makeup, and predicament of the "group."

The combination of Koselleck and Bourdieu promises to be fruitful: the former brings an interpretive focus on texts and sources, the latter a relational framework within which to locate the producers and consumers of those texts, and to trace their practical repercussions. Together they pave the way for a *structural hermeneutics* of the "underclass."

1. Reinhart Koselleck, "*Begriffsgeschichte* and Social History" (1982), p. 411, and idem, *The Practice of Conceptual History: Timing History, Spacing Concepts* (2002). See also Niklas Olsen, *History in the Plural: An Introduction to the Work of Reinhart Koselleck* (2012).
2. Reinhart Koselleck, Javiér Fernández Sebastián, and Juan Francisco Fuentes, "Conceptual History, Memory, and Identity: An Interview with Reinhart Koselleck" (2006), p. 125.
3. Reinhart Koselleck, "The Historical-Political Semantics of Asymmetric Counterconcepts," in *Futures Past: On the Semantics of Historical Time* (2004), pp. 155–91.
4. Pierre Bourdieu and Loïc Wacquant, *An Invitation to Reflexive Sociology* (1992), pp. 36–47.
5. Pierre Bourdieu, *Science de la science et réflexivité* (2001), and idem, "The Scholastic Point of View" (1990), and "Participant Objectivation: The Huxley Medal Lecture" (2003).
6. Gaston Bachelard, *La Formation de l'esprit scientifique. Contribution à une psychanalyse de la connaissance objective* (1938), and Georges Canguilhem, *Connaissance de la vie* (1952). A lucid and compact presentation of the tenets of "historical epistemology" is Hans-Jörg Rheinberger, *On Historicizing Epistemology: An Essay* (2010 [2007]). Bourdieu's indebtedness to historical epistemology is fully documented in his book (with Jean-Claude Chamboredon and Jean-Claude Passeron), *Le Métier de sociologue. Préalables épistémologiques* (1968, 2nd ed. 1973).
7. Pierre Bourdieu, *Fields of Cultural Production* (1993c).
8. Pierre Bourdieu, "The Peculiar History of Scientific Reason" (1991), and idem, *La Noblesse d'État. Grandes écoles et esprit de corps* (1989), Part 4; Pierre Bourdieu and Loïc Wacquant, "From Ruling Class to Field of Power" (1993); and Pierre Bourdieu, "Champ du pouvoir et division du travail de domination" (2011).

Prologue

Through two decades of heated debate initiated by the Harlem blackout riots of 1977, the "underclass" remained a stubbornly incoherent, heterogeneous, and specular notion, plagued by a host of semantic ambiguities, logical deficiencies, and empirical anomalies. Its spectacular, if fleeting, success expressed first and foremost the class fear and caste horror of the educated middle classes and state managers in the face of the deteriorating condition of the black precariat, and the desire to affix blame for mounting urban ills on this outcast category.[7] Its sudden demise in public debate in the mid-1990s (contrasting with its continued silent circulation in social science as a descriptive stand-in for a variety of subalterns) reveals the fundamental *heteronomy of the category*: after the "welfare reform" of 1996, policy-makers abruptly pivoted to other worrisome populations and conditions, and social scientists followed suit, finding new problem subgroups to study and shepherd: "fragile families" expected to transition "from welfare to work," parolees going through "prisoner reentry," and inner-city residents redistributed in space through housing subsidies and "moving-to-opportunity"-type programs.

Through the reflexive sociology of the rise and fall of the "underclass," I offer a critique, not just of the normal science of "race and poverty" in the American "inner city," but of a particular style of sociology one might call *normalized empiricism*. This sociology is empiricist in that it borrows its categories unfiltered from the social world, it is driven by data collection and mining, and, paradoxically, it is maximally distant from the phenomenon. This sociology is normalized in that its parameters, tools, and sources are embraced as a matter of course, without systematic examination or explicit

---

[7] By *precariat*, I mean the *precarious* fraction of the black *proletariat*, in the technical sense of sellers of labor power. Members of this class fraction have minimal or no "market capacity" (in the language of Max Weber) in regard of the dualized division and flexibilization of labor. They are locked out of wage work or locked in unstable and underpaid jobs that are vectors of *social insecurity* (extending to the gamut of life spheres: family, housing, health, education, etc.). I trace the genealogy and elaborate the concept of precariat in the second part of the book, *infra*, pp. 162–8.

Prologue

justification. In that regard, the present book is an extension of, and a complement to, my earlier critique of *moral empiricism* in the normal practice of urban ethnography in America.[8]

I use the strange career of the "underclass" to raise several questions that can shed light on the trials and tribulations of other concepts. What accounts for the "lemming effect" that drew a generation of scholars of race and poverty over a scientific cliff? What are the conditions for the formation and bursting of "conceptual speculative bubbles"? What is the role of think tanks, journalism, and politics but also academic reproduction in imposing "turnkey problematics" soaked in moral doxa upon social researchers? And what are the special quandaries posed by the naming of destitute and stigmatized categories in scientific discourse? Answering these questions constitutes an exacting exercise in epistemic reflexivity in the tradition of Bachelard, Canguilhem and Bourdieu.[9] This exercise leads me to elaborate a minimalist set of criteria for what makes a good concept in social science, liable to minimizing epistemic troubles such as those epitomized by the "underclass."

In conclusion, I draw on these epistemological criteria to tackle the most ductile and flammable category of them all: "race." I propose to *rethink race as veiled or denegated ethnicity*, a pure form of symbolic violence through which a classificatory schema trading on the correspondence between natural and social hierarchies is turned into reality – inscribed in the subjectivity of socialized bodies (habitus) and in the objectivity of institutions (social space).[10] The dialectic of classification and stratification based on quantum of honor sup-

---

[8] Loïc Wacquant, "Scrutinizing the Street: Poverty, Morality, and the Pitfalls of Urban Ethnography" (2002). Christopher Bryant calls this brand of research "instrumental positivism," in contradistinction with the French lineage of positivism initiated by Auguste Comte and with the logical empiricism of the Vienna Circle (Carnap, Hempel, Gödel). I prefer the idiom of empiricism for its opposition to the rationalism of historical epistemology. Christopher G.A. Bryant, *Positivism in Social Theory and Research* (1985).

[9] The exemplary study here is Georges Canguilhem, *La Formation du concept de réflexe aux XVIIe et XVIIIe siècles* (1955).

[10] Pierre Bourdieu, "Le mort saisit le vif" (1980b).

Prologue 9

plies the core of an analytic of race and distinguishes it from other bases of division (class, gender, age, etc.). I advocate for breaking down ethnoracial phenomena into the *elementary forms of racial domination* that compose them: categorization, discrimination, segregation, ghettoization, and violence. Reversely, I spotlight the dangers of lumpy notions such as "structural racism" as guides for knowledge production and civic action.

At multiple junctions in this inquiry, I sound a *clarion call against epistemic promiscuity* – the tendency of scholars to deploy a mix of instruments of knowledge and criteria of validation circulating in different universes (science, journalism, philanthropy, politics and public policy, everyday life), without duly checking their origins, semantic span, logical coherence, and the social unconscious they carry. *The Invention of the "Underclass"* will have fulfilled its mission if it increases the epistemological vigilance of its readers and assists them modestly in the "perpetual reconstruction of those concepts through which we seek to comprehend reality."[11]

Chasing after an urban chimera

In his reflections on the philosophy of science, Max Weber stresses that every social scientist "operates with the conceptual stock-in-trade of [their] time" and that "concept-construction depends on the setting of the problem, and the latter varies with the content of culture itself."[12] In other words, the formulation of a problematic in the social sciences – in contradistinction to the natural sciences – is *doubly* influenced by the state of the scientific field *and* by the state of the surrounding society. As a French citizen landing in Chicago

---

[11] Max Weber, "Objectivity in Social Science and Social Policy" (1947 [1904]), p. 105. At key junctures in my excavation, I call on the ghosts of past observers of urban marginality (and contemporary scholars caught red-handed in the act of myth-making) in the form of boxed quotes to illustrate the ironic permanence of the representations and concerns of "poverticians" over a century and more.

[12] Weber, "Objectivity in Social Science and Social Policy," pp. 105 and 106.

10   Prologue

in the summer of 1985 to pursue a doctorate in the Mecca of
American sociology, I was initially attracted to the intellectual
stream drawn by the "underclass." The emerging notion was
a hot intellectual commodity that promised to energize urban
sociology, extend class theory, and nourish bold arguments
across the academy and the policy world. Its dramatic tenor
seemed to match the lunar landscape of black dispossession
surrounding on all sides the rich white enclave of Hyde Park,
home of the University of Chicago.

My novice fervor for this thematics, lasting about a year,
came from a close reading of William Julius Wilson's *The
Declining Significance of Race*, in which the term designates
a fraction of the working-class marginalized by the forward
march of capitalism.[13] It was further stimulated by Bill's infec-
tious passion for the study of the social transformation of the
ghetto, correlated with the shift of the flashpoint of ethnoracial conflict from the economy to the polity. So, when he
offered me the opportunity to work closely with him on his
new team study of the topic, I eagerly accepted. Class, racial
domination, ghetto, state: those were the categories that I
naively associated with the term "underclass." I soon discovered that the keywords of the emerging debate on the topic
were welfare dependency, female-headed family, teenage
pregnancy, concentrated poverty, high school dropout, and
violent criminality.

My initial enthusiasm thus turned quickly into a cautious
stance of principled skepticism. My intellectual training in a
European tradition at once more theoretical and more historical than the American alerted me to the danger of characterizing as novel and unprecedented a phenomenon that must
surely have had historical precedents or analogues. Indeed,
the comparative social history of marginality in the industrial city, as represented by such classic studies as Friedrich
Engels's *The Condition of the Working Class in England*,
Louis Chevalier's *Classes laborieuses, classes dangereuses*, and Gareth Stedman Jones's *Outcast London*, readily
revealed that the intersection of capitalist industrialization

---

[13] William Julius Wilson, *The Declining Significance of Race: Blacks
and American Institutions* (1978, exp. 1980 ed.). I dissect Wilson's
use of the "underclass" in chapter 3.

Prologue   *11*

and urbanization had repeatedly destabilized laboring populations and spawned the belief, among the coalescing bourgeoisie, that the city's underbelly harbored culturally distinct, socially secluded, and vicious populations.[14] The notion that the festering of these categories, *Lumpenproletariat*, underworld, *bas-fonds*, whatever the designation, posed an urgent moral and physical threat to the social order that called for innovative public policies designed to thwart it was not news either: had not the wave of beggars and vagrants that flooded the burgeoning cities of Northern Europe at the end of the sixteenth century led to the twin invention of poor relief, on the one side, and the penal prison, on the other?[15]

My European skepticism grew into a gnawing American suspicion about the "underclass" when I turned to the arc of race, class, and space in Chicago over a century. Here I benefited from the fact that the Windy City is the most studied metropolis in America (if not the world), and so I delved into the rich lineage of historical inquiries that recapitulate the trajectory, structure, and experience of "Bronzeville." Monographs on the topic cover a full century. Allan Spear's pioneering *Black Chicago: The Making of a Negro Ghetto, 1890–1920* recounts the birth of the "black city within the white," while James Grossman's *Land of Hope* probes the springs and consequences of the Great Migration of black Southerners to Chicago in the interwar years. St Clair Drake and Horace Cayton's monumental *Black Metropolis* dissects the structure and experience of African-American social life at the apogee of the communal ghetto around the mid-twentieth-century point. Arnold Hirsch's *Making the Second*

---

[14] Friedrich Engels, *The Condition of the Working Class in England* (1993 [1845]); Louis Chevalier, *Classes laborieuses et classes dangereuses à Paris pendant la première moitié du XIXe siècle* (1958); Gareth Stedman Jones, *Outcast London: A Study in the Relationship between Classes in Victorian Society* (1971). A fascinating long-term history of the making of the urban "underworld" in the collective imaginary of Western society is Dominique Kalifa, *Les Bas-fonds. Histoire d'un imaginaire* (2013).

[15] Georg Rusche and Otto Kirchheimer, *Punishment and Social Structure* (2003 [1939]); Catharina Lis and Hugo Soly, *Poverty and Capitalism in Pre-industrial Europe* (1979); Bronislaw Geremek, *La Potence ou la pitié. L'Europe et les pauvres du Moyen Âge à nos jours* (1978).

12   Prologue

Ghetto picks up the story of race, housing, and politics for
the period 1940–60, focusing on the revamping of the dark
ghetto from above via city, state, and federal policies. Bill
Wilson's watershed book, *The Truly Disadvantaged*, maps
the hollowing out of the black inner city under the press of
deindustrialization and class bifurcation after 1970.[16]

Put together, these studies suggested permanence, recurrence, and novelty in the making of the "underclass."
Permanence of the sharp social and spatial division of the city
by race; recurrence of phases of class consolidation and dissolution that caused tectonic shifts in city politics; novelty in the
virulence of the territorial stigma draped over the remnants
of the dark ghetto, amplified by the sulfurous corona of the
"underclass" said to have emerged in their midst.

I grew frustrated as my efforts to articulate clearly what
the "underclass" was designating confusedly proved vain: the
more I read on the topic, the less it seemed to make sociological sense. My suspicion soon morphed into full-scale alarm
as I attended the working seminars, think-tank meetings, and
policy conferences on the topic to which Bill Wilson took me
or dispatched me in his stead. Between 1987 and 1990, I was
placed in the eye of the "underclass" storm and given a minor
insider role in what the historian Alice O'Connor nicely
christens "the poverty research industry" that was then in a
state of intellectual flux and organizational recomposition.[17]
Armed with my foreign lenses and cushioned by historical

---

[16] Allan H. Spear, *Black Chicago: The Making of a Negro Ghetto,
1890–1920* (1967); James R. Grossman, *Land of Hope: Chicago,
Black Southerners, and the Great Migration* (1989); St. Clair Drake
and Horace R. Cayton, *Black Metropolis: A Study of Negro Life in a
Northern City* (1993 [1945]); Arnold R. Hirsch, *Making the Second
Ghetto: Race and Housing in Chicago 1940–1960* (1983, new exp.
ed. 1998); and William Julius Wilson, *The Truly Disadvantaged:
The Inner City, the Underclass, and Public Policy* (1987, new exp.
ed. 2012). There existed no monograph on race, class, and space in
Chicago in the 1960s, the decade which I will argue proved pivotal
to the tale of the "underclass."

[17] Alice O'Connor, *Poverty Knowledge: Social Science, Social Policy,
and the Poor in Twentieth-Century US History* (2001), ch. 9. This
book is a must-read for any serious student of poverty in America,
whatever their discipline.

Prologue 13

reservations, I carried out rough fieldwork on the constitution of the mixed problematic of the "underclass" by scholars and experts based at the Brookings Institution, the Ford Foundation, the Rockefeller Foundation, Mathematica Policy Research Inc., the Joint Center for Political and Economic Studies, and the Urban Institute, as well as by researchers from leading universities across the country.

When the Rockefeller Foundation disbursed $6 million to the Social Science Research Council (SSRC) to launch a "Program of Research on the Urban Underclass" in 1988, I was invited to the two planning meetings. At the first meeting, the historian Michael Katz and I kept raising the question of the origins, meaning, and (mis)uses of the term "underclass." The two program officers coordinating the Committee's work were visibly embarrassed; they kept punting and would not so much as provide a working definition of the central notion motivating our presence. Other participants were stoically uninterested in dispelling the semantic fog around the "underclass" and were quite content to carry on with their mission regardless. Over a three-year period, I got to meet, hear, and engage the leading students of the topic; to bump into and tussle with top government experts and policy luminaries (including a vitriolic clash with none other than Daniel Patrick Moynihan that dismayed Bill Wilson); and to discover first-hand the concerns, styles, and strategies of the policy institutes and philanthropies taking the lead in constituting the academic-cum-policy nebula of the "underclass."

I was also shocked to discover that the vast majority of the country's leading experts on the question had never set foot in a poor black neighborhood and were constantly stuffing the gap between their macro-level data and everyday reality with racial commonplaces that are part of a national common sense I did not share. This discovery convinced me that, in order to break with what W.E.B. Du Bois calls "car-window sociology,"[18] I needed to start from scratch

---

[18] W.E.B. Du Bois, *On Sociology and the Black Community* (1978), p. 37. This expression refers to caricatural knowledge of African American society and culture produced by white scholars in the Jim-Crow south, based on distant and circumstantial observation (such as can be carried out while riding a Pullman car on a vacation trip).

14   Prologue

through a historical-analytical reconstruction of the ghetto, on the one side,[19] and from close-up observation of social relations at street level, on the other. For this, I resolved to find an observation post inside the hyperghetto to figure out from the ground up how the realities of class, race, and space shaped the social strategies and experience of young black men caught in the undertow of economic restructuring and state abandonment.

A series of chance circumstances led me to land in a boxing gym on the devastated thoroughfare of 63rd Street in Woodlawn, only two blocks from my home at the southern border of Hyde Park – but as distant experientially as another planet.[20] I signed up to learn how to box as a conduit to get to know the club members; to my own surprise, I was drawn into the sensual and moral coils of pugilism and ended up apprenticing in the craft for three years.[21] I followed my gym mates in their daily round and observed how they dealt with the labor market, family, welfare state, and police. This prompted me to question root and branch the existing conceptual apparatus of the sociology of caste and class in the American metropolis. Here was a cluster of men who, *on paper*, matched most definitions of the urban "underclass" and yet displayed a personal sense of order, a love of family, respect for authority, the pursuit of long-term goals, and an iron-clad work ethic. Pierre Bourdieu turned out to be right when he told me at the time that this boxing gym and its members would teach me more about the sociology of the (hyper)ghetto than all the tomes on the "underclass" I could read.

During the period when my intellectual distance from the ductile discourse on the "underclass" gradually grew, Bill Wilson and I had countless breakfasts and dinners during which we hashed out our epistemological, theoretical, and

---

[19] Loïc Wacquant, "A Janus-Faced Institution of Ethnoracial Closure: A Sociological Specification of the Ghetto" (2012a).

[20] A fuller account of my biographical and intellectual pathway into and inside the South Side is Loïc Wacquant, "The Body, the Ghetto and the Penal State" (2009a).

[21] Loïc Wacquant, *Body and Soul: Notebooks of an Apprentice Boxer* (2004 [2000], exp. anniversary ed. 2022).

Prologue 15

policy differences. It was an advanced tutorial in sociology the likes of which no university offers. He, patient, stolid, and confident in his ability to bend the policy debate to his scholarly arguments; I, irreverent, frenetic, and stubborn in my call of scientific purity above all. With his trademark intellectual generosity, in spite of our disagreements, Bill offered me to co-author with him the sequel to *The Truly Disadvantaged*, set to be entitled *The American Underclass* (the book that became *When Work Disappears*).[22] This was an enormously alluring offer to an impecunious graduate student, considering the mirific advance offered by the publisher Knopf. But I demurred, insisting that we first find out whether we could agree on the answer to this question: should we use the "underclass" as a *tool for* analysis, a formal construct with which to explore and parse the empirical world, or as an *object of* analysis, a historically dated discursive formation and collective belief about the remnants of the dark ghetto and its inhabitants? The present tome is a continuation of that dialogue and a closing of that chapter. This is why it is dedicated to Bill Wilson, with gratitude and affection.

Anti-urbanism and the fear of the (black) city underbelly

To elucidate the full meaning and mechanisms of the invention of the "underclass" in the late twentieth century, it is *essential to historicize* them, in this case to set them against two staggered backdrops that reveal analogues and precursors of the category. The first and deeper backdrop is a centuries-long strand of *abiding anti-urbanism* in American culture and politics, with roots in the country's origin as an agrarian settler colony and the steadfast desire to distinguish itself from Europe and its great cities – which Thomas Jefferson famously viewed as "pestilential to the morals, the health and the liberties of man." For this national tradition, the metropolis is an engine of class conflict, ethnic promiscuity, social disintegration, and moral perdition, as exemplified

[22] William Julius Wilson, *When Work Disappears: The World of the New Urban Poor* (1996).

16   Prologue

by the shrill denunciations of the "wicked city" that flour-
ished in the mid-nineteenth century.[23]

The second backdrop is a more recent historical vision that
recentered urban fear and fulmination onto the dark "inner
city" during the postwar decades, making *race as blackness
the paramount prism of public perception and policy* in the
metropolis. This inflection of anti-urbanism, provoked by the
ghetto uprising of the 1960s, portrayed poor blacks as agents
of violence, disorder, and immorality, and the city itself as
an ungovernable sociospatial form doomed to crisis, breakdown, and irreversible decline.[24] Both backstories suggest
that the impulse to sociomoral control in the metropolis has
a long and recurrent history; and that this impulse drives the
symbolic delineation of the target populations viewed as dese-
crating the values of the Anglo middle and upper classes – and
not the other way around.

In the collective imaginary of the United States, and especially among its educated elite, the emergence of the first
urban centers in the 1830s was experienced as a mortal
threat to the young nation and its exceptional character, as
it undermined the mythic pioneer virtues of independence
and self-sufficiency. The city was considered the dissolute
redoubt of the "three Ms," mongrels, mobs, and money, a
dumping ground for the dregs of European society, a foul
and sinful place that made a dignified life impossible.[25] The
flourishing of urban-reform societies rooted in Evangelical
Christianity at mid-century, with their missionary visitors,
tract associations distributing bibles, and Sunday schools
aiming to revive the moral order of the village, was no match
for the surging urban masses at once "vicious, abandoned,
debased." Tidal waves of migration and working-class formation soon triggered trepidation over the "replication of

---

[23] Morton Gabriel White and Lucia White, *The Intellectual Versus the
City: From Thomas Jefferson to Frank Lloyd Wright* (1962); Andrew
Lees, *Cities Perceived: Urban Society in European and American
Thought, 1820–1840* (1985); Steven Conn, *Americans Against the
City: Anti-Urbanism in the Twentieth Century* (2013), ch. 1.

[24] Robert A. Beauregard, *Voices of Decline: The Postwar Fate of US
Cities* (1993).

[25] White and White, *The Intellectual Versus the City.*

Prologue   *17*

> ## "The refuse of Europe"
>
> "The refuse of Europe ... congregate in our great cities and send forth wretched progeny, degraded in the deep degradation of their parents – to be the scavengers, physical and moral, of our streets. Mingled with these are also the offcast children of American debauchery, drunkennesss, and vice. A class more dangerous to the community ... can scarcely be imagined."
>
> American Bible Society, *Annual Report*, 1857

European conditions" and alarm at the spread of "popery" and "pauperism."[26]

By the 1870s, the idiom of wilderness was transferred from the Western frontier to the urban frontier, and the inner ring of cities portrayed as an abyss of anonymity, depravity, and artificiality, whose "semi-barbarous" residents threatened to capsize the societal edifice *in toto*. Theories of hereditary degeneracy and moral delinquency were combined to develop the doctrine and practice of "scientific philanthropy" based on the partitioning of the urban poor into worthy and vicious.[27] Of particular concern was the size, growth, and menace of a submerged stratum of the urban proletariat known as the *residuum* – a notion borrowed from Charles Booth's mammoth survey of the London poor[28] – nested in the most squalid tenements of the metropolis. Criminality, casual work, moral dissolution, and family disintegration were the defining features of this fearsome and unreformable population, which makes it a close ancestor to the "underclass."

---

[26] Paul S. Boyer, *Urban Masses and Moral Order in America, 1820–1920* (1978), p. 57.

[27] David Ward, *Poverty, Ethnicity, and the American City, 1840–1925: Changing Conceptions of the Slum and the Ghetto* (1989), pp. 53–61.

[28] Christian Topalov, "The City as *Terra Incognita*: Charles Booth's Poverty Survey and the People of London, 1886–1891" (1993 [1991]).

18   Prologue

During the Gilded Age, the anxiety of the Anglo-Saxon
bourgeoisie took on hysterical proportions in the face of "the
triple menace of class warfare, alien radicalism, and urban
mass violence."[29] Colossal demographic changes turned the
old urban centers into the province of foreign migrants splin-
tered by language and religion, spawned the squalor of the
slums, and fueled the growth of patronage politics. Religious
groups, such as the Salvation Army and its "slum brigades,"
and the charity organization movement sprang into action,
based on "the assumption that the urban poor had degen-
erated morally because the circumstances of city life had cut
them off from the elevating influence of their moral betters"
– shades of the lament that the "underclass" lacks proper
"mainstream role models" a century later.

To battle indolence and ameliorate the character of the
poor required investigation, visitation, and the compiling of
dossiers made available to prospective landlords, employers,
banks, and even the police.[30] Imported from London, the settlement house movement led by Jane Addams favored envi-
ronmental remedies over individual solutions and made the
neighborhood the focus of inquiry and remediation, antici-
pating its adoption by the Chicago school of sociology two
decades later. The urban reform of the 1890s thus followed
two tracks: a coercive approach seeking to rein in the immoral
behavior of the poor through surveillance and supervision in
their own best interest (Jacob Riis summed up this perspective
with the formula, "Those who would fight *for* the poor must
fight the poor to do it"), and an environmentalist approach
aiming to ameliorate the tenements with bathhouses, parks,
and playgrounds suited to restoring the moral health of the
proletariat.[31]

---

[29] Boyer, *Urban Masses and Moral Order in America, 1820–1920*,
p. 126.
[30] Boyer, *Urban Masses and Moral Order in America, 1820–1920*,
p. 153. The practice is a precursor to the public systematization and
private diffusion of criminal records in the late twentieth century
as dissected by James B. Jacobs, *The Eternal Criminal Record*
(2015).
[31] Boyer, *Urban Masses and Moral Order in America, 1820–1920*,
p. 176.

Prologue 19

Faced with the pestilence and violence of the teeming immigrant working class, the bourgeoisie fled to the emerging suburbs, also imported from England and consciously crafted as the sociomoral opposite of the city. Inspired by Puritanism, the ideal of urbane living among the American bourgeoisie has always been suburban, that is, socially homogeneous, ethnically exclusive, spatially separate, and bucolic.[32] The suburb promoted and protected middle-class ideals of property, familial privacy, and moral propriety; it allowed the gracious single-family home, set in its large green lawn and drained of profane concerns, to function as the cradle of domesticity and religiosity. It expressed, not just the desire for self-seclusion, but also the fear of the class and ethnic other as well as trepidation at the rapid social changes wrought by the market.[33] The suburb thus defined itself through a series of homological oppositions that systematically devalued the first term: city/suburb, industry/family, poor/rich, ethnic promiscuity/ethnic purity, paganism/religiosity, artificial/natural, and depravity/morality. It is a key "asymmetric counterconcept" of America's urban imagination.[34]

During the Progressive Era, the taming of the city, viewed as a continued menace to the state and the nation, took two forms. The first strand extended the coercive and moralistic approach to stimulate crusades against such ills of urban life as sexual deviancy (the brothel) and intemperance (the saloon). The second, with Jane Addams as its figurehead, drew on a more sanguine view of the metropolis; it embraced positive environmentalism to remake the urban setting in ways believed to nourish sound habits and good conduct among the laboring class. The development of tenement reform, parks and playgrounds, civic pageants, and municipal art, not to forget "temperance saloons" offering masculine

---

[32] Robert Fishman, *Bourgeois Utopias: The Rise and Fall of Suburbia* (1988). This is in sharp contrast to the bourgeoisie of continental Europe, which viewed the city as the fount of civilization and civility and aspired to reside at its historic center.

[33] Robert M. Fogelson, *Bourgeois Nightmares: Suburbia, 1870–1930* (2007), part 2.

[34] Reinhart Koselleck, "The Historical-Political Semantics of Asymmetric Counterconcepts." (2004).

20   Prologue

camaraderie with no alcohol, partook of this approach. So did the teaching of English, ethnic crafts, and occupational and domestic skills. Such settlement work, moreover, had the virtue of reducing the isolation of the urban poor from their social betters which, together with congestion, was believed to be the main source of their moral condition.[35]

"The peril of this republic"

"The vices of cities have been the undoing of past empires and civilizations. It has been at the point where the urban population outnumbers the rural people that wrecked republics have gone down ... The peril of this republic likewise is now clearly seen to be in her cities. There is no greater menace to democratic institutions that the great segment of an element which gathers its ideas of patriotism and citizenship from the low grogshop."

Anti-Saloon League, *Yearbook*, 1914.

Importantly, urban reform was henceforth predicated on scientific knowledge and technical expertise. It drew on statistics and sociological inquiry to characterize the negative features of the city environment in need of remediation. Early American sociology arose to satisfy this interest in studying problem populations so as to better manage them.[36] The shift from "moral purity" to "social hygiene" marked the secularization and professionalization of sociomoral control in the metropolis. It fostered the birth of city planning as the profession devoted to creating the new environment fit to nourish moral unity and civic pride, and thereby recreate in the metropolis the imagined social and cultural cohesion of the village. For a brief moment in American history, the city appeared capable of producing the remedies to its own ills and elevating the social standards of the teeming masses.

---

[35] Michael B. Katz, *In the Shadow of the Poorhouse: A Social History of Welfare in America* (1996), p. 166.

[36] Boyer, *Urban Masses and Moral Order in America, 1820–1920*, pp. 200, 222–32.

Prologue   21

This urban optimism did not extend to the other territory of worry and mystery that mushroomed at the core of the metropolis alongside the European immigrant slums between 1910 and 1930: "the Black Belt and its offshoots [which] were slums, [but] they were something more: ghettos, where confinement was complete and based on color and not class."[37] The material and moral conditions of the coalescing ghetto were appalling, with rates of overcrowding, morbidity, mortality, illegitimacy, and delinquency topping the city charts, but these would have to be tackled by separate settlement houses and service agencies run by middle-class colored women. For the goal of white middle-class reformers, when it came to Bronzeville, prioritized *containment over improvement*.[38] The means to implement rigid ethnoracial enclosure included restrictive covenants, racial steering by real estate agents, pressure by white property-owners associations to prevent the renting or selling of houses to Negros, assaults by white "athletic clubs" on the street and the bombing of African-American homes, climaxing with periodic pogroms, such as the race riots of the "Red Summer" of 1919, when whites attacked the colored districts in three dozen cities to enforce their boundaries.[39]

Despite modest achievements in reforming schools and courts, work conditions, sanitation and food safety, housing and city administration, the politicians and professionals of the Progressive era failed to convince the citizenry that cities were wholesome places and municipal government a force for public good. During the interwar years, the "decentralists," such as Lewis Mumford, Frank Lloyd Wright, and Ralph

---

[37] Thomas Lee Philpott, *The Slum and the Ghetto: Neighborhood Deterioration and Middle-Class Reform* (1978), p. x.

[38] Philpott, *The Slum and the Ghetto*, pp. 346–7; Spear, *Black Chicago*, pp. 169–79; Drake and Cayton, *Black Metropolis*, ch. 8.

[39] William M. Tuttle, *Race Riot: Chicago in the Red Summer of 1919* (1970); Lee E. Williams, *Anatomy of Four Race Riots: Racial Conflict in Knoxville, Elaine (Arkansas), Tulsa, and Chicago, 1919–1921* (2008). See also Chicago Commission on Race Relations, *The Negro in Chicago: A Study of Race Relations and a Race Riot* (1923), one of the most remarkable accounts of the nexus of race, class, and space ever written (largely by sociologist Charles S. Johnson).

22 Prologue

Borsodi, gained the upper hand in advocating for the dispersal of population and industry as the solution to the problems of congestion, poverty, and social mixing in crowded city centers, as well as the means to reign in an intrusive government.[40] The New Deal drew on the ideas of the decentralists and trained its transformative power on rural regions and small-town society viewed as a wholesome setting in which to ground civic virtues. Thus, Roosevelt, who was "a child of the country," was especially enthused by the Civilian Conservation Corps because "it offered urban men that chance not just for a job but also for the restorative effects of being in the country, close to the earth."[41] The Resettlement Administration was similarly tasked with the rehabilitation of rural America and the planning of greenbelt towns bringing to reality Ebenezer Howard's blueprint of the Garden City, a self-sufficient settlement built in open countryside far from the slums and the smoke of the metropolis.[42]

Immediately after World War II, unabated anti-urbanism dominated city and regional planning as well as federal policy. The massive public subsidy of suburban development provided homes and transportation for the millions of whites fleeing city centers as black migrants from the South moved in. Top-down schemes of "slum clearance" and "urban renewal" pursuant to the Housing Act of 1949 failed to staunch the exodus of middle-class households and factories, even as they tore through the fabric of black neighborhoods declared "blighted" to try and salvage white ones, boost property values, and rebuild the tax base.[43]

Then, in the 1960s, a *double racial wave* hit the American metropolis full force and gave a new color to anti-urbanism: a wave of black migrants streaming in from the South as part of the second Great Black Migration and a wave of riots fueled

---

[40] Conn, *Americans Against the City*, ch. 3.

[41] Conn, *Americans Against the City*, pp. 94–5.

[42] Peter Hall, *Cities of Tomorrow: An Intellectual History of Urban Planning and Design Since 1880*, 4th ed. (2014), ch. 4.

[43] Kenneth T. Jackson, *Crabgrass Frontier: The Suburbanization of the United States* (1987), chs. 11 and 12; Jon C. Teaford, *The Rough Road to Renaissance: Urban Revitalization in America, 1940–1985* (1990).

Prologue 23

by the "urbanization" of the Civil Rights Movement and the refusal of African Americans to stay further confined inside the perimeter of the crumbling ghetto. This double wave redirected white middle-class *Angst* over the metropolis from the multiethnic "wicked city" to the black "inner city," and it planted the seeds of the loathsome imagery of the "underclass" that would blossom over the ensuing two decades.

The mass exodus of whites to the suburbs and the surging influx of blacks from the South caused alarm at the threat this posed to the established ethnoracial order. Thus, between 1950 and 1960, 678,000 whites moved out of Chicago while 153,000 African Americans moved in; based on this trend blacks could be expected to hold a numerical majority by 2000, not just in the Windy City, but in eight of the country's ten largest cities, thus establishing "Negro control" over urban America. And there was no stopping this demographic tumble so long as the presence of blacks in the metropolis was "associated in white minds with crime, drug addiction, juvenile delinquency and slums."[44]

Alarm turned into outright panic as a wave of racial clashes swept through the country, igniting cities from coast to coast. In the decade from 1963 to 1972, the United States recorded over 750 black riots, affecting more than 525 cities, including nearly every city with an African-American population exceeding 50,000. What the historian Peter Levy calls *The Great Uprising* marked an unprecedented historical rupture in the arc of caste domination,[45] and it inflicted unspeakable *symbolic trauma* upon the white citizenry of the country. It frontally attacked their sense of ethnoracial preeminence and it activated dormant representations of the "bad nigger" descended from the days of chattel slavery and Jim Crow subjugation – unruly, fierce, violent, the Negro who does not know and keep his "place." Thus, after 1966, noted a liberal political scientist who worked for presidents Kennedy and Johnson, "the image of the Negro was no longer that of the praying, long-suffering nonviolent victim of southern sheriffs; it was a defiant young hoodlum shouting 'black power'

[44] Beauregard, *Voices of Decline*, p. 137.
[45] Peter B. Levy, *The Great Uprising: Race Riots in Urban America during the 1960s* (2018).

24   Prologue

and hurling 'Molotov cocktails' in an urban slum."[46] Replace violent political threat with an equally violent but nihilistic criminal menace on the streets and you get a first approximation of the "underclass." Thence the "Urban Crisis" and the "Negro Question" would be indissolubly entwined.

The sprouting of Black Power activists in cities across the country inspired sheer racial terror. With their militant rhetoric of black separatism, strident hostility toward "whitey" and "pigs," invocations of Marxist revolution and colonial subjugation, and calls for armed struggle "against Ameri-KKK-a," they seemed to corroborate the worst anxieties about the city as crucible of social violence and hellish dissolution. For many of its participants, especially young black men on the borders of the world of work, the rebellion produced a vivid, if fleeting, collective sentiment of agency, racial pride and unity.[47] In the eyes of whites, the meshing of black power slogans and street riots portended a racial apocalypse; for government officials, it threatened a civic cataclysm unseen since the Civil War.

The "spiral to urban apartheid"

"If the Negro population as a whole developed an even stronger feeling of being 'penned in' and discriminated against, many of its members might come to support not only riots, but the rebellion now being preached by only a handful. If large-scale violence resulted, white retaliation could follow. This spiral could quite conceivably lead to a kind of urban *apartheid*, with semi-martial law in many major cities, enforced residence of Negroes in segregated areas, and a drastic reduction of personal freedoms for all Americans, particularly Negroes."

The Kerner Report: The 1968 Report of the National Advisory Commission on Civil Disorders, 1989 [1968].

---

[46] Cited in Thomas Byrne Edsall and Mary D. Edsall, *Chain Reaction: The Impact of Race, Rights, and Taxes on American Politics* (1991), p. 52.

[47] Thomas J. Sugrue, *Sweet Land of Liberty: The Forgotten Struggle for Civil Rights in the North* (2008), pp. 334–51; William L. Van Deburg, *New Day in Babylon: The Black Power Movement and American Culture, 1965–1975* (1992).

Prologue   25

Paradoxically, America's obsession with urban pathology became fixated onto the black "ghetto" *just as the latter was imploding* under the press of deindustrialization, demographic transformation, and black protest – so that the term itself turned into the pejorative designation of an urban area of social disintegration, contrary to its *dual* historical reality as instrument of ethnoracial closure by whites *and vector of African-American social cohesion and advancement* for a half-century.[48] As they spread, the riots came to frighten, not just whites in and out of the city, but also the African-American bourgeoisie committed to pressing for peaceful and gradual change through institutional means, and so they opened a social fissure between the black middle and working classes that would widen in subsequent decades.[49] With buildings ablaze, rampant looting, reported sniper fire, rolling street clashes, and tanks patrolling its thoroughfares, it is no wonder the metropolis was diagnosed as acutely "sick," downright "unheavenly," and, to sum it all up, yet again "in crisis."[50] Foreboding invocations of "jungle," "wilderness," "lawlessness," "psychological enfeeblement," and "depravity" returned with a vengeance and crowded public discussion of the city's fate while the country shuddered at the prospect of an all-out "race war" fought in the streets of its major urban centers.

As ingrained anxiety over the metropolis turned into scornful hostility, quiet rage, and vociferous antagonism toward disorderly blacks, state policies of "benign neglect" of race and urban inequality gave way to a comprehensive campaign of workfare disciplining, punitive containment, and brutal

---

[48] Wacquant, "A Janus-Faced Institution of Ethnoracial Closure," pp. 10–12.

[49] Eldridge Cleaver, *Soul on Ice* (1968); Robert M. Fogelson, "White on Black: A Critique of the McCone Commission Report on the Los Angeles Riot." (1967), pp. 363–4. Read the condemnation of the "separatist charade" as "a carbon copy of white supremacy" and a "Lorelei of black racism" by Kenneth B. Clark, "The Black Plight, Race or Class?" (1980).

[50] Beauregard, *Voices of Decline*, pp. 185–216. A flood of scholarly and journalistic books with the words "urban crisis" in their title gushed out in the 1960s and 1970s.

26 Prologue

criminal sanction converging on (hyper)ghetto residents.[51] The collective white trauma of the exploding city of the mid-1960s was reactivated by the Los Angeles riots of 1992 following the acquittal of the policemen responsible for the savage beating of motorist Rodney King.[52] By then, "urban crisis" had become a polite scholarly and policy synonym for the volatile yet inextricable intersection of caste segregation, African-American marginality, and street violence. It expressed the growing "Fear of a Black Planet" – to borrow the title of the 1990 album by the Compton rap group Public Enemy – lodged at the heart of the decaying metropolis, a fitting fin-de-siècle avatar of the long American tradition of anti-urbanism.[53] This *fear is the collective emotion that propelled the "underclass"* from the shadow of the race riots to the forefront of the academic and public debate.

[51] Lillian B. Rubin, *Quiet Rage: Bernie Goetz in a Time of Madness* (1986); Katz, *In the Shadow of the Poorhouse*, ch. 11; Michael Tonry, *Malign Neglect: Race, Crime and Punishment in America* (1995); Loïc Wacquant, *Punishing the Poor: The Neoliberal Government of Social Insecurity* (2009b), chs. 2–3 and 7.

[52] Robert Gooding-Williams (ed.)., *Reading Rodney King, Reading Urban Uprising* (2013).

[53] For an analysis of how rappers both play on and amplify the imagery of anti-urbanism as anti-blackness, see Tricia Rose, *Black Noise: Rap Music and Black Culture in Contemporary America* (1994), ch. 4.

PART ONE

THE TALE OF THE "UNDERCLASS"

"Nothing is so firmly believed as that which we least know."
Michel de Montaigne, *Essais*, 1580

"The tendency has always been strong to believe that whatever received a name must be an entity or being, having an independent existence of its own. And if no real entity answering to the name could be found, men did not for that reason suppose that none existed, but imagined that it was something particularly abstruse and mysterious."
John Stuart Mill, *Analysis of the Phenomena of the Human Mind*, 1829

Entry

A new social animal burst upon the American urban landscape at the close of the 1970s and soon sowed fear and loathing among the citizenry as well as caused spiking worry among public officials. Its discovery triggered a veritable media tsunami: major national outlets devoted lurid articles, fulminating editorials and alarming reports on the noxious and predatory behaviors alleged to characterize it. Politicians of every stripe rushed to denounce its sinister presence at the heart of the metropolis, in which they detected now the symptom, now the cause of the unraveling of the derelict districts that disfigured the nation's major cities. Social scientists and public policy experts were summoned to establish its geographic location, to specify its social habitat, to enumerate its ranks, and to elucidate its mores, so that the means by which to contain its malignant proliferation might be urgently devised. Legislative hearings were held, academic conferences organized, and scholarly tomes and popular accounts proliferated apace.[1]

---

[1] It would take a booklet to simply list all the print articles, television reports, and academic publications devoted to the "underclass" during the two decades covered here (1977–1997). A quick tour giving the reader an idea of the intensity and diversity of concerns covered by this umbrella term in journalism includes Ken Auletta, *The Underclass* (1982); Chicago Tribune, *The American Millstone: An Examination of the Nation's Permanent Underclass* (1986); Myron Magnet, *The Dream and the Nightmare: The Sixties Legacy to the Underclass* (1993); and Peter Davis, *If You Came This Way: A Journey Through the Lives of the Underclass* (1995). A panel of scholarly views is Christopher Jencks and Paul E. Peterson (eds.), *The Urban Underclass* (1991); William Julius Wilson (ed.), *The Ghetto Underclass: Social Science Perspectives* (1993a); Michael B. Katz (ed.), *The "Underclass" Debate: Views from History* (1993a); and William A. Kelso, *Poverty and the Underclass: Changing Perceptions of the Poor in America* (1994). The tortuous interface between academic, journalistic, and policy views is captured live in Joint Economic Committee, *The Underclass, Hearing Before the Joint Economic Committee of the 101st Congress of the United States* (1989), which I dissect in chapter 2.

Figure 1 Cover of *Time Magazine* in the wake of the "Harlem blackout riot" of August 1977

That animal is the urban "underclass," a term with woolly contours and sulfurous connotations (see box "A nebulous term" on pp. 31–2) that is best kept in quotation marks since it refers to a sociosymbolic constellation peculiar to the United States of the two decades following the New York City blackout riots of July 1977 that prompted *Time Magazine* to devote its cover to this fearsome "minority within a minority" (see figure 1). As we shall see, it has no real precedent in American history due to the *triple stigma of class, caste, and place* it carries and no counterpart in Western European countries owing to the deep differences in the manner in which these two continents conceive urban marginality and treat it politically.[2]

---

[2] Alberto Alesina and Edward L. Glaeser, *Fighting Poverty in the US and Europe: A World of Difference* (2004), and Jonas Pontusson, *Inequality and Prosperity: Social Europe vs. Liberal America* (2005).

Entry   *31*

Indeed, the "underclass" is neither the "subproletariat" of Marxist theory (for the term itself is misleading on that count; it is not a class), nor the "fourth-world" of the sociology of poverty inspired by reformist Catholicism (it is the object of scorn and terror rather than compassion), nor the "new poor" or the "excluded" figuring prominently in the contemporaneous European debates on urban inequality (the first term was briefly in fashion at the start of the 1960s, the second is largely absent from the American vocabulary on the topic).[3] It is a diffuse and motley aggregate – "a mishmash of social misfits," concludes sociologist Carole Marks upon conducting a broad-ranging survey of extant scholarly studies on the question[4] – composed of fundamentally incongruous categories that owe being lumped together thus to the simple fact that they are *perceived as a menace*, at once physical, moral, and fiscal, for the integrity of urban society.

A nebulous term with "evil" connotations

"The term is powerful because it calls attention to the conjunction between the characters of individuals and the impersonal forces of the larger social and political order. 'Class' is the least interesting half of the word. Although it implies a relationship between one social group and another, the terms of that relationship are left undefined until combined with the familiar word 'under'. This transformation of a preposition into an adjective has none of the sturdiness of 'working', the banality of 'middle', or the remoteness of 'upper'. Instead, 'under' suggests the lowly, passive, and submissive, yet at the same time the disreputable, dangerous, disruptive, dark,

---

[3] On the "subproletariat," see Pierre Bourdieu, *Algérie 1960. Structures économiques et structures temporelles* (1977); the concept of "*quart-monde*" is elaborated by Jean Labbens, *Le Quart-monde. La condition sous-prolétarienne* (1969), and idem, *Sociologie de la pauvreté. Le tiers-monde et le quart-monde* (1978). The parallel rising popularity of "exclusion" in Europe is attested by Graham Room (ed.), *Beyond the Threshold: The Measurement and Analysis of Social Exclusion* (1995), and Serge Paugam, (ed.), *L'Exclusion. L'état des savoirs* (1996).

[4] Carole Marks, "The Urban Underclass" (1991), p. 462.

evil, and even hellish. Apart from these personal attributes, it suggests subjection, subordination, and deprivation. All these meanings are perhaps best brought together in Richard Wagner's *The Ring of the Nibelung*. Wotan goes under the earth to wrest the ring from the malicious Alberich, who had used it to enslave a vile and debased subhuman population."

Paul Peterson, Henry Shattuck Professor of Government at Harvard University and Chair of the Committee for Research on the Urban Underclass at the Social Science Research Council, reporting approvingly the findings of a major conference on the topic (in Jencks and Peterson, *The Urban Underclass*, 1991, p. 3).

1

Between concept and myth: Genealogy of a shifty category

~

Described alternatively as a "ferocious subculture," a "hotbed of deviance," and a "tangle of pathology," or as a "contagion of disorder" and a "nation apart" on the verge of forming "permanent enclaves of poverty and violence" (so many expressions that one finds indiscriminately under the pen of journalists and in leading scholarly publications), the "underclass" does not encompass all the poor, nor even the most marginal of those dwelling at the urban margins. In keeping with the Victorian distinction between the virtuous and the vicious poor inherited from the nineteenth century,[1] it came to designate the *"undeserving" and threatening black poor from the dilapidated remnants of the historic Bronzeville.* By dint of their "antisocial" behaviors, "dysfunctional" lifestyle, and "deviant" values, those destitute African Americans trapped in the hyperghetto would be responsible for their own piteous fate as for the decline of the metropolis, which they saddle with a string of "social dislocations" that seem consubstantial to them: persistent joblessness and long-term

---

[1] Robert Castel, "La 'guerre à la pauvreté' et le statut de l'indigence dans une société d'abondance" (1978); Michael B. Katz, *In the Shadow of the Poorhouse: A Social History of Welfare in America* (1996); and Stephen Pimpare, *The New Victorians: Poverty, Politics, and Propaganda in Two Gilded Ages* (2004).

34 Part One: The Tale

reliance on public aid, marital dissolution and sexual anomie, educational failure and cultural deviation, drug trafficking and consumption, street delinquency and violent criminality, topped off by repeat incarceration.

Dangerousness and *immorality* in the city, along with membership in a *stigmatized ethnoracial category* (African Americans and, for some authors, Puerto Ricans), are the distinctive characteristics that motivate the authoritative (nay authoritarian) allocation to this "group" of the poor, whose emergence would explain the continued deterioration of the "ghettos" of the American metropolis. But we shall see that this collective *exists as such only on paper*, or in the minds of those who invoke it to spotlight a population they find violates their sense of sociosymbolic propriety.

A statistical artefact born of the arbitrary lumping of populations pertaining to disparate social relationships and mechanisms – ethnicity, the labor market, the family, geography, and state action on the social and penal fronts – the "underclass" is a *lurid location* in symbolic, social and physical space, a reviled and shunned entity perceived from afar (and above) and upon which each can project his racial and class fantasies.[2] Rather than a sociological category serving knowledge production, it is a *social categoreme* (from the Greek *katégoreisthai*): an instrument of "public accusation."[3] The "underclass" thus enters into the sociology of urban marginality not as an analytic *tool* but as an *object* of study: a collective belief (or rhetorical mirage) to be elucidated, a confused yet consequential classification that impacts urban reality by twisting its collective representation, a trope

---

[2] I use the masculine advisedly: nearly all the leading writers on the "underclass" are men who write from a masculinist perspective, assuming, for instance, that the patriarchal nuclear household is the normal form of the family.

[3] Pierre Bourdieu, *Sociologie générale. Cours du Collège de France 1981–1983* (2015), vol. 1, pp. 35–6. "The public prosecutor is someone who classifies and who says: 'You are sentenced to so many years', 'You are demoted', etc., and his classification carries the force of law. Someone classified by a public accusator, mandated by the whole group, and who pronounces his verdict in front of the whole group in the name of the group, has no right to argue. He is objectively stigmatized."

Between concept and myth 35

of incrimination that reveals more about those who deploy it than about those whom it ostensibly designates.

Whence comes this turbid notion of "underclass," how is the semantic space it describes configured, and what are the reasons for its sudden, if short-lived, success at the cutting edge of urban and policy research? And what lessons can be garnered from its strange career for the sociology of caste and class in the polarizing metropolis? An abbreviated genealogy takes us from the world of scholarship, to philanthropy and policy institutes, to journalism and the bureaucratic state, and back to think tanks and the university, each cluster of protagonists finding symbolic profit in the endorsement of the category by the others, so that the fiction of *the "underclass" gains credibility by circulating across the boundaries of the academic, political-policy-philanthropic and journalistic fields.*[4]

Issued from the scholarly and public debates of the 1960s that fueled the launching of President Johnson's "War on Poverty," the term was coined in 1963 by the Swedish economist Gunnar Myrdal in a book alerting America to the ominous formation of a stratum of the working class that was being permanently marginalized by postindustrialization.[5] Myrdal used the term to refer to a new position in the labor market and class structure. But the "underclass" failed to make a mark in university, media, and government circles because two rival notions captured the public imagination at that time: Daniel Patrick Moynihan's "tangle of pathology" and Oscar Lewis's "culture of poverty." Applying Koselleck's prescriptions for conceptual history, we must grasp these three notions in their interrelationships as part of a single "historical arrangement" of mental constructs emerging in the political turmoil of the mid-1960s. And, consistent with Bourdieu's theory of classification struggles, we must spotlight

[4] On the triadic exchanges between these three spaces of symbolic production and their contribution to the fabrication of "social problems," see Pierre Bourdieu, "Champ politique, champ des sciences sociales, champ journalistique" (1996).

[5] Gunnar Myrdal, *Challenge to Affluence* (1963). I discuss the substance of Myrdal's argument as well as rival concepts of the "underclass" in the next chapter. Here, I flag the main stages of its travels.

36 Part One: The Tale

the contest to establish one or another label as the right diagnosis for the ills of the collapsing ghetto.

The explosive expression "tangle of pathology" was not Moynihan's; it was coined by the renowned black psychologist Kenneth B. Clark in a report to Harlem Youth Opportunities Unlimited, a community action program, that served as basis for his book, *Dark Ghetto: Dilemmas of Social Power*, published to considerable acclaim in 1965 amidst the race riots shaking the country from coast to coast. In that book, Clark wrote somberly:

> The dark ghetto is institutionalized pathology, it is chronic, self-perpetuating pathology; and it is the futile attempt by those with power to confine that pathology so as to prevent the spread of its contagion to the "larger community." ... Not only is the pathology of the ghetto self-perpetuating, but one kind of pathology breeds another.[6]

Clark also used the expression "tangle of antisocial activities dominated by apathy and despair" in reference to delinquent youths at the center of his inquiry, and he repeatedly resorted to the biological idiom of illness and epidemic to describe social conditions.[7] Indeed, we will see in the next chapter that Clark's enumeration of the woes of the ghetto, "low aspiration, poor education, family instability, illegitimacy, unemployment, crime, drug addiction and alcoholism, frequent illness and early death," was a prescient anticipation of the tale of the "underclass."[8]

The tag "tangle of pathology" was seized upon by Daniel Patrick Moynihan, then an Assistant Secretary of Labor advisor in the Johnson administration, and used to frame a White House report on *The Negro Family: The Case for National Action*.[9] Before it could even be released, the 76-page

[6] Kenneth B. Clark, *Dark Ghetto: Dilemmas of Social Power* (1965), p. 81.

[7] Clark, *Dark Ghetto*, p. 87.

[8] Clark, *Dark Ghetto*, p. 27.

[9] Daniel Patrick Moynihan, *The Negro Family: The Case for National Action* (1965). Moynihan, who had received undergraduate degrees in sociology and diplomacy and a doctorate in history, and previously taught at Syracuse University, would go on to serve as advisor

Between concept and myth 37

document, full of statistics and cautious language stressing class bifurcation among African Americans, lit a policy and scholarly firestorm.[10] Its central thesis was that the crumbling of the black family – taking the form of forced matriarchy as a result of slavery and Jim Crow – was undermining the black community from within and threatening to undo the racial progress presaged by the freshly voted civil rights legislation ending the legal basis for segregation and discrimination.[11] Moynihan sketched a dire profile of the Negro family as measured by the dissolution of marriages in the city (23% versus 8% among whites), the rise of illegitimate births (eight times the white ratio), the increase in the proportion of single-parent families (one-quarter compared to 7% for whites) and "a startling increase in welfare dependency."[12] Set in the patriarchal context of American society, the female-centered family was dysfunctional. Together with "the racist virus in the American blood stream," it marginalized black men, disoriented black youths, and caused school failure. Unless the federal government launched a frontal attack to establish the patriarchal family among Negros, matriarchy would reproduce itself and consign the black lower class to utter social devastation: "The present tangle of pathology is capable of perpetuating itself without assistance from the white world."[13]

Even though it was never released, the Moynihan report triggered a furious political and intellectual backlash. Critics insisted that it made the "disorganized family," headed by the single mother with her illegitimate children, "the principal source of most of the aberrant, inadequate, or antisocial

---

to President Nixon, ambassador, Harvard professor, and senator. He was already well known at the time as co-author, with Nathan Glazer, of the contentious book, *Beyond the Melting Pot: The Negroes, Puerto Ricans, Jews, Italians and Irish of New York City* (1963), which argued that the urban crucible had failed to melt ethnicity.

[10] Lee Rainwater and William L. Yancey (eds.), *The Moynihan Report and the Politics of Controversy* (1967).

[11] Moynihan, *The Negro Family*, prefatory note, unpaginated.

[12] Moynihan, *The Negro Family*, pp. 10–17.

[13] Moynihan, *The Negro Family*, p. 47.

38   Part One: The Tale

behavior" perpetuating black marginality in the urban core,[14] all but making poor black men the victims of poor black women. No less problematic was the remedy proposed, which consisted in establishing patriarchy among African Americans so that black men could fulfill their seemingly natural roles as bread-winner and disciplinarian. Overnight, the vitriolic controversy remade the public and academic debate on race and urban poverty in America, effectively deterring sustained empirical research on the hyperghetto for the better part of two decades.[15]

Regardless of the report's caveats and merits, the language of pathology had the effect of turning the policy focus away from the economic and political causes of the deteriorating condition of the black precariat – the racially skewed functioning of the labor and housing markets, for instance, was not labelled pathological. It enabled Moynihan to fudge the difference between empirical observation and moral adjudication, and to treat the nuclear white middle-class family as an absolute norm by which to judge and remake the African-American family in the hyperghetto. In this anticipation of the discourse of the "underclass," the asymmetric counterpart to the disorganized black lower class in the city was out in the open.

The controversy over the Moynihan report established the "tangle of pathology" as a keyword in the dominant approach to racialized poverty in the postindustrial metropolis. Indeed, the expression reemerged two decades later under the pen of the black sociologist William Julius Wilson in *The Truly Disadvantaged* (1987).[16] Echoing analysts of the 1960s, Wilson maintained that it was necessary "to discuss in candid terms the social pathologies of the inner city" – among them violent crime, "family dissolution and welfare dependency" – in order to draw attention from policy makers and to press for public interventions aiming to interrupt the involutive course of the black precariat. The Chicago sociologist

[14] Moynihan, *The Negro Family*, p. 30.
[15] James T. Patterson, *Freedom Is Not Enough: The Moynihan Report and America's Struggle over Black Family Life* (2010).
[16] William Julius Wilson, *The Truly Disadvantaged: The Inner City, the Underclass, and Public Policy* (1987), pp. 21–9.

Between concept and myth 39

attributed the waning influence of the liberal perspective in the public debate on race and urban poverty to the reluctance of progressive scholars to "describe any behavior that might be construed as unflattering or stigmatizing to ghetto residents" and to their refusal to use the term "underclass," even though the latter was needed to grasp "a reality not captured in the more standard designation lower class."[17]

The storm over the "tangle of pathology" was still raging when another concept arose to occupy the intellectual scene at the intersection of academy and policy, and prevented the "underclass" from taking hold: the "culture of poverty." The anthropologist Oscar Lewis fashioned the notion to account for what he saw as the self-perpetuating dynamic of destitution in Western nations. Based on a field study of the everyday life of five families in a Mexican village and a team ethnography of Puerto Rican families in San Juan and New York City, Lewis claimed that the poor in capitalist societies develop a distinct "subculture" or lifestyle in "an effort to cope with feelings of hopelessness and despair" arising from "the improbability of their achieving success" according to the prevailing values.[18] Born as "an adaptation and a reaction to their marginal position in a class-stratified, highly individuated, capitalistic society," this subculture tends to lock them into marginality across generations because it is transmitted to their children even as "it goes counter to the cherished ideals of the larger society."

Lewis listed some 70 traits characterizing this "design for living" of the poor that stressed "the inexorable repetitiousness and the iron entrenchment of their lifeways." Among these traits, "the low level of organization," "the disengagement from the larger society," and "hostility to [its] basic institutions," including the police, seemed to fit well poor blacks then rioting in American cities from coast to coast.[19] But the thesis that the latter obey a distinctive life design

---

[17] Wilson, *The Truly Disadvantaged*, pp. viii, 8, and 6.

[18] Oscar Lewis, "The Culture of Poverty" (1966b), pp. 19 and 21; idem, *Five Families: Mexican Case Studies in the Culture of Poverty* (1959), and *La Vida: A Puerto Rican Family in the Culture of Poverty, San Juan and New York* (1966a).

[19] Lewis, "The Culture of Poverty," p. 23.

40   Part One: The Tale

perpetuating their dispossession seemed to disregard material forces keeping them down and to make (hyper)ghetto residents responsible for their own parlous fate – what the psychologist William Ryan would later call "blaming the victim" in his cutting critique of the Moynihan report and assorted middle-class nostrums deployed in denial of the realities of caste and class.[20]

As a result, the "culture of poverty" became the epicenter of a second venomous debate among social researchers, much as the "tangle of pathology" fixated discussion among policy-oriented scholars. These two notions worked in tandem to fasten attention on the *internal* properties of the (hyper) ghetto and its inhabitants, effectively obscuring the web of *external* relations linking the latter to the broader structure of the city, the economy, and the state. In particular, these two notions obfuscated the continuing significance of caste as an active principle of social vision and division bisecting social and physical space in the metropolis. Myrdal's "underclass" did not enter into the academic, journalistic, and policy vocabulary because it went against the grain of both rival notions: "tangle of pathology" consecrated race over class, but race construed as a substantialist property as opposed to a relational construct;[21] "culture of poverty" prioritized culture over structure. Class receded into the background of both scholarly-policy disputes; the state as generator of marginality all but vanished.

But the "underclass" did not disappear so much as go underground, and it gained currency a decade later among philanthropic foundations. The latter seized on the notion as the rhetorical device ideally suited to relegitimizing their action in the face of the alleged failure of the "War on Poverty" to ameliorate conditions in the inner city. The "underclass" identified for them a new target population seemingly impervious to traditional means of poverty remediation and therefore requiring a renewed enterprise in observation and intervention. Two decades later, a senior

---

[20] William Ryan, *Blaming the Victim* (1971); see also Charles A. Valentine, *Culture and Poverty* (1968).
[21] Mustafa Emirbayer and Matthew Desmond, *The Racial Order* (2015).

staff member of the Rockefeller Foundation in charge of the "underclass" program under the aegis of the foundation's Equal Opportunity Division, would confide to sociologist Herbert Gans that "poverty didn't sell" anymore whereas "underclass" was an "energizing" term.[22]

The key role here was played by Mitchell Sviridoff, the Vice-President for national affairs at the Ford Foundation and later a professor of urban policy at the New School for Social Research. As early as 1966, Sviridoff provided a large grant to launch and support the Vera Institute of Justice to carry out "demonstration projects in the field of criminal justice and the underclass" – the first mention of the category referenced in the foundation's archives.[23] He was then the architect behind the creation of the Manpower Development Research Corporation (MDRC) in 1974. The MDRC's mission was to establish and evaluate employment and job training programs showcasing incremental change carried out in cooperation with the US Department of Labor. This was motivated by Sviridoff's view that "'the activist experimentation' of the 1960s had gone 'too far, too fast'"; that poverty was best tackled by teaching poor individuals good "work habits" and by clearing paths to self-sufficiency; and that, to moderate the liberal agenda, it was best "to avoid direct confrontation with the issue of race."[24] The first training program administered by the MDRC targeted the "chronically unemployed," chiefly welfare recipients, recently released criminal convicts and drug addicts, viewed by Sviridoff as making up "the core of a new 'underclass'."[25] This move laid the groundwork for the Ford Foundation's forceful intervention into research on

---

[22] Cited by Herbert J. Gans, *The War Against the Poor: The Underclass and Anti-Poverty Policy* (1995), p. 51.

[23] This is the title of the grant listed in the Ford Foundation archives (https://dimes.rockarch.org/xtf/, accessed July 29, 2020). Biographical data on Sviridoff comes from his obituary in the *New York Times*, October 23, 2000, and from a foundation profile.

[24] Alice O'Connor, *Poverty Knowledge: Social Science, Social Policy, and the Poor in Twentieth-Century US History* (2001), p. 232.

[25] O'Connor, *Poverty Knowledge*, p. 232. The word "underclass" is used in the annual report of MDRC for 1977. It is the term the corporation employed to define its target "clients."

42   Part One: The Tale

the urban "underclass" a decade later, after the latter had
made its way into America's social imaginary by way of the
popular media.

The "underclass" burst onto the public stage in the summer
of 1977 via a *Time* magazine cover and feature article that
warned the country about the portentous presence of this
newfound group:

> Behind the [ghetto's] crumbling walls lives a large group of
> people who are more intractable, more socially alien and
> more hostile than almost anyone had imagined. They are the
> unreachables: the American underclass ... Their bleak envi-
> ronment nurtures values that are often at odds with those
> of the majority – even the majority of the poor. Thus the
> underclass produces a highly disproportionate number of the
> nation's juvenile delinquents, school dropouts, drug addicts
> and welfare mothers, and much of the adult crime, family dis-
> ruption, urban decay and demand for social expenditures.[26]

The article notes that, borrowed from the Swede Gunnar
Myrdal, "the term itself is shocking to striving, mobile
America" (it wrongly states that the term has "long been used
in class-ridden Europe"). Yet, despite a strong labor market
and billions of dollars in public spending to fight poverty,
"the underclass remains a nucleus of psychological and material destitution" stuck at the bottom that defies government
intervention. Indeed, an assistant secretary of Housing and
Urban Development warns that "the underclass presents our
most dangerous crisis, more dangerous than the Depression of
1929, and more complex."[27] This threat is made more urgent
still by the boiling envy that the "underclass" is said to feel
toward successful blacks who left the ghetto and its aggressive resentment toward the affluent society that ignores them.
This much had been demonstrated a month earlier when New
York City lost power for 25 hours, during which time black
rioters set off some thousand fires in 31 neighborhoods and
looters ransacked over 1,600 stores, leading to 4,500 arrests,

---

[26] George Russell, "The American Underclass: Destitute and Desperate
in the Land of Plenty" (1977), p. 16.
[27] Cited in Russell, "The American Underclass: Destitute and
Desperate," p. 17.

Between concept and myth   43

in what *Time* magazine called a "night of terror."[28] The blackout mutiny of New York City made the headlines around the country and the globe, announcing to the world the coming out of the American "underclass."

Alarmed at the sighting of the group, public officials from coast to coast at every level of government asked in unison, "How big is it? Who is in it? What motivates its members?" The article answers by coursing through the demographic, social, and psychic makeup of the "underclass," adorned by a dozen dramatic photos all displaying sullen and beaten black men, women, and children amidst physical chaos and social detritus.[29] Special attention is accorded to men who have never held jobs and terrorize the streets, and to women who receive more from welfare than what they would earn working: "Welfare dependency means that for many members of the underclass, the concepts of income and jobs are barely related," and "for many women in the underclass, welfare has turned illegitimate pregnancy into a virtual career."[30]

Given the failure of the War on Poverty to contracept the "underclass," the path to salvation is said to rest on "new efforts by the underclass themselves" and by private business, along with a reallocation of social spending to improve public education, toughen policing, expand courts and jails, and subsidize low-paying jobs. As an example of remedy, the article vaunts a job-training program, sponsored by the Ford Foundation, "aimed at long-term welfare mothers, ex-drug addicts and ex-convicts," providing intense supervision and stringent work discipline for its participants. Whatever the

[28] *Time*, "The Blackout: Night of Terror," cover picture and featured story, July 25, 1977.

[29] The captions read: "Young, unemployed blacks reflect frustration and resentment from the confines of a ghetto basement"; "Three generations on welfare"; "Nowhere to go, an elderly woman surveys the litter of her inner-city surroundings from atop a trash can"; "High in hand, a glue-sniffer takes his ease – alcohol, heroin also abound"; "A jobless man gazes through a shattered tenement window in one of the many abandoned dwellings in New York City slums"; "Washing at a neighborhood fire hydrant – jealousy can make you hate"; "Down and out on a bleak inner-city street in Harlem, two men take dispirited refuge in whiskey and sleep on a summer afternoon."

[30] Russell, "The American Underclass: Destitute and Desperate," p. 21.

44 Part One: The Tale

combination of public, private, and philanthropic efforts, to tame the "underclass" promises to take not years but a whole generation.

The article had an immediate impact on politicians, who quickly repeated its claims almost word for word. Thus Senator Edward Kennedy, the standard bearer for the progressive wing of the Democratic Party, alerted the country in a 1978 address to the National Association for the Advancement of Colored People:

> The great unmentioned problem of America today: the growth, rapid and *insidious*, of a group in our midst, perhaps more *dangerous*, more bereft of hope, more difficult to confront than any for which our history has prepared us. It is a group which *threatens* to become what America has never known – a permanent underclass in our society.[31]

The *Time Magazine* portrait primed the *turn toward a racialized and behavioral vision of the "underclass"* that was accelerated by the book, *The Underclass*, by the New York journalist Ken Auletta. In 1982, Auletta was a staff writer and weekly columnist at the *Village Voice*, weekly political columnist for the *New York Daily News*, political commentator on WCBS-TV, and a regular contributor to *The New Yorker*, all but guaranteeing the high visibility of his investigation. Serialized in *The New Yorker* just before its release, *The Underclass* was an instant hit and drew myriad reviews in the mainstream media, including a laudatory front-page review by the political scientist Andrew Hacker in the *New York Review of Books*. Remarkably, it was also reviewed in *Contemporary Sociology* as if it were a scholarly tome.[32] It

---

[31] Cited in James T. Patterson, *America's Struggle Against Poverty in the Twentieth Century* (2000), p. 210, my italics.

[32] Andrew Hacker, "The Lower Depths," *New York Review of Books*, August 12, 1982. Hacker is uneasy about the terminology but bows to the emerging consensus: "I confess to mixed feelings about this phrase: it suggests a sociological perspective which may not in fact be there. However, since I lack a better term ('lumpenproletariat' has special connotations), I will go along with underclass, and without quotation marks." Morris L. Fried endorses the term and the book with no qualms in *Contemporary Sociology* (1983, p. 461): "*The*

Between concept and myth

popularized the term "underclass" among the educated public and political personnel, and it quickly established itself as a central reference invoked by other journalists as well as by academics and think tankers alike as evidence of the existence of the group.[33]

"Something different was happening among the poor"

"The idea [for the 1981 articles in *The New Yorker* that became the book *The Underclass*] formed from my observations that something different was happening among those we classify as poor. The number of people classified as having dropped out of the labor force rose. Where once most murders were among those who knew each other, the 'murder by stranger' category jumped. On the subways and streets [of New York City] I was struck by the growing number of the homeless and drugged individuals. Welfare rolls were populated by those on welfare a long time who now seemed permanently dependent. I visited my editor and said, 'Mister Shawn – everyone called him mister – I think *something significant is happening*,' and explained. He encouraged me to pursue the idea but cautioned that it sounded like a 'sociological yak piece,' and I needed to find a vehicle to tell this story."

Journalist Ken Auletta, personal communication, May 2021

The Underclass centers on a supported-work training and evaluation program similar to the one flagged by the 1977 *Time* article, devised by Sviridoff and run by the MDRC with funding from the Ford Foundation. Auletta spent seven months embedded with a cohort of 26 trainees attending daily

---

Underclass should be required reading for students in courses in social problems and the structure of American society." An early dissenting view, appropriately published in *Dissent*, is William Kornblum, "Lumping the Poor: What is the Underclass?" (1984).

[33] "Ken Auletta was not the first to use the term [underclass] but he was largely responsible for making it part of middle-class America's working vocabulary" (Christopher Jencks, "Is the American Underclass Growing?," [1991], p. 28).

46   Part One: The Tale

classes in "life-skills" aiming "to instill the habit of work and
to expunge bad habits." He initially approached his topic
with trepidation: "As a white journalist, I worried about the
racial freight the subject carried. At first, I used the word
underclass [by which the MDRC designated its 'clients'] gin-
gerly, fearful that it was somewhat racist. I worried whether
a focus on crime, welfare, and pathological behavior might
present a distorted picture of the American poor." But he was
soon enough reassured:

> I quickly learned that among students of poverty there is little
> disagreement that a fairly distinct black and white underclass
> does exists; that this underclass generally feels excluded from
> society, rejects common values, suffers from *behavioral* as
> well *income* deficiencies. They don't just tend to be poor; to
> most Americans, their behavior seems aberrant.[34]

Auletta stresses that, for the vast majority of America's
30 million poor, "poverty is not a permanent condition" as
it can and will be overcome "in a generation or two." But
"an estimated 9 million Americans do not assimilate" in
this fashion – no source is given for this numerical estimate.
"They are the underclass," of which Auletta offers a florid
enumeration that deserves to be quoted *verbatim et literatim*:

> (a) the *passive poor*, usually long-term welfare recipients; (b)
> the *hostile* street criminals who terrorize most cities, and who
> are often school dropouts and drug addicts; (c) the *hustlers*,
> who, like street criminals, may not be poor and who earn their
> livelihood in an underground economy, but rarely commit
> violent crimes; (d) the *traumatized* drunks, drifters, homeless
> shopping-bag ladies and released mental patients who fre-
> quently roam or collapse on city streets.[35]

[34] Auletta, *The Underclass*, pp. xiii–xiv, original italics. Four decades
later, Auletta confirms: "I did not receive very much pushback on my
use of the term. There were some who thought I was suggesting this
was a permanent condition, a notion I took care to debunk both in
the original 1982 book and in the 1999 Introduction. And I recall
one reviewer described me as a 'redneck'" (personal communication
with Ken Auletta, May 2021).

[35] Auletta, *The Underclass*, p. xvi, original italics. This folk typology
was derived from the administrative categories eligible for the

Between concept and myth 47

This view of the "underclass" as a collection of social parasites, refuse, and predators whose deviant behaviors explain their dereliction is validated by the participants in the work program: these aver that "most welfare clients stay on the dole most of their lives" because they are "loafers who don't want to work," that they prefer "their side hustle" to regular employment, "accept the garbage and dirt" in their buildings, do not care about their neighborhood, and are skilled at "getting something for nothing."[36] Members of the "underclass" fall into alcoholism, drug abuse, and crime, not just because of deprivation, but also due to their lack of self-confidence, passivity, and ingrained hostility toward society. Participants in the training program agree with "the experts" that the female-headed family is responsible for the "welfare mentality" and teenage pregnancy which join to feed a cycle of dependency and destitution.[37] This *agreement between folk and expert constructs is taken as empirical validation* of the notion of "underclass."

What explains the stunning success of Auletta's book and the metamorphosis of a scholarly structural proto-concept into a journalistic behavioral one? The *Begriffsgeschichte* of Reinhart Koselleck invites us to pay special attention to the *timing* of conceptual innovation and to the changing *semantic charge* of keywords as they circulate. In the prosperous 1960s, the structural construct of the "underclass" forged by Myrdal did not catch on, and thus went into intellectual hibernation, because the public stage of the War on Poverty was occupied by the controversies around the "culture of poverty" and the "tangle of pathology" of the (hyper)ghetto. These controversies raged against the backdrop of the mobilization of the poor, the spectacular expansion of public assistance, and the general reduction in caste and class inequality that made the coalescence of an immobile fraction of the working class seem implausible.[38]

MDRC supported-work program (personal communication with Ken Auletta, May 2021).

[36] The quotations are the words of program participants, in Auletta, *The Underclass*, pp. 52–3, 57, 61, 90, 124–5.

[37] Auletta, *The Underclass*, pp. 73–4.

[38] Patterson, *America's Struggle Against Poverty in the Twentieth Century*, chs. 3 and 4, and Frances Fox Piven and Richard A.

48 Part One: The Tale

A decade later, when the "underclass" resurged in behavioral garb to establish itself as pressing public menace and target for focused social research and government intervention, the "inner city" was said to be in crisis and the landscape of intellectual and political positions had changed dramatically. The 1980s brought, not only a sweeping backlash against racial equality and a frontal attack on the welfare state by the Reagan administration after a decade of stagflation, but also a sea change in the space of production and consumption of what the historian Alice O'Connor calls "poverty knowledge."[39]

With the pullback of government subsidies, liberal policy institutes such as the Institute for Research on Poverty and the Urban Institute, which had prospered since their founding in the 1960s, faced an existential crisis and became more dependent on foundation grants just as a new crop of conservative think tanks, among them the Heritage Foundation, the Cato Institute, and the Manhattan Institute (established in 1973, 1977, and 1978, respectively), were gathering intellectual steam, media visibility, and political authority.[40] Philanthropies, for their part, recalibrated their project and discourse to adapt to the sharp rightward shift of the policy debate, which required further eliding structural factors and euphemizing caste in the genesis of urban marginality. "The poverty research industry survived through the crash of the early 1980s by becoming more entrepreneurial and political in the search for research funds."[41]

This meant accepting the newly dominant social policy problematic centering on the twin priorities of ending "welfare dependency" and enforcing "individual responsibility," to the neglect of the continuing deterioration of the low-wage labor market, the shrinking of the social safety net, and the sharp

---

Cloward, *Poor People's Movements: Why they Succeed, How they Fail* (1977).

[39] O'Connor, *Poverty Knowledge*; on the racial and class backlash of the long 1980s, see Sean Wilentz, *The Age of Reagan: A History, 1974–2008* (2008).

[40] The swift transformation of the space of "think tanks" during this pivotal period of growth and consolidation is mapped by Thomas Medvetz, *Think Tanks in America* (2012), ch. 3.

[41] O'Connor, *Poverty Knowledge*, p. 245.

Between concept and myth   49

rise in class inequality. There is thus a direct affinity between Auletta's racialized enumeration of behavioral misfits and the individualistic and moralistic conception of social problems adopted by policy institutes in their effort to remain relevant. Indeed, we will see later that economists from the center-left Urban Institute played the lead role in "behavioralizing" the technical definition of the "underclass." In taking this path, O'Connor writes, liberal policy analysts "actively participated in what they hitherto had been trying to avoid: they repauperized the poverty problem and heightened the distinction between the 'undeserving' and the 'deserving' poor," and they fostered "the revival of a frankly pathologized vision of poverty" in the guise of the "underclass."[42]

Philanthropic foundations contributed decisively to the diffusion of the "underclass" as scholarly object and policy objective: once the term had perked up in public debate, they pounced on it and swiftly financed the investigative infrastructure that made it an academic household name.[43] The sudden profusion of funding, research programs, fellowships, conferences, and databases, in turn, seemed to offer proof positive of the existence of the group. Thus, in 1989, Peter Goldmark, the new president of the Rockefeller Foundation, made a media splash by announcing that the foundation was launching a major new program of research and intervention targeted at America's "underclass":

> These are the people government and everyone wants to forget
> ... We are talking about the one or two million Americans

[42] O'Connor, *Poverty Knowledge*, p. 244.

[43] On the role of philanthropies as conservative "clearing houses" for public common sense and vectors of epistemic consensus in policy debates, see Donald Fisher, "The Role of Philanthropic Foundations in the Reproduction and Production of Hegemony: Rockefeller Foundations and the Social Sciences" (1983); Joan Roelofs, *Foundations and Public Policy: The Mask of Pluralism* (2003), ch. 6; Ellen Condliffe Lagemann, *The Politics of Knowledge: The Carnegie Corporation, Philanthropy, and Public Policy* (1992), esp. "Scientific Philanthropy," pp. 29–84 and ch. 9; Alice O'Connor, *Social Science for What? Philanthropy and the Social Question in a World Turned Rightside Up* (2007), part II; and David L. Seim, *Rockefeller Philanthropy and Modern Social Science* (2013).

50   Part One: The Tale

alienated from all the mainstream institutions. They don't just
do badly in school; they are out of school. Many are not on
welfare; they are hustlers. Many are responsible for much of
the antisocial behavior that goes on in our cities.

There was an urgent need for up-close empirical investigation, because "the underclass is not a topic to pursue from
the library. *You get out and look for them.*" A major plank
was to draw top researchers to the topic, which they must
approach with a definite sense of mystery and foreboding:

> They are a *very special group* within the poor community . . .
> *Nobody knows who they are, what they do, how they stay
> alive* or why they are so totally cut off from institutions of
> American life. The only institution they come in contact with
> is the criminal-justice system.[44]

"It is not easy to say how they live"

"[They] consist mostly of casual labourers of low character,
and their families, together with those in a similar way of life
who pick up a living without labour of any kind. Their life is
the life of savages, with vicissitudes of extreme hardship and
occasional excess. . . . It is not easy to say how they live. . . .
These are the worst class of corner men who hang around the
doors of public houses, . . . the ready materials for disorder
when occasion serves. They render no useful service, they
create no wealth: more often they destroy it. They degrade
whatever they touch, and as individuals are perhaps incapable
of improvement."

Charles Booth, *Life and Labour of the
People in London* (1892), p. 38

In addition to stimulating social research, the Rockefeller
foundation planned to fund "community development corporations" to work on neighborhood renewal from within

---

[44] Peter Goldmark, cited in Kathleen Teltsch, "Charity to Focus on
Underclass" (*New York Times*, 1989), my italics.

Between concept and myth 51

and groom a generation of grassroots leaders because "what typifies the underclass neighborhood is total absence of leadership, total absence of role models, absence of anything positive." A first multi-million-dollar subsidy would go to the Local Initiatives Support Corporation, an organization spawned in 1980 by the Ford Foundation.

From 1988 to 1993, the Rockefeller Foundation allocated $6 million in support of a multifaceted program at the Social Science Research Council (SSRC) "designed to stimulate interdisciplinary research on the origins and persistence of concentrated urban poverty in the United States" and "to create a cadre of young scholars that can further advance the state of knowledge about the urban underclass." This endeavor was spearheaded by a committee of distinguished scholars (chaired by Harvard political scientist Paul Peterson), leading working groups tasked with sponsoring workshops and conferences and with commissioning studies on the low-wage labor market, drugs and crime, and families in very poor neighborhoods as well as on "the historical origins of the underclass." In 1992, the foundation was pleased to report on the success of the SSRC Committee for Research on the Urban Underclass in its *Annual Report*:

> When the Foundation asked the SSRC to mount this effort, there were only four major academic centers of research on poverty issues in this country, and only 36 of 250 students completing dissertations in relevant areas between 1980 and 1986 described their research as being concerned with the urban underclass. Since 1988, SSRC has awarded 70 undergraduate assistantships, 35 slots in summer dissertation workshops, 23 dissertation awards, and 15 postdoctoral fellowships. Today there is a community of over 100 senior scholars, and as many young scholars, doing research at more than 60 universities. The intellectual output to date includes 16 research studies, 26 commissioned papers, 45 research articles, and an urban underclass database containing over 6,000 social, economic, demographic, and health indicators that has been used already by the U.S. Department of Housing and Urban Development in preparing a major report to the President on national urban policy.[45]

---

[45] Rockefeller Foundation, *Annual Report 1992*, p. 42.

52   Part One: The Tale

For the year 1992 alone, the Rockefeller foundation issued $1.2 million to the Social Science Research Council "to continue support for the SSRC's five-year program to mobilize the academic community for interdisciplinary research on the underclass," including $625,000 to provide fellowships and training "aimed at developing a cohort of younger scholars concerned with the study of persistent poverty and the underclass"; $260,000 to the Joint Center for Political and Economic Studies, an established black-issues think tank, to "continue support for its policy analysis and dissemination activities on issues of persistent poverty and the underclass"; and $6.8 million to the Urban Institute "to continue support for its policy research on the urban underclass and dissemination of the findings to policy makers, community leaders and the media."[46]

Not to be outdone, in 1998 (at a time when the shine of the question was fading), the Ford Foundation launched the Research and Training Program on "Poverty, the Underclass, and Public Policy," based at the University of Michigan in Ann Arbor, with joint support from the university's Presidential Initiatives Fund Award, offering two-year "postdoctoral fellowships to American minority scholars in all the social sciences." The fellows would start by taking a course crosslisted in social work, public policy, and political science, SW486, taught by professor Mary Corcoran, entitled "Poverty, the Underclass and Public Policy" probing the questions "What is poverty? Who is in the underclass? Why is poverty so persistent? Why are poverty and unemployment rates for minorities so high?" Another generation of doctoral students would thus get indoctrinated in the category and help it endure in the academy.

---

[46] Rockefeller Foundation, *Annual Report 1992*, p. 42.

2

"The tragedy of the underclass": Policy theater and scholarship

~

From scholarship to philanthropies to journalism back to philanthropies: the next stage in the journey of the "underclass" was its adoption by state managers and elected politicians. The recognition of the category by official bodies of government gives it the imprimatur of the paramount symbolic agency, the state as "central bank of symbolic capital" and guarantor of the power of naming.[1] By designating it as an urgent "social problem" mandating public attention and intervention, the state ratifies the existence of the "underclass" and makes it part of the civic doxa of the moment.

The hearing held by the Joint Economic Committee of the 101st Congress in May 1989 provides a theatrical representation of the work of *symbolic fabrication of the "underclass" through officialization*. In it, we witness how scholars, think tankers, and politicians engage one another and collectively sustain the taken-for-granted belief in the existence of the group by debating its traits, origins, and possible treatments in a formal government setting, according to a set public choreography, before a body of representatives

---

[1] On the power of naming and ratification of the state, see Pierre Bourdieu, "Esprits d'État. Genèse et structure du champ bureaucratique" (1993a), p. 56.

54   Part One: The Tale

attesting to the concern of the nation.[2] The president of the
Joint Committee formed by ten congressmen and ten senators
opens the session by setting the stage for the "tragedy of the
underclass":

> Many Americans – in fact, most Americans – probably never
> visit underclass neighborhoods. They are unaware of the ter-
> rible human toll that the breakdown of social convention has
> taken. They are unaware of the real face of economic depri-
> vation, but highly visible manifestations of the tragedy of the
> underclass, like soaring teenage pregnancies, drug murders,
> chaotic schools, have alerted the Nation as a whole to the fact
> that the problem affects us all. If compassion did not prompt
> us to seek solutions to these problems, certainly enlightened
> self-interest, both individual and societal, would.[3]

The three expert witnesses, two of them African American,
represent the three disciplines of economics, political science,
and sociology, and span the continuum between policy think
tank and university. In accordance with the public image of
these three social sciences, the first testimony offers a positivist operationalization of the "underclass," the second moral
exhortation about its forlorn civic obligations, and the third
close-up ethnographic vignettes on the street-level conduct
and feelings of its presumed members.

First to appear on stage, the young black economist
Ronald Mincy (PhD from MIT, 1987) is a research associate at the Urban Institute, where he is a part of a cluster
of think-tank scholars, known as the "Underclass Research
Project," involved in a diligent enterprise of technical codification of the "underclass" as a behavioral construct.[4]
Mincy mentions the structural concept of Gunnar Myrdal in

---

[2] All five ingredients of Burke's "pentad of dramatism" are present
in this happening: act, agent, agency, purpose, and scene. Kenneth
Burke, "Dramatism" (1968).

[3] Joint Economic Committee, *The Underclass, Hearing Before the
Joint Economic Committee of the 101st Congress of the United
States* (1989), p. 1.

[4] Ronald Mincy is the (co-)author of a series of articles defining and
measuring the underclass discussed in the next chapter, including
"The Underclass: Concept, Controversy, Evidence" (1994).

"The tragedy of the underclass" 55

his opening but, without further explication, proffers a mixed behavioral-cum-spatial definition pegged on "four indicators: high-school dropout rates, female headship, welfare dependency, and nonwork." Then he further narrows this definition to concentrate on black inner-city districts beset by "multiple social problems" because this fits "conventional description."[5] The behavioral specification of the "underclass" is thus laid down as the unquestioned common ground for the discussion to follow.

Armed with this definition, Mincy presents a sobering picture of the spatial fixation of the group in the urban core: "We discovered that there were 243 underclass areas in 1970, but by 1980 that number of neighborhoods had risen to 880, and the population in all underclass areas was about 750,000 people in 1970 and it had grown to 2.5 million in 1980." The economist acknowledges that "the problem of working poverty in rural areas is severe," but the rural poor do not belong to the "underclass" because they "tend not to exhibit the same dysfunctional behaviors that the underclass area population does."[6] The impeccable scientific rhetoric and the apparent neutrality of the measurements give an air of unimpeachable verisimilitude to the testimony.

The second expert queried by the congressmen is the political scientist Lawrence Mead (PhD from Harvard, 1973), a professor at New York University who was previously speechwriter to Henry Kissinger and Director of Research for the Republican National Committee, well known for his advocacy for the "obligations of citizenship" that the dependent poor should fulfill in return for public aid.[7] Like Mincy before him, Mead posits *ab initio* that "there is no serious disagreement about the definition" of the "underclass" since "everyone uses this term to mean people who are poor and who have problems in functioning."[8] Among "the various dysfunctions

---

[5] Mincy in Joint Economic Committee, *The Underclass*, pp. 3, 4, 6.

[6] Mincy in Joint Economic Committee, *The Underclass*, pp. 2, 4.

[7] Lawrence M. Mead, *Beyond Entitlement: The Obligations of Citizenship* (1986), and *The New Politics of Poverty: The Nonworking Poor in America* (1992), on which his testimony draws.

[8] Lawrence Mead in Joint Economic Committee, *The Underclass*, pp. 21 and 28. "To explain the underclass means, in essence, to

56   Part One: The Tale

that define the "group," Mead is particularly perturbed by
what he calls "nonwork" among the residents of the hyperghetto, where "an alien subculture opposed to self-reliance has
arisen that may be feeding on itself." He sees nonwork as a
product of "social isolation, permissive welfare, and attitudes
contrary to work," whereby young men "reject available jobs
as beneath them" while welfare mothers are "defeatist" and
"overwhelmed by the demands of working."[9]

"The greatest danger" to America's future

"The greatest danger [to America's future] is the existence
of an ignorant, debased and permanently poor class in the
great cities. ... The members of it come at length to form
and separate population. They embody the lowest passions
and the most thriftless habits of the community. They corrupt
the lowest class of working-poor who are around them. The
expense of police, of prisons, of charities and means of relief,
arise mainly from them."

Charles Loring Brace, *Second Annual Report*
of the Children's Aid Society, 1855

According to this mish-mash of rational choice, magazine
psychology, and cultural determinism, the "underclass" is
made up of individuals who are devoid of "economic competence"; they do not "seek to get ahead and seize opportunities
and go to work without prompting" or "we wouldn't have an
underclass in the first place."[10] It follows that the state should
design policies aiming to "liberat[e] the will to get ahead in
these people" by forging economic competence rather than
presuming it. Mead expounds: "So we have to be willing to

---

explain the demoralized mindset that leads to the functioning problems of the group, which in turn usually cause its poverty. The puzzle
is to explain why people engage in behaviors, such as illegitimacy,
crime, and nonwork, which are irrational for the individual's long-
term interest, let alone society's" (p. 30).

[9] Mead in Joint Economic Committee, *The Underclass*, pp. 33, 24, 34.
[10] Mead in Joint Economic Committee, *The Underclass*, p. 24.

"The tragedy of the underclass" 57

be tutelary. We have to be willing to set up a structure to some extent paternalist. I don't see any alternative to that." Such paternalist oversight would take the form of diligent law enforcement to prevent inner-city men from escaping into the criminal economy and compelling single mothers receiving welfare to work at low-wage jobs.

The third expert witness is Elijah Anderson (PhD from Northwestern, 1976), a leading African-American sociologist and professor at the University of Pennsylvania whose ethnographic work focuses on the social peregrinations of young black men in and out of the hyperghetto.[11] Anderson takes the "underclass" as defined in prior testimony and zeroes in on the demise of an institution that he deems historically central to the black community, namely, the mentoring relation between "old heads" and youths. This relationship used to "socialize young men to meet their responsibilities with regard to the work ethic, family life, law, common decency." In the olden days, the old head could be a minister, a teacher, an athletic coach, a policeman, or a corner man. He acted as a "kind of guidance counselor and moral cheerleader who preached anticrime and antitrouble messages to his charges." But the old head has been undermined by the disappearance of stable working-class jobs and consigned to social irrelevance by the rise of the drug economy. He is now being supplanted by his living antithesis, the successful narcotics dealer who leads a "fast life" of crime, vice, and conspicuous consumption on the street.[12]

Anderson is not fully at ease with the behavioral definition of the "underclass" he is set up to work from, because his research requires him to engage face-to-face with the human beings presumed to belong to it, and he cannot but be disquieted by the deprecatory cast of the notion – at one point, he slips and refers to one of the subjects of his ethnography as "a young man of the so-called underclass." Anderson is at pains to stress that "even in the most destitute neighborhoods, decent people continue to believe in the infinite value of work,

---

[11] Anderson is about to publish *Streetwise: Race, Class, and Change in an Urban Community* (1990).

[12] Anderson in Joint Economic Committee, *The Underclass*, pp. 43 and 46.

58   Part One: The Tale

even for jobs that are increasingly unavailable."[13] But the very
opposition between "decent" and "street" people he invokes
to salvage the worthy residents of "underclass areas" reac-
tivates the same moral cleavage between the dysfunctional
and the deserving poor that Mincy and Mead had laid down
for him. His call for public policies designed to bring back
the "old heads" sounds like nostalgic yearning for a bygone
era of caste relations and his micro-focus on social relations
internal to the hyperghetto undercuts the plausibility of his
advocacy for job-training programs.

Remarkably for a committee ostensibly tasked with clari-
fying economic issues, the debate following expert testimony
turns entirely on race and welfare in the inner city. Estimates
of the size of the "underclass" are weighed (they range from
2 to 10 million or one-third of all poor Americans). Mead
reasserts that the inability of the group "to function" is
rooted "in lifestyle rather than in the structure of things" and
bemoans "the breakdown of social authority involving the
schools, involving the welfare system, involving law enforcement." When representative Solarz asks him, "Why do they
prefer to be on welfare rather than to work?," the political
scientist confesses: "I don't know. *That is really the ultimate
mystery.*"[14] The chair of the proceedings closes them by
beseeching the experts: "Before we adjourn this hearing – and
it has been a most interesting, if somewhat depressing hearing
– can somebody say something of an upbeat nature that will
leave us with some hope?"[15]

The upshot of the hearing was contained in its title and
opening: *the "underclass" exists* since state officials can hold
a public meeting about it and inquire into its features; experts
can measure it, detect its moral failings, and even encounter its members on the streets. Objective data reveal that it
is growing; it resides in the decaying urban core; it is overwhelmingly if not exclusively African American (motivating
the selection of two black witnesses out of three); it threatens

[13] Anderson in Joint Economic Committee, *The Underclass*, pp. 58,
   47.
[14] Mead in Joint Economic Committee, *The Underclass*, pp. 50, 52, 67
   (my italics).
[15] Joint Economic Committee, *The Underclass*, p. 75.

"The tragedy of the underclass" 59

to become permanent; it is a burden and a menace to society due to its dysfunctional behaviors. The sense of foreboding and mystery enshrouding the category in contemporaneous media portrayals is not dispelled but reinforced by the three experts – who agree that more research is urgently needed. The latter's authority is boosted by the fact that the hearing is finely calibrated to achieve political equilibrium, with Mincy occupying a neutral mid-point between the conservative Mead and the liberal Anderson.

This bureaucratic ceremonial involving protagonists drawn from the academic, think tank, and political fields who are convinced of its reality has the effect of elevating the "underclass" to the rank of official "social problem" officially worthy of state concern and public intervention.[16] It is easy to imagine how different the outcome of such a hearing would have been if the committee had invited the sociologist William Julius Wilson (a proponent of a neo-ecological approach to the "underclass," stressing the effects of concentrated joblessness), the social historian Michael Katz (a dogged critic of the notion), or the Marxist political scientist Adolph Reed (a caustic debunker of the category and its political uses).

Ratified by government publications and hearings, the hybrid (re)construction, part policy-philanthropic and part journalistic, of the "underclass" as social menace in the hyperghetto then *reentered the academic field* to impact social research, by ensuring that the works of those who adopted it as their framing category garnered lavish foundation support, professional attention, and media interest. So much so that the notion quickly superseded the hackneyed problematic of the "culture of poverty" and attained hegemonic status.[17] By the close of the 1980s, it was virtually impossible to write about race and poverty in the American metropolis without coming to terms with the "underclass," if only to quarrel over

---

[16] The invention, design and staging of bureaucratic commissions, and their role in the social construction of public issues calling for public remedies, are discussed in Pierre Bourdieu, *Sur l'État. Cours du Collège de France, 1989–1992* (2012), pp. 47–54.

[17] Michael Morris, "From the Culture of Poverty to the Underclass: An Analysis of a Shift in Public Language" (1989).

60   Part One: The Tale

its features, wrangle over its definition, or dispute its existence and disown the term altogether.

Between 1987 and 1995, a rapid-fire succession of major
scholarly publications anointed the "underclass" as *category du jour*: William Julius Wilson published *The Truly
Disadvantaged: The Inner City, the Underclass, and Public
Policy* (1987) to considerable acclaim and impact (the book
garnered a full-page review in *Time* magazine as well as a
shout-out from President Clinton, and shortly afterward
Wilson received a McArthur Foundation "genius" award);
the *Annals of the American Academy of Social and Political
Science* released a thematic issue on the "underclass" (republished as a book a couple of years later), as did *The Black
Scholar*, the *International Journal of Urban and Regional
Research*, *Urban Geography* and *Focus*, the periodical of
the Institute for Research on Poverty (a special issue made
possible by a special grant from, who else, the Rockefeller
Foundation); and the *Annual Review of Sociology* devoted
an article to the topic, while interest in the debate and puz-
zlement at the category diffused into neighboring disciplines:
demography, anthropology, psychology, criminology, social
work, medicine, psychiatry, and even pediatrics. The intellectual excitement (or reticence) about the "underclass" across
disciplines was such that the *Chronicle of Higher Education*
published not one but three lengthy reports on it in successive
years.[18]

In 1991, the Brookings Institution released a canonical
volume soberly entitled *The Urban Underclass* (1991), resulting from a three-day conference, organized in 1989 by the
SSRC with funding from the Rockefeller Foundation and the
Ford Foundation, gathering a Who's Who of normal scholars
of poverty, and launched by a Washington press conference

---

[18] Chris Raymond, "Scholars Examining the Plight of the Urban Poor
Broaden Scope of Research on the 'Underclass'," notes that "once
confined to economics, studies now include fields from cultural
anthropology to politics" (1989); idem, "American Underclass Grew
from 1970 to 1980, Study Indicates" (1990); and Karen J. Winkler,
"Researcher's Examination of California's Poor Latin Population
Prompts Debate over the Traditional Definitions of the Underclass"
(1990).

"The tragedy of the underclass" 61

covered by *The Wall Street Journal*. In 1992, a group of black philosophers led by Bill Lawson joined the fray to engage *The Underclass Question* (1992) – "the first collective written intervention on a specific topic by black philosophers in U.S. history." The same year, Douglas Massey and Nancy Denton subtitled their landmark book on *American Apartheid, Segregation and the Making of the Underclass* (1992), even though they do not bother to define the category in it, while Christopher Jencks published an opportunistic collection of review essays under the title, *Rethinking Social Policy: Race, Poverty, and the Underclass* (1992).[19]

A counter-attack soon ensued: in 1992, the black political scientist Adolph Reed dissected "The 'Underclass' as Myth and Symbol" in *Radical America*, arguing that the academic success of the category resided in its "appeal to hoary prejudices of race, gender, and class." A year later, a group of eminent historians led by Michael Katz (who was official archivist for the SSRC Research Committee on the Urban Underclass) questioned the notion in *The "Underclass" Debate: The View from History* (1993), moving the analytic focus from individual and family pathology to the transformation of institutions, politics, and the state. They were following in the footsteps of Jacqueline Jones's critique in *The Dispossessed: America's Underclasses from the Civil War to the Present* (1992), which stressed the agency of the poor, black and white, rural and urban, in the face of a century of labor repression, political disenfranchisement, racial domination, and structural dislocation. Two years later Herbert Gans released his biting deconstruction of the "underclass" in *The War Against the Poor: The Underclass and Antipoverty Policy* (1995), cataloguing the manifold sociopolitical functions

[19] William Julius Wilson, *The Truly Disadvantaged: The Inner City, the Underclass, and Public Policy* (1987); Carole Marks, "The Urban Underclass" (1991); Christopher Jencks and Paul E. Peterson (eds.), *The Urban Underclass* (1991); Bill E. Lawson (ed.), *The Underclass Question* (1992, Preface by William Julius Wilson); Douglas Massey and Nancy A. Denton, *American Apartheid: Segregation and the Making of the Underclass* (1993); Christopher Jencks, *Rethinking Social Policy: Race, Poverty, and the Underclass* (1992).

62   Part One: The Tale

played by the vituperation of the urban poor in American society and history.[20]

At about the same moment, across the Atlantic, European scholars caught notice of the American furore. They labored to puzzle out the sudden eruption of scholarly publications about the "underclass" and the perplexing plural meaning of this new term – and how to translate it.[21] They wondered about its relationship to the problematic of "exclusion," then dominant across the continent thanks to the policy endorsement and research funding of the European Commission (which played for "exclusion" a role analogous to that of American philanthropies for the "underclass"). They turned to asking whether there was a French, German, Dutch, British, Irish, or Polish "underclass" emerging in their polarizing cities, by which they meant some combination of the working poor, the long-term unemployed, postcolonial migrants, and the residents of marginalized neighborhoods – absent any behavioral or moral features. So much so that a Danish scholar was prompted to ask in 1995, "The Underclass Debate: A Spreading Disease?"[22] And when, that same year, a

---

[20] Adolph L. Reed, "The 'Underclass' as Myth and Symbol: The Poverty of Discourse about Poverty" (1992); Jacqueline Jones, *The Dispossessed: America's Underclasses from the Civil War to the Present* (1992); Michael B. Katz (ed.), *The "Underclass" Debate: Views from History* (1993a); and Herbert J. Gans, *The War Against the Poor: The Underclass and Anti-Poverty Policy* (1995).

[21] In the French translation of Wilson's 1987 book, *Les Oubliés de l'Amérique* (Desclée de Brouwer, 1994), the sociologist Ivan Ermakoff (mis)translates "underclass" by *sous-prolétariat*. In French journals of sociology, the term is kept in italics in the English original.

[22] John Andersen, "The Underclass Debate: A Spreading Disease?" (1995). A panorama of European studies of/on the "underclass" is Barbara Schmitter Heisler, "A Comparative Perspective on the Underclass" (1991); Sako Musterd, "A Rising European Underclass?" (1994); Nicolas Herpin, "L'*urban underclass*' chez les sociologues américains: exclusion sociale et pauvreté" (1993); Cyprien Avenel, "La question de l'*underclass*' des deux côtés de l'Atlantique" (1997); Jean-Charles Lagrée, "Exclusion sociale ou formation d'une *underclass*?" (1995); Jens S. Dangschat, "Concentration of Poverty in the Landscapes of 'Boomtown' Hamburg: The Creation of a New Urban Underclass?" (1994); Hartmut Häußermann, "Armut in den

"The tragedy of the underclass" 63

distinguished left-wing Italian sociologist assembled a collection of contemporary essays on urban inequality, marginality, and policy on the two sides of the Atlantic, he was *forced* by the British publisher Basil Blackwell to include the word "underclass" in the title, and then denied the pressing request of the contributors to the book that the term be put in quotations marks, evidence that the notion had become part of the Newspeak of American categories circulating around the globe, thanks to the unrivaled symbolic power of the United States to naturalize its historical peculiarities (here the nexus of caste, class, and state in the postindustrial metropolis) by falsely universalizing them.[23]

During this pivotal period, the accelerating circulation of the "underclass" across the frontiers of academic research, policy think-tanks and politics, and journalism solidified its place in the social and scholarly imaginary of America. It also *blurred the distinctions between the three discursive varieties* and facilitated the sharing of references and the tacit transfer of meaning and imagery from one field to the other, so that one cannot grasp the social scientific, policy-philanthropic, and media signification of the "underclass" except *in relation to one another*, as elements of a triadic semantic constellation.

Großstädten: eine neue städtische Unterklasse?" (1997); Martin Kronauer, "Armut, Ausgrenzung, Unterklasse" (1998); Robert C. Kloosterman, "The Making of the Dutch Underclass? A Labour Market View" (1990); Theo Roelandt and Justus Veenman, "An Emerging Ethnic Underclass in the Netherlands? Some Empirical Evidence" (1992); John Westergaard, "About and Beyond the 'Underclass': Some Notes on Influences of Social Climate on British Sociology Today" (1992); Paul Bagguley and Kirk Mann, "'Idle Thieving Bastards'? Scholarly Representations of the 'Underclass'" (1992); Lydia D. Morris, "Is There a British Underclass?" (1993), and *Dangerous Classes: The Underclass and Social Citizenship* (1994); Christopher T. Whelan, "Marginalization, Deprivation, and Fatalism in the Republic of Ireland: Class and Underclass Perspectives" (1996); and Elżbieta Tarkowska, "In Search of an Underclass in Poland" (1999).

[23] Enzo Mingione (ed.), *Urban Poverty and the Underclass: A Reader* (1995); Pierre Bourdieu and Loïc Wacquant, "On the Cunning of Imperialist Reason" (1999 [1998]).

64   Part One: The Tale

Reflecting on this period of symbolic frenzy in 1993, Douglas Massey observes that "empirical studies of the underclass carried out by social scientists have mirrored the popular media stereotypes" according to which persistent urban poverty is a "*Black* problem" epitomized by "jobless young Black men and unwed Black welfare mothers." He gives a good account of the *lemming effect* that sent scholars in droves over a conceptual precipice and propelled the category to the top of the research agenda without regard for its constitutive ambiguity and moral import:

> With foundation budgets being earmarked for underclass initiatives, with conferences on the underclass being held every few months, with committees on the underclass being formed at the Social Science Research Council and elsewhere, with congressional hearings on urban poverty going full steam, and with the press vigorously pursuing the "underclass debate", it seemed sensible to insist that Latinos be included.

It was wise to adopt the problematic predetermined by journalistic vogue and policy dictates. In "a time of growing scarcity and increasing competition for resources," the decision to "climb aboard the underclass bandwagon" seemed the more reasonable one. So Hispanics tried to "muscle their way in the poverty limelight."[24] Among the products of this rush figured a working group, a conference, and an edited volume sponsored by the Russell Sage Foundation showing that the notion of "underclass" was *not* useful to grasp poverty patterns among Latino groups.[25]

The existence of the "underclass" was thus established through a classic form of *argumentum ad populum*, the logical fallacy of "appealing to the people" (sometimes called the bandwagon fallacy), whereby one takes a belief to be true because many others accept it (the epistemic variant), or one gains assent to a proposition by arousing the feelings of the multitude (the emotive variant).[26] Scholars referring

---

[24] Douglas S. Massey, "Latinos, Poverty, and the Underclass: A New Agenda for Research" (1993), p. 450.

[25] Joan Moore and Raquel Pinderhughes (eds.), *In the Barrio: Latinos and the Underclass Debate* (1993).

[26] Benjamin W. McCraw, "Appeal to the People" (2018).

"The tragedy of the underclass" 65

to Ken Auletta's book in which Auletta himself refers to a putative consensus among scholars or think-tank officials is an example of the former; the political scientist and conservative advocate James Q. Wilson illustrates the latter when he erupts:

> Despite the efforts of some to discourage the use of the word "underclass," it is nonsense to pretend that such a group does not exist or is not a threat. The reason why it is called an underclass and why we worry about it is that its members have a bad character: they mug, do drugs, desert children, and scorn education.[27]

---

[27] James Q. Wilson, "Redefining Equality: The Liberalism of Mickey Kaus" (1992), p. 103.

3

Anatomy: The three faces of the "underclass"

~

Now that I have retraced the genealogy of the "underclass," I can turn to its anatomy. Rather than partition the various uses of the term by the putative political leanings of their proponents – conservative, liberal, or radical – I propose to cluster them, on an analytic basis, into three broad families depending on whether they emphasize the *structure* of the economy and labor market, the *behavior* and cultural proclivities of the individuals incriminated, or the social characteristics of the *neighborhood* and proximate human milieu in which they evolve. Of these three conceptions, the structural, the behavioral and the neo-ecological, it is the second, whose semantic charge is shock-full of degrading associations, that occupied the front and center of the intellectual and political stage at the acme of the "underclass" debate.[1] It enjoyed a near complete hegemony, scarcely dented by the proponents

---

[1] This is attested by Robert Aponte, "Definitions of the Underclass: A Critical Analysis" (1990); Christopher Jencks, "Is the American Underclass Growing?" (1991); Ronald B. Mincy, "The Underclass: Concept, Controversy, and Evidence" (1994); Joel A. Devine, and James D. Wright, *The Greatest of Evils: Urban Poverty and the American Underclass* (1993), chs. 4 and 6; and Herbert J. Gans, *The War Against the Poor: The Underclass and Anti-Poverty Policy* (1995), ch. 2.

The three faces of the "underclass"   67

of a neo-ecological approach intent on integrating structural, spatial, and individual factors.

1. At the origins, the "under-class" as structural position

The first use of the word "underclass" recorded by the *Oxford English Dictionary* is by the Scottish revolutionary socialist John Maclean (1879–1923) who, during his trial for sedition in 1918, asserted that "the whole history of society has proved that society moves forward as a consequence of an under-class overcoming the resistance of a class on top of them." The term did not catch on among British communists already equipped with the full class taxonomy furnished by Marx. As a contemporary keyword of public debate, we owe this terminological innovation to the Nobel Prize economist Gunnar Myrdal in his 1963 book *Challenge to Affluence*, which he wrote as a manner of sequel and complement to his classic 1944 tome on *An American Dilemma*. Whereas *Dilemma* tackled the explosive but nonetheless improving "Negro problem" of the United States, *Challenge* warns about the overlooked yet worsening issue of class inequality and rising marginality facing the same country as a result of changes in economic structure and functioning.[2]

Going against the grain of the ambient optimism prevalent at the start of the 1960s – John Kenneth Galbraith was celebrating the advent of "the affluent society" and Daniel Bell heralding "the end of ideology"[3] – Myrdal debunks the fiction of a "free and open" American society in which anyone can rise up the socioeconomic ladder and prosper if only they have the will to do so. He sounds the alarm at the emergence of "an 'under-class' of unemployed and, gradually,

[2] Gunnar Myrdal, *Challenge to Affluence* (1963). Remarkably, Myrdal does not use the term "underclass" even once in the fifteen hundred pages of *An American Dilemma: The Negro Problem and Modern Democracy* (1944).

[3] John Kenneth Galbraith, *The Affluent Society* (1958), and Daniel Bell, *The End of Ideology: On the Exhaustion of Political Ideas* (1960).

68   Part One: The Tale

unemployable and underemployed persons and families at the bottom of a society" who are "not really an integrated part of the nation but a useless and miserable substratum."[4]

To dramatize this peril for "the very tenets of American society" that he reveres, Myrdal is inspired by the Swedish term *underklass* which, in nineteenth-century literary language, designated the lower stratum and delineated the opposition between the bottom and the top tiers of the class spectrum, with the latter bearing the name of *överklass*. Myrdal introduces the notion with this caveat:

> The word "under-class" does not seem to be used in English. In America where, as opinion polls over several decades show, the great majority reckon themselves as "middle class," this is particularly understandable on ideological grounds. Nevertheless, the term will be used in this book as the only one adequate to the social reality discussed.[5]

A novel term is necessitated by the brute fact that, while "abject destitution for millions of people is nothing new" in the United States, until now "there has been no under-class of hopeless people, conditioned to living apart from the rest of the nation" by the "closing of opportunities" at the foot of the social hierarchy.[6]

This worrisome trend has two main springs, according to Myrdal: the continual rise of labor productivity through technological upgrading and automation, on the one hand, and the steady opening of access to higher education, on the other. These two factors are combining to destroy unskilled jobs by

[4] Myrdal, *Challenge to Affluence*, pp. 34–5.
[5] Myrdal, *Challenge to Affluence*, p. 34n. This anticipates almost word for word the justification that Wilson will give a quarter-century later for his use of the term in *The Truly Disadvantaged* (1987, p. 7). Notably, the Americanization of the term by Myrdal effaced its original negative moral valence: "With a certain aplomb, Myrdal had picked up the old, somewhat disreputable and politically incorrect Swedish word *underklass*, employed mostly in bourgeois circles, particularly in the early and mid-twentieth century, to refer to conduct lacking in good manners and knowledge of etiquette." Ulf Hannerz, "Afterword: Soulside Revisited" (2004), p. 213.
[6] Myrdal, *Challenge to Affluence*, pp. 36, 11, 16.

The three faces of the "underclass"   69

the millions and effectively render obsolete a growing segment of the working class residing in the inner cities and the rural hinterland. For the most dispossessed, a *caste-like barrier* is being erected, as eviction from the productive sphere due to postindustrial innovation is entrenched by the corporatist stance of unions and public policies favoring the enlargement of the middle class. Thus, whereas most of America enjoys increased social and economic mobility through higher education, "beneath that level a line is drawn to an 'under-class'. That class line becomes demarcated almost as a caste line, since the children in this class tend to become as poorly endowed as their parents."

In the absence of corrective policies, social marginality amidst plenty becomes self-perpetuating according to the mechanism of "circular cumulative causation" that Myrdal had famously introduced in *An America Dilemma* to explain the continued subordination of African Americans: because of its economic deprivation, the underclass will be "forced to live in slums" where "the schools will be bad" while "the whole way of life" is "destructive for the will and ability to advance in life."[7] Myrdal predicts that the crystallization of a hardened core of the permanently unemployed will be accompanied by the rise and spread of anomie, social isolation and criminality, but also by the growing demoralization of families sacrificed on the altar of economic modernization. For, in a wealthy society dominated by a Puritan ethic centered on occupational competition, being shorn of employment strips one of the means of acquiring self-respect and social dignity. The absence of political representation closes the "vicious cycle of circular causation" in which America's new social outcasts find themselves locked out of national prosperity: "Poor people in America are mute, inarticulate, and inactive" on the electoral front, "with the result that they have not gotten a fair deal" and are now "facing the greatest dangers."[8]

Myrdal invokes the term "under-class" but with parsimony and prudence – and when he does, he takes pain to spell it with a hyphen and to enclose it in quotation marks.

[7] Myrdal, *Challenge to Affluence*, pp. 38 and 42.
[8] Myrdal, *Challenge to Affluence*, p. 99.

70   Part One: The Tale

In his view, such a collective is less a firmly established reality than a "new threat" looming on the horizon of postindustrial society.[9] Its presumed configuration is nonetheless clear: it rests on a *position at the very bottom of the class structure*; it is rural as well as urban, and black and Hispanic as well as white. The circular interlock of joblessness and inferior living conditions is particular potent among African Americans – Myrdal sees it as the "greatest danger threatening the gratifying upward trend in race relations in America" – but it also affects Puerto Ricans and Mexicans as well as "poor white people everywhere in America who will be pressed down, and by the vicious circle held down."[10]

Finally, the volume and fate of the underclass are directly impacted by public policies with regards to education, job training, housing, public assistance, and urban development. For Myrdal, it is the very character of the economy, and more specifically slow growth combining with the upgrading of the occupational distribution leading to a widening "structural discrepancy between labor demand and labor supply"[11] at the bottom, that is the driving causal factor, and not the character of individuals, their everyday conduct, or the culture of the groups to which they belong. The critical element is the slackened or broken link to the world of wage labor, and the only true remedy for the "curse of permanent joblessness" is "vigorous public policies" across the board stimulating growth and producing full employment.

Myrdal's analysis of the social implications of the "sluggish and jerky development of the American economy" for class structure, mobility, and politics at the bottom was in many respects prescient: it anticipated by two to three decades crucial debates on the growth of inequality, the polarization of life chances, the rising premium granted to college credentials on the labor market, the resurgence of the informal and criminal economy in the metropolis, and the demoralizing effects of long-term economic redundancy, whether in

[9] Myrdal, *Challenge to Affluence*, pp. 37–9. The use of the hyphen is notable here, as it is clearly intended to stress the term's social relationality.
[10] Myrdal, *Challenge to Affluence*, p. 45.
[11] Myrdal, *Challenge to Affluence*, p. 16.

The three faces of the "underclass"　　71

the form of joblessness or job precariousness; and it foretold the incapacity of Keynesian policies to accelerate economic growth and ameliorate these problems.[12] Yet it failed to make either an academic or a policy mark. In his biography of the Swedish scholar and statesman, Walter Jackson notes that "most American reviewers failed to appreciate the originality and breadth of vision of *Challenge to Affluence*" because, due to his fame and frequent engagements with broader publics, researchers "had begun to see Myrdal more as a prophet and a social critic than a technical economist."[13]

On the policy front, the impact of *Challenge to Affluence* was preempted by the publication a year earlier of Michael Harrington's *The Other America*, which captured the attention of journalists and the fancy of progressive politicians thanks to its vivid human vignettes and the more palatable claim that American poverty was residual and somewhat extraneous to the national body, rather than a phenomenon on the rise woven deep into its economic makeup as asserted by Myrdal.[14] As we saw earlier, the concept of "culture of poverty" forged by the anthropologist Oscar Lewis also monopolized the attention of social scientists concerned with urban marginality and poverty policy.

The scholars who made analytical use of the structural concept forged by Myrdal are few and far between, and they are, moreover, almost never cited in the subsequent American debate on caste and poverty in the city. For example, the highly regarded monograph by Lee Rainwater, *Behind Ghetto Walls*, a three-year team field study of black tenants in a St. Louis low-income project published in 1970, concludes on a somber warning that "the relative deprivation of the underclass is at the heart of their marginality and their

---

[12] The chapter on "Unemployment and poverty" containing the core discussion of the "under-class" is reprinted in full in the selection of key texts by Myrdal, *The Essential Gunnar Myrdal* (2005), pp. 133–143.

[13] Walter A. Jackson, *Gunnar Myrdal and America's Conscience: Social Engineering and Racial Liberalism, 1938–1987* (1990, new ed. 2014), p. 347.

[14] Michael Harrington *The Other America: Poverty in the United States* (1962).

72   Part One: The Tale

alienation." In line with Myrdal, and against the theme of
the "other America," Rainwater insists that America's elite
had better "stop deluding themselves about the underclass.
It is the product of an economic system so designed that it
generates a destructive amount of income inequality."[15] But,
when *Behind Ghetto Walls* is invoked in later discussions, it
is for its portrayal of the family life and economic strategies
of poor blacks, not its inadvertent income-based definition
of an "underclass." Similarly, in 1977, the economist Frank
Levy of the Urban Institute in Washington followed a neo-
Myrdalian track in a working paper entitled "How Big Is the
American Underclass?"[16] Levy used data from the Michigan
Panel Study of Income Dynamics to estimate the size of the
population that was persistently poor, that is, falling below
the official "poverty line" during five of the seven years
between 1967 and 1973. He computed that about 9 million
individuals were persistently poor, a group that was 70%
non-white and made up of children for 70%. But his estimate did not draw interest among analysts of urban poverty,
even in the world of policy institutes. It came too early for
that.

One has to migrate to the United Kingdom to find the
term flourishing a decade after Myrdal's coinage under the
pen of the young English sociologist Anthony Giddens, in his
noted 1973 book on *The Class Structure of the Advanced
Societies*.[17] Giddens proposes that we are in the presence of

[15] Lee Rainwater, *Behind Ghetto Walls: Black Family Life in a Federal
Slum* (1970), pp. vii and 323–4. A year earlier, Rainwater had edited
an issue of the social science magazine *Trans-Action* on the "urban
underclass" but none of the articles in it elaborated the notion and it
went unnoticed.

[16] Frank Levy, *How Big Is the American Underclass?* (1977). The paper
was originally written in 1974 while Levy was at Berkeley's School
of Public Policy. It remained unpublished (it was unsuccessfully submitted to the *Journal of Human Resources*). Personal communication
with Frank Levy, September 3, 2020.

[17] At the time, Giddens had yet to morph into an abstract social theorist
and displayed an abiding interest in issues of elite and class formation. His book addresses current topics in class theory, particularly
the need to supplement discredited Marxist accounts of structural
dualization and working-class impoverishment with a neo-Weberian

The three faces of the "underclass" 73

an "underclass" whenever "ethnic differences act as a 'disqualifying' market capacity, such that those in the category in question are heavily concentrated in the lowest paid occupations, or are chronically unemployed or semi-employed."[18]

According to this definition, the "underclass" represents the most precarious segment of the working class due to the intersection of economic and ethnic cleavages. It is causally related to the growing dualization of the labor market, between a "primary" set of protected jobs at the core of the economy and a "secondary" set of "insecure occupations yielding only a low rate of economic return" and filled by a floating workforce.[19] The presence of a "vast, highly structured underclass" composed of urban blacks emerges as a central feature of American social and political life by the early 1970s. In European countries, by contrast, the foundation of the "underclass" is both narrower and more fragile owing to its recent recruitment amongst immigrant workers from the Third World.[20] Whereas Myrdal used the term "underclass" to spotlight a marginalized segment of the postindustrial working class irrespective of the makeup of its occupants, Giddens makes membership in a subordinate ethnic category one of its two constitutive features.

This dual structural conception of the underclass as *class position inflected by ethnicity* was picked up and further developed by another of Britain's leading sociologists, the South African John Rex, as a key component of a neo-Weberian theory of ethnic domination and class formation. In *Colonial Immigrants in a British City: A Class Analysis* (1979), a landmark study of immigrant incorporation in Birmingham conducted with Sally Tomlinson, Rex asks "whether there is any tendency at all for the formation of specifically important underclass groupings marked by a separate fate and by the

---

analysis of embourgeoisement. The question of the bases, composition, size, and political proclivities of the middle class(es) was then salient in the study of inequality (e.g., Nicholas Abercrombie and John Urry, *Capital, Labour, and the Middle Classes* [1983]).

[18] Anthony Giddens, *The Class Structure of the Advanced Societies* (1973), p. 113.

[19] Giddens, *Class Structure of the Advanced Societies*, p. 289.

[20] Giddens, *Class Structure of the Advanced Societies*, pp. 216–18.

74 Part One: The Tale

emergence of incipient immigrant labour organisation."[21] He proposes that the "underclass" is a class position situated below and apart from the working class due to the systematic bifurcation of South Asian and Caribbean laborers from the native working class, not just in employment, but also in housing and education. Brought to England by the collapse of the imperial social structure, those immigrants have sought to adjust to British society but they have been met with prejudice, stigma, and discrimination, such that they have not merged into the homegrown working class. Yet Rex does not adopt Myrdal's model wholesale and he does not share his pessimism as regards the future of the "underclass."

First, the institutional context of class formation in the United Kingdom is not the competitive individualism of the marketplace of the United States but the achievement of basic social and economic rights guaranteed by the welfare state. Second, for Rex, the West Indian and Asian populations of England are not "a despairing mass" that has "rotted in the ghetto for several generations" as have African Americans, and so they are not beset by demoralization and social involution.[22] Stuck in unskilled and low-paid jobs, concentrated in inferior and separate housing, funneled into segregated schools, Asians and West Indians have been compelled to develop their own labor and political outfits. The result is that they are forming, not just an "underclass-in-itself," defined by exclusion from the social benefits granted to the working class by the state, but also an "underclass-for-itself," endowed with "its own form of organization, culture, political goals and ideology."[23] This growing subjective consciousness of occupying a distinctive position in both industry and the city among the children of Third-World immigrants promises, not further marginalization, but a growing ethno-class conflict and political struggles for full equality, of which the riots of 1981 sparked by clashes between immigrant youths and the police were one oblique manifestation.

---

[21] John Rex and Sally Tomlinson, *Colonial Immigrants in a British City: A Class Analysis* (1979), p. 9.

[22] John Rex, *The Ghetto and the Underclass: Essays on Race and Social Policy* (1988), p. 29.

[23] Rex, *The Ghetto and the Underclass*, p. 113.

The brewing American debate on the "underclass" never engaged these British works; it developed in complete isolation from the rest of world research, in keeping with the doxic parochialism of the national social science that makes it acceptable to ignore germane investigations conducted in other countries, even when these are published in English. But one can draw two lessons from this brief British detour. The "dual model" of the underclass throws into relief two tacit presumptions made by all analysts of the "underclass" in the United States: that the market is a natural and fair mechanism for the allocation of persons to positions and that the state has but a limited capacity to provide essential goods to its population. Next, the work of British scholars demonstrates that *Myrdal's structural concept was viable when inserted into a neo-Weberian class theory* centered on market capacities and it did not have to devolve into a behavioral term of vituperation. Indeed, this neo-Weberian notion was further developed and debated in the 1990s by British sociologists when the "underclass" made its way back to the intellectual foreground as a result of the importation of the American discussion.[24]

Returning to the United States, the analyses of Douglas Glasgow in *The Black Underclass: Poverty, Unemployment, and the Entrapment of Ghetto Youth*, published in 1980, fit the mold of this expanded structural conception – Douglas explicitly credits Myrdal in the opening pages of his book.[25] They are rarely cited and never discussed, because they appeared just before the moral panic of the "underclass" took off to reach national proportions and likely because they come from social work, a practical discipline situated at the periphery of the standard circles of social science debate.

---

[24] A recapitulation of this second British debate on the "underclass" triggered by American imports is Robert Moore, "Rediscovering the Underclass" (2014).

[25] Douglas Glasgow, *The Black Underclass: Poverty, Unemployment, and Entrapment of Ghetto Youth* (1980), p. 3. The book is based on dissertation research conducted into the mid-1970s. Douglas went on to become professor of social work at Howard University; he later helped found the Black Men's Development Center and the National Association of Black Social Workers.

76   Part One: The Tale

Drawing on a study of the social trajectories and strategies of participants to the 1965 Watts riots, Glasgow maintains that the "underclass" is an incontrovertible social fact, a permanent location in the urban class structure occupied by black youths trapped in the dispossessed districts of the crumbling ghetto. Three interrelated mechanisms fuel its consolidation:[26] first, racial exclusion, brutal and overt prior to the revolts of the 1960s, more subtle and disguised since; next, the systematic practices of rejection by official institutions, prominent among them the school, which mutilates the life chances of the youths of poor black districts and consigns them to social failure; lastly, eviction from the wage-labor sphere, which spawns a large supernumerary population whose control redounds to the police as well as to the welfare and medical sectors of the state.

For Glasgow, however, the "underclass" is best differentiated from the lower class by its *social immobility*. The label, as he uses it, "implies no connotation of undeservingness," and no attribution of any psychological flaw or cultural incapacity. Regardless of whether they adopt mainstream orientations or seek refuge in a "culture of survival" that clashes with dominant norms, the residents of America's urban Bantustans are condemned to unremitting relegation. It follows that Glasgow forcefully denounces the three pernicious "myths" according to which hyperghetto youths would be indifferent to social striving and success, unmotivated to work, and eager to join the ranks of the welfare-dependent.[27] It is remarkable that, even though he dealt frontally with all the issues that would preoccupy American students of the "underclass" in the closing decades of twentieth century, including the need for welfare reform, job training, school upgrading, and the political mobilization of the poor, Glasgow's work was generally ignored by them.

Another tome on the "underclass" was widely read by sociologists of penality and criminologists, among whom it quickly acquired the status of a mini-classic, but, again, failed to attract the notice of policy-oriented scholars due to disciplinary blinders: John Irwin's *The Jail: Managing the Underclass*

---

[26] Glasgow, *The Black Underclass*, pp. 1–11.
[27] Glasgow, *The Black Underclass*, pp. 178–81.

The three faces of the "underclass"

in American Society (1985), an ethnography of the processing of inmates in three San Francisco detention facilities inspired by the microsociology of Erving Goffman.[28] Irwin argues that the jail, whose population doubled nationally over the preceding decade, does not serve to fight crime so much as to regulate and reproduce "the rabble," which he characterizes as those urban poor who are both socially detached and disreputable. It subjects its clientele to social disintegration, cultural disorientation, and personal degradation, and inadvertently increases the size and solidifies the status of the rabble. Irwin stresses that the regular clients of the jail suffer from ethnic discrimination and structural unemployment, as well as from "changes in the economy, immigration patterns, government policies, and a shift in cultural values," as a result of which they are in the process of joining a "permanent and large underclass, whose members for all intents and purposes are outside society."[29]

Irwin borrows the term "underclass" from the black Berkeley sociologist Troy Duster, who – even as he cites journalist Ken Auletta – deploys a neo-Myrdalian conception stressing how the rise of structural unemployment and multiplying contact with the criminal justice system are propelling an increasing number of black youths "toward permanent placement at the base of the economic order," permanency being the new and distinctive mark of an "underclass."[30] By pointing to the merging of the "rabble" into the "underclass," *The Jail* is a pioneering study in that it discloses a pivotal linkage between urban marginality, ethnoracial division, and penal institutions two decades before the topic rose to the forefront of the study of punishment and inequality.[31] Incarceration is indeed one of the ways in which the

[28] John Irwin, *The Jail: Managing the Underclass* (1985).
[29] Irwin, *The Jail*, pp. 103–4.
[30] Troy Duster, "Crime, Youth Unemployment, and the Black Urban Underclass" (1987), p. 303.
[31] Bruce Western, *Punishment and Inequality in America* (2006); Devah Pager, *Marked: Race, Crime, and Finding Work in an Era of Mass Incarceration* (2007); and Loïc Wacquant, "Marginality, Ethnicity, Penality: An Analytic Cartography" (2014). The stimulative historical study of regimes of parole in California over a century by Jonathan

78   Part One: The Tale

state reaches deep into the life of the urban precariat and its consistent omission in studies of the "underclass" (however defined) is a gaping hole in the empirical and theoretical specification of urban marginality at century's close.

2. The dominant schema of the "underclass" as assortment of "antisocial behaviors"

It is ironic that the three misconceptions that Douglas Glasgow warned against – that the residents of the hyperghetto do not care to get ahead, lack the work ethic, and wish to lead a life of indolence on the welfare rolls – constitute the cornerstones of the hegemonic notion of "underclass" that reemerged at the crossroads of the philanthropic, journalistic, and academic fields in the mid-1980s, following a *semantic metamorphosis* that turned it into a keyword in the regressive discourse on social policy dominating that decade. "In a ten-year period, the underclass [was] transformed from surplus and discarded labor force into an exclusive group of black urban terrorists."[32] Its members were no longer detected by their lack of income, employment opportunities, or socio-economic (im)mobility, but by an assortment of "anti-social behaviors" that caused them to diverge from and menace the "mainstream" of American society (another vague and highly malleable category). The following vignette of the "underclass" offered by the reporters of the *Chicago Tribune*, in a book gloomily entitled *The American Millstone*, illustrates the mutation undergone by the term:

> A new class of people has taken root in America's cities, a lost society dwelling in enclaves of despair and chaos that threaten the communities at large. The group defies most conventional label and definitions. . . . Its members don't share traditional values of work, money, education, home, and perhaps even

---

Simon similarly spotlights the link between the penal institution and changing forms of marginality, but, like all historical work, it was quietly ignored by the main contributors to the "underclass" debate. Jonathan Simon, *Poor Discipline: Parole and the Social Control of the Underclass, 1890–1990* (1993).

[32] Carole Marks, "The Urban Underclass" (1991), p. 454.

The three faces of the "underclass" 79

of life. This is a class of misfits best known to more fortunate Americans as either victim or perpetrator in crime statistics.

Over the last quarter-century in America, this sub-culture has become self-perpetuating. It devours every effort aimed at solving its problems, resists solutions both simple and complicated, absorbs more than its share of welfare and other benefits and causes social and political turmoil far out of proportion to its numbers.[33]

Similar sensationalistic portraits were drawn in reports proliferating in *Newsweek*, *Fortune Magazine*, *US News and World Report*, the *Atlantic Monthly*, and *Reader's Digest*, as the assault on the welfare state intensified under the successive administrations of Ronald Reagan and George Bush the father.[34] The demonic tale of the behavioral "underclass" reactivated the national anti-urban impulse and reprised the themes of disorganization and exoticism long dominant in the national vision of the city. It unfolded at the confluence of three reactionary movements in American politics: a *class reaction* against the advances made by the working class into the 1960s (when the minimum wage and the share of wages in national income both reached their postwar peak), taking the form of anti-union campaigns, fiscal austerity, and labor market deregulation; a *racial reaction* against the gains achieved by African Americans as a result of collective mobilization, civil rights legislation, and affirmative action programs; and an *anti-statist reaction* against taxation and remedial poverty policy, taking the paradoxical form of simultaneous calls to decrease welfare *and* increase punishment. Disciplinary "workfare" and neutralizing "prisonfare" thus became the two complementary planks of public action directed at the "underclass" according to a gendered division of the work of domination, restrictive social policy handling

---

[33] Chicago Tribune, *The American Millstone: An Examination of the Nation's Permanent Underclass* (1986), p. 3. The book was previously serialized in 29 episodes published over three months in the newspaper.

[34] Frances Fox Piven, Richard A. Cloward and Fred Block, *The Mean Season: The Attack on the Welfare State* (1987), and Paul Pierson, *Dismantling the Welfare State? Reagan, Thatcher and the Politics of Retrenchment* (1994).

80   Part One: The Tale

poor women (and their children), and expansive penal policy targeting (their) men in the hyperghetto.[35]

This triple reaction found its expression in the space of production of poverty knowledge in the rise of right-wing foundations and openly ideological think tanks providing an institutional home for a conservative "counterintelligentsia" engaged in a crusade to dismantle the social state and establish the rule of the "free market."[36] The rightward tilting of the political field was thus accompanied by a homological drift in the space of philanthropies and policy institutes that altered the terms and parameters of the debate on caste, class, and state in America. For what then worried the citizenry first and foremost was not the crushing destitution or truncated life chances of its most vulnerable citizens, but the disorders and threats emanating from the hyperghetto, including violent criminality symbolized by black street gangs, the alleged moral depravation of the poor incarnated by the uncontrolled sexuality of teenage mothers, and the fiscal burden, deemed intolerable, of the social programs established under the press of the protest movements of the 1960s.

The notion of "underclass" thus lost its structural mooring: position in the relations of production or market capacity (the two properties determining class location in the Marxist and Weberian traditions, respectively)[37] vanished, to be replaced by a litany of "behaviors" deemed contrary to the civic standards of national morality. By the same token the geographical location of the "underclass" became fixated onto the remnants of the ghetto and its racial dimension hardened while being euphemized: the term effectively names and shames poor blacks in the hyperghetto without for that being overtly "colored." The institutional and political underpinnings of the group it is supposed to designate are further obscured by

---

[35] Loïc Wacquant, *Punishing the Poor: The Neoliberal Government of Social Insecurity* (2009b).

[36] Alice O'Connor, *Social Science for What? Philanthropy and the Social Question in a World Turned Rightside Up* (2007), p. 6, and Thomas Medvetz, *Think Tanks in America* (2012), ch. 5, on the shift "from deprivation to dependency" in expert discourse on welfare.

[37] Erik Olin Wright (ed.), *Approaches to Class Analysis* (2005), chs. 1 and 2.

The fact that it is now defined in extension, *via enumeration*, rather than in intension, by enunciating the necessary and sufficient sociological principles that confers it its unity. And this for a good reason: there are no such principles, aside from the scorn for, and fear of, dispossessed and dishonored populations trapped in the cracks and crevices of the imploding ghetto in this period of social upheaval and economic uncertainty.[38]

"I'll point to a member of the underclass"

"Sheldon Danziger of the Wisconsin Poverty Institute cares less for the term 'underclass.' He believes it is similar to appreciating good art. He knows it when he sees it. 'Take me out and I'll point to a member of the underclass,' he said recently, but the academic words now in vogue are just too vague. 'There is a notion of antisocial behavior and there is a notion of poverty . . . Where those two cross is the underclass.'"

Sheldon Danziger, liberal economist and director of the Institute for Research on Poverty (now President of the Russell Sage Foundation), cited in Chicago Tribune, *The American Millstone* (1986), p. 11

The scientific uses of the "underclass" that boomed during the decade after 1985 are *invariably contaminated by the common-sense prenotions* whose catalog was drawn up by journalist Ken Auletta. A comparative examination of academic and journalistic writings reveals that there is hardly a scholarly definition of the category that does not include some "behavioral" ingredient issued from ordinary perception (see box "A heterogeneous and fearsome scarecrow 'group'" on pp. 90–3). To have a child outside of marriage and to receive public aid as a single parent, to leave high school without graduating, and being unemployed while of sound mind and body are all treated as so many "underclass-specific

---

[38] The suffusive class resentment and simmering ethnic fear of that decade are beautifully captured by Lilian B. Rubin, *Quiet Rage: Bernie Goetz in a Time of Madness* (1986).

82   Part One: The Tale

behaviors," as soon as they are observed within the bounded perimeter of the hyperghetto.[39]

The most remarkable fact about the behavioral conception of the "underclass" is that *it is not conservative think tanks but experts in liberal policy institutes that proffered and promoted it*, with the support, now reluctant, now enthusiastic, of liberal social scientists in the university. No authors exercised more influence on this front than the trio of economists from the Urban Institute composed of Isabel Sawhill and her two younger African-American colleagues Ronald Mincy and Erol Ricketts. Together, they worked diligently on the Underclass Project (funded by the omnipresent Rockefeller Foundation) and produced a string of overlapping papers that codified the behavioral definition and measurement of the "underclass."[40] While remaining "agnostic about the fundamental causes of these behaviors," Ricketts and Sawhill proposed "to move beyond qualitative or journalistic descriptions of the underclass to concrete definition and measurement." In the abstract for the article, they write:

> Research on the underclass has been hampered by the absence of a clear definition of the term. In this article we develop an operational definition of the underclass that is consistent with the emphasis of most of the underclass literature on behavior rather than poverty. Using this definition, we analyze data for all census tracts in the United States in 1980. According to our definition, about one percent of the U.S. population lived in

[39] Christopher Jencks and Paul E. Peterson (eds.), *The Urban Underclass* (1991), pp. 30, 155–6, 172, 301, 322–3, 397.

[40] Erol R. Ricketts and Isabel V. Sawhill, "Defining and Measuring the Underclass" (1988); Isabel V. Sawhill, "What About America's Underclass?" (1988); Ronald B. Mincy, "Paradoxes in Black Economic Progress: Incomes, Families, and the Underclass" (1989); Erol R. Ricketts and Ronald B. Mincy "Growth of the Underclass: 1970–80" (1990); Ronald B. Mincy, Isabel V. Sawhill and Douglas A. Wolf, "The Underclass: Definition and Measurement" (1990); Ronald B. Mincy, "Underclass Variations by Race and Place: Have Large Cities Darkened Our Picture of the Underclass?" (1991); Erol R. Ricketts, "The Underclass: Causes and Responses" (1992); and Ronald B. Mincy, "The Underclass: Concept, Controversy and Evidence" (1994).

The three faces of the "underclass"   *83*

"underclass areas" in 1980, and this group was overwhelmingly concentrated in urban areas. It was also disproportionately made up of minorities living in the older industrial cities of the Northeast.[41]

In addition to being perfectly circular, this operational definition of the "underclass" is based on two conceptual sleights of hand. The first consists in passing a *social and economic status* (e.g., being unemployed) or a *demographic characteristic* (e.g., household composition) off as a *behavior*. Workers who are laid off or cannot find gainful employment amidst an economic recession (like the 1981–2 downturn triggered by a tight monetary policy) would be surprised to learn that their joblessness is an individual behavior, and not a consequence of the behavior of their employer or of the anemic state of the labor market. The second trick is to move *from individual to area*: because microdata on individual conduct are not available, Ricketts and Sawhill resolve to measure the "underclass" by the spatial incidence of a set of social statuses redefined as "behaviors." And so it is that, just as there exists "underclass behaviors," declining cities become instantly dotted with – and burdened by – "*underclass neighborhoods.*" Ricketts and Sawhill baptize as such any census tract containing a high proportion (over one standard deviation above the national average for each variable) of adults without high school degrees, jobless men, welfare recipients, and single-parent households.

One surprising consequence of this operationalization is that working residents who graduated from high school, do not receive public aid, or live in two-parent families, find themselves lumped into the "underclass" by virtue of dwelling in an "underclass neighborhood" – as if their less fortunate neighbors somehow contaminated them. Based on these measurements, Ricketts and Sawhill ascertain that there exist 880 census tracts (out of some 70,000), harboring about 2.5 million people (70% of them black or Hispanic), where such violations of American norms were "commonplace," a phenomenon they present as irrefutable *proof* for the "reality

---

[41] Ricketts and Sawhill, "Defining and Measuring the Underclass," p. 316.

84   Part One: The Tale

of the underclass."[42] This proof seemed to them all the more solid inasmuch as this "behavioral definition" agrees with the scholarly literature and with the "common uses" (i.e., journalistic invocations) of the term. Indeed, how could it be otherwise when the former was directly inspired by the latter?

This behavioral construct of the "underclass" spawned by the Urban Institute was actively diffused by think tanks and proselytized to officials in government bodies. In March of 1987, the Joint Center for Political Studies convened a meeting intended to hammer out a consensual definition of the category. The participants included 16 academic researchers, scholars from the Institute for Research on Poverty and the Urban Institute, and envoys from the Brookings Institution, Public Advocacy Inc., and the Rockefeller Foundation. "The centerpiece of the meeting" was an early draft of the paper by Rickett and Sawhill dissected above. By "majority opinion," their behavioral definition of the "underclass" became the conventional if not the universally accepted conception.[43]

The behavioral conception crafted by journalists and marginalist economists was then disseminated among political personnel by way of print, meetings, and expert testimony, such as the conversation on the topic with the economist Sawhill, the political scientist Mead and the sociologist Jencks staged in 1989 in Washington by the General Accounting Office of the US Government – entrusted with providing "fact-based, nonpartisan information to Congress" – and published in the quarterly journal sponsored by that office. The editors of the periodical introduce the dialogue with this note: "Most *GAO Journal* readers have become acquainted with the term 'underclass' through the popular media. In February GAO invited three leading social policy analysts to discuss the concept of underclass and portray both the possibilities and the difficulties surrounding its application."[44]

---

[42] Ricketts and Sawhill "Defining and Measuring the Underclass," pp. 321–4, cite p. 321.

[43] Robert Aponte (a doctoral student of Wilson's), who attended it along with William Julius Wilson, gives an account of the meeting in "Definitions of the Underclass: A Critical Analysis" (1989), pp. 125–6 and 135.

[44] Christopher Jencks, Lawrence M. Mead, and Isabel Sawhill, "GAO Features: The Issue of Underclass" (1989), p. 15.

The three faces of the "underclass"

The three scholars concur that "the definition ought to be behavioral" (Jencks), even though this is arbitrary; that "to be squeamish about recognizing the existence of the underclass is to ignore a very real phenomenon" (Mead); that "the geographic dimension is useful" because it allows analysts to capture "the contagion effect of living in an underclass neighborhood," although such effect "hasn't yet been proven" (Sawhill); that a behavioral definition is warranted since "to the public, aberrant behavior is much more important than income" (Mead), even if this means "setting [the 'underclass'] apart from those who are commonly viewed more sympathetically" (Jencks); that the "main problem is defeatism" (Mead), which "can eventually create a counterculture" (Jencks) and derail public policies.[45]

The *civic moralism* entailed by the behavioral definition of the "underclass" is neither implicit nor discreet; on the contrary, it is forthrightly claimed by its proponents. In 1990, the National Research Council (an arm of the National Academy of Sciences) published an assessment of *Inner-City Poverty in the United States* in which it asked "whether ghetto poverty actually causes the development of an underclass." The report was frank about the moral(izing) import of the inquiry: "This volume directly addresses this issue: does ghetto poverty in central city cause or reinforce *behaviors deemed socially unacceptable* that, in turn, lead to long-term or persistent poverty among affected residents, and especially among children."[46]

Similarly, in an article for the interdisciplinary journal *Science*, Mincy, Sawhill, and Wolf clarify that the "underclass" is formed by "people who engage in bad behavior or a set of bad behaviors" or "behavior that is individually and socially harmful." They see the fact that their approach "coincides with common sense" as validating their operational construct.[47] Conversely, if definitional criteria lead to

[45] Jencks, Mead, and Sawhill, "GAO Features: The Issue of Underclass," pp. 15, 16, 20.

[46] Laurence E. Lynn and Michael G.H. McGeary (eds.), *Inner-City Poverty in the United States* (1990), p. 12.

[47] Mincy, Sawhill, and Wolf, "The Underclass: Definition and Measurement," pp. 450, 451.

86   Part One: The Tale

"findings that do not accord with common sense notions of the underclass," then they are rejected. The turn to neighborhood data is justified, "not because class and geography are synonymous but because there may be not defensible, practical alternative," and because "neighborhoods are tangible physical entities, which can be directly observed and used as basis for targeting various forms of assistance."[48] Bad people in bad neighborhoods: the operationalization of the "underclass" is not derived from a theoretical model of the phenomenon but a *pragmatic precipitate of ordinary moral concerns and available bureaucratic data.*

Reflecting back upon her work on the "underclass" a dozen years after its bloom, Isabel Sawhill, now a senior scholar at the Brookings Institution, confirms that she took the term from the Rockefeller Foundation and affirms that she consciously sought to replace an income-based conception with a behavioral one, pegged on the violation of the norms of an idealized middle class:

> My own involvement in this debate began in the late 1980s, when the Rockefeller Foundation established a program of research on *what it called "the underclass."* The underclass was *commonly* defined as those families living in areas of concentrated poverty, *usually* in neighborhoods where at least 40 percent of all households were poor. At the time, I was a scholar at the Urban Institute, a Washington think tank, and *I suggested an alternative definition, one that was more behaviorally oriented.* It was based on the idea that in order *to achieve* a middle-class life, an individual must do a few specific things: graduate from high school, defer having a baby until marriage, and obtain steady employment.
>
> With the help of several colleagues, I estimated the number of people who lived in neighborhoods *where the basic norms of middle-class life had eroded* to the point where a large fraction of residents had failed to do these three things. Our research showed that the underclass, thus defined, was still quite small, heavily concentrated in large urban areas, dispro-

[48] Mincy, Sawhill and Wolf, "The Underclass: Definition and Measurement," pp. 451, 452. This article was flagged for a broad academic audience by the *Chronicle of Higher Education*: Chris Raymond, "American Underclass Grew from 1970 to 1980, Study Indicates" (1990).

The three faces of the "underclass"   87

portionately made up of racial minorities, and, at the time, growing.[49]

In Sawhill's marginalist vision, the class structure is not rooted in the differential distribution of species of capital and attendant life chances but the aggregate result of the singular choices and the self-determining conducts of individuals, and increasing class inequality is a product of an increase in the "perverse and antisocial behavior" among the poor.

> Not only does behavior matter, it matters more than it used to. Growing gaps between rich and poor in recent decades have been exacerbated by a divergence in the behavior of the two groups. No feasible amount of income redistribution can make up for the fact that the rich are working and marrying as much or more than ever while the poor are doing just the reverse. Unless the poor adopt more mainstream behaviors, and public policies are designed to move them in this direction, economic divisions are likely to grow.[50]

As for the advantage in class background between rich and poor, it resides in a difference in "parental behavior" such as "encouraging children to do well in school, providing them with a structured routine, reinforcing good behaviors, or simply having good genes."

Sawhill maintains that the worsening behavior of the poor requires a paradigm shift in social policy, from supportive measures designed to raise living standards and secure opportunities to programs aiming to straighten out the wayward ways of the "underclass": "We should not pretend that money alone is going to change significantly the lives of these families," and we can no longer afford to "disregard the unpleasant facts about their behavior." The failure to work full time

---

[49] Isabel Sawhill, "The Behavioral Aspects of Poverty" (2003), my italics.

[50] "Most academics, myself included, feel considerable sympathy for those who are poor or disadvantaged. We understand that none of us is perfect; and that while bad habits and poor discipline are widespread, they are more consequential for those living on the margin, where any slip-up may tumble someone over the edge" (Sawhill, "The Behavioral Aspects of Poverty").

88 Part One: The Tale

is the gravest offense, since jobs that are "low-paying and disagreeable" are readily available to those who would take them, as recent immigrants toiling away demonstrate. The failure to postpone having babies until one can marry and support them is also incomprehensible and inexcusable given the wide availability of contraception.[51] "What is needed is what some have called 'tough love'," that is, "strong measures to change these *poverty-inducing behaviors* at the bottom and ward off the damage they inflict upon the next generation," measures tailored to "*link assistance to a change in behavior* ... Not only will these 'tough love' policies be more effective than the cash welfare policies of the past, but they will be more popular with the public."[52]

Between an atomistic-individualist and a relational-structuralist conception of inequality and marginality, Sawhill and her co-authors made a clear choice that put them in fundamental agreement with neo-conservative detractors of the "underclass" who wished to either abandon them outright or place them under stern state tutelage so as to correct their errant conduct.[53] For the Urban Institute economist, class position is *achieved* through personal exertion, self-discipline and cultural ascesis. Public policy should therefore aim at building character, altering cultural norms, and manip-

---

[51] "Liberals, in their eagerness to help, have been much too willing to *ignore or excuse the cultural underpinnings of poverty*" and to tolerate errant behavior. As concerns having children, "to a young woman, the new system says, 'Full-time motherhood at public expense is no longer an option', and to young men it says, 'If you father a child, you will be expected to contribute to that child's support'" (Sawhill, "The Behavioral Aspects of Poverty," my italics). For a subtle analysis of why destitute young men become early parents that belie this crude behaviorism, see Timothy Black and Sky Keyes, *It's A Setup: Fathering from the Social and Economic Margins* (2020).

[52] Sawhill, "The Behavioral Aspects of Poverty," my italics. Elsewhere Sawhill calls this "tough-minded compassion," that is, "compassion tempered by concern about the willingness of the poor to help themselves, the cost of any new effort, and its likely effectiveness." Sawhill, "What About America's Underclass?," p. 36.

[53] See, respectively, Charles Murray, *Losing Ground: American Social Policy, 1950–1980* (1984), and Lawrence M. Mead (ed.), *The New Paternalism: Supervisory Approaches to Poverty* (1997).

The three faces of the "underclass" 89

ulating micro-incentives to impact behavior, not endeavor to change structures of opportunity (or, quite simply, redistribute income). In short, it should leave institutions alone and work to implant an abstemious middle-class mind inside a profligate lower-class body. Government measures designed to expand collective life chances are an exercise in futility – a classic reactionary trope[54] – unless and until the "underclass" mends its wayward ways and stops creating its own troubles by its "poverty-inducing behaviors."

This is to forget, first, that there are social and economic conditions of production of the frugal, strategic, forward-looking dispositions characteristic of the petty-bourgeois that Sawhill presents as an inborn property of the middle class.[55] Such dispositions are highly unlikely to take root in the conditions of extreme material penury and endemic social insecurity characteristic of the hyperghetto. Next, this is to deny that an individual trajectory through social space is a function, not just of one's subjective dispositions, but also of one's endowment in economic, cultural, social, and symbolic capital and of the objective chances offered (or refused) by institutions of social reproduction and mobility, including the school system, the labor market, the marriage market, laws of property and inheritance, and the provision of public goods by the state. Lastly, this is to disregard the immense capacity of the state to both reduce inequality and remedy urban marginality as demonstrated by the patterned variations in social policy and poverty among advanced nations.[56] The claim that the best way to fight entrenched poverty is to "ameliorate" the poor one person at a time is simply outlandish when

[54] Albert O. Hirschman, *The Rhetoric of Reaction: Perversity, Futility, Jeopardy* (1991).

[55] Pierre Bourdieu, *Algérie 60. Structures économiques et structures temporelles* (1977), ch. 1, and idem, *La Distinction. Critique sociale du jugement* (1979), chs. 2 and 3.

[56] Gøsta Esping-Andersen, *The Three Worlds of Welfare Capitalism* (1990); Benjamin I. Page and James R. Simmons, *What Government Can Do: Dealing with Poverty and Inequality* (2002); Alberto Alesina and Edward L. Glaeser, *Fighting Poverty in the US and Europe: A World of Difference* (2004); David Brady, *Rich Democracies, Poor People: How Politics Explain Poverty* (2009); and Gorän Therborn, *The Killing Fields of Inequality* (2014), ch. 9.

90   Part One: The Tale

taken outside of the narrow confines of the American policy debate on urban marginality.

A heterogeneous and fearsome scarecrow "group"

"They are the underclass: the people who prey on our communities committing the senseless, heinous murders, rapes and muggings that haunt the news every day; the thieves who break into our homes night after night; the hard-core unemployed; the hustlers of the underground economy – the peddlers of loot, the 'gentlemen of leisure', the prostitutes, the drug pushers; the passive poor who are unable to cope in the workaday world; the single mothers living chronically on welfare; the strung-out junkies and the aimless juvenile delinquents; the deranged vagrants and the homeless and helpless shopping-bag ladies. These new millions of social dropouts . . . account for a disproportionate amount of the street crime, long-term welfare dependency, chronic unemployment and antisocial behavior in America today. Both traditional poverty programs and the penal system have so far failed to socialize these increasingly desperate, often virulent members of our society."

Ken Auletta, *The Underclass* (1982), inside flap-jacket text

"In American society circa 1980, it is expected that children will attend school and delay parenthood until at least age 18, that adult males (who are not disabled or retired) will work at a regular job, that adult females will either work or marry, and that everyone will be law abiding. The underclass, in our definition, consists of people whose behavior departs from these norms and in the process creates significant social costs. An underclass area is one where the proportion of people engaged in these costly behaviors departs significantly from the mean for the U.S. population as a whole."

Erol Ricketts and Isabel Sawhill, "Defining and Measuring the Underclass," *Journal of Policy Analysis and Management* (1988), pp. 319–20

"One cannot deny that there is a heterogeneous grouping of inner-city families and individuals whose behavior contrasts

The three faces of the "underclass" 91

sharply with that of mainstream America. . . . Included in this group are individuals who lack training and skills and either experience long-term unemployment or are not members of the labor force, individuals who are engaged in street crime and other forms of aberrant behavior, and families that experience long-term spells of poverty and/or welfare dependency. These are the populations to which I refer when I speak of the *underclass*. I use this term to depict a reality not captured in the more standard designation *lower class*.

In my conception, the term underclass suggests that changes have taken place in ghetto neighborhoods, and the groups that have been left behind are collectively different from those that lived in these neighborhoods in earlier years. It is true that long-term welfare families and street criminals are distinct groups, but they live and interact in the same depressed community and they are part of the population that has, with the exodus of the more stable working- and middle-class segments, become increasingly isolated socially from mainstream patterns and norms of behavior. It is also true that certain groups are stigmatized by the label underclass, just as some people are stigmatized by the term ghetto or inner city, but it would be far worse to obscure the profound changes in the class structure and social behavior of ghetto neighborhoods by avoiding the use of the term underclass."

William Julius Wilson, *The Truly Disadvantaged*
(1987), pp. 7–8, original italics

"The old lower class has grown larger and perhaps more isolated from mainstream society. In my judgment these changes are not large enough to justify substituting the term underclass for the term lower class. But *since almost everyone else now talks about the underclass rather than the lower class, I will do the same.*

Poverty may be a necessary condition for inclusion in the underclass, but few observers think it sufficient. The term caught on because it focused attention on *those who were poor because they violated mainstream rules of behavior. . . .*

Journalists, politicians, cab drivers, and graduate students are all convinced that violent crime has increased over the past generation, especially in poor black areas. Indeed, one reason

92   Part One: The Tale

the underclass hypothesis *appeals* to many Americans is that *it seems to explain the breakdown of law and order* in those areas. . . .

The term 'middle class' evokes someone who has attended college, holds a steady job, earns an adequate income, got married before having children, and has never murdered, raped, robbed, or assaulted anyone. 'Underclass', in contrast, conjures up a chronically jobless high school dropout who has had two or three children out of wedlock, has very little money to support them, and probably has either a criminal record or a history of welfare dependence."

> Christopher Jencks, "Is the American Underclass Growing?," in *The Urban Underclass* (1991), pp. 28, 36, 74, and 96, italics added

"We prefer a definition of 'the' underclass as persons living in urban, central city neighborhoods or communities with high and increasing rates of poverty, especially chronic poverty, high and increasing levels of social isolation, hopelessness, and anomie, and high levels of characteristically antisocial or dysfunctional behavior patterns. No one factor is sufficient to create an underclass; all must be simultaneously present."

> Joel A. Devine and James D. Wright, *The Greatest of Evils* (1993), pp. 88–9

"In 1984, *Losing Ground*'s argument that a growing number of poor people were engaged in self-destructive personal behavior that would keep them at the bottom of society pro-voked angry retorts that I was blaming the victims. Today no major figure in either academia or public life argues against the existence of such a group. It even has an accepted, uncon-troversial name: the underclass . . .

As years went by, what had always been obvious to social workers and police officers who worked in underclass neighborhoods – that a lot of people in those neighborhoods were indeed living by a very different set of values from those of mainstream society – became incrementally more obvious in a wide variety of behavioral ways."

> Charles Murray, *Losing Ground: American Social Policy, 1950–1980* (1984 ed.), pp. xvi and xvii

The three faces of the "underclass" 93

> "We should not ignore the behavioral problems of the underclass, but we should discuss and react to them as if we were talking about our own children, neighbors, and friends. This is an American tragedy, to which we should respond as we might to an epidemic of teen suicide, adolescent drunken driving, or HIV infection among homosexual males – that is, by embracing, not demonizing, the victims.
>
> Glenn Loury, "An American Tragedy: The Legacy of Slavery Lingers in our Cities' Ghettos" (1998)

3. The neo-ecological conception, or the neighborhood as multiplier of marginality

The structural conception of Myrdal locates the "underclass" in a hierarchical system of objective positions rooted in the economy; it invites a relational vision of the novel stratification order spawned by postindustrialism. The behavioral approach turns the category rightside up and issues an atomistic enumeration of individual conducts in violation of the proclaimed moral norms of middle-class society. The third perspective, forged by the sociologist William Julius Wilson, seeks a *via media* between the structural and the behavioral conceptions by embedding the "underclass" in the "ghetto neighborhood" construed as multiplier of advanced marginality.

It is generally believed that Wilson first broached the topic of the "underclass" in his blockbuster book *The Truly Disadvantaged* published in 1987 to counter the ascendancy of conservative views on the nexus of race, poverty, and welfare in the inner city. But, in fact, the Chicago sociologist used the notion extensively a decade earlier in his controversial tome on *The Declining Significance of Race*, in which the word "underclass" appears no fewer than 27 times, starting on the very first page of the book, on which Wilson evokes "a vast underclass of black proletarians – that massive population at the very bottom of the social class ladder, plagued by poor education and low-paying, unstable jobs."[57] Wilson's

[57] William Julius Wilson, *The Declining Significance of Race: Blacks and American Institutions* (1978, exp. 1980 ed.), p. 1.

94 Part One: The Tale

early conception is couched in Marxist-sounding language but it is Myrdalian in substance. Like the Swedish economist's, it stresses structural location in the economy and changing technology, and it makes no mention of untoward behavior or neighborhood type: the "new set of obstacles [which] has emerged from structural changes in the economy" are "impersonal" yet "even more formidable"; they "create hardships especially for the black underclass" which, for this reason, is "in a hopeless state of economic stagnation, falling further and further behind the rest of society."[58]

Again the early Wilson echoes Myrdal when he contends that economic expansion is "not likely to reverse the pattern of unemployment, under-employment, poverty, welfare, and female-headed households." Neither will affirmative action programs that disproportionately benefit the black middle class endowed with the means to compete for credentialed jobs.[59] Wilson does add one major causal variable to Myrdal's model, the legacy of white domination: "A history of racial discrimination and oppression created a huge black underclass, and the technological and economic revolutions have combined to insure its permanent status."[60] But while blacks are disproportionately stuck at the bottom rung of the dualizing class structure, "underclass whites, Hispano-Americans, and native Americans are all victims, to a greater or lesser degree, of class subordination under advanced capitalism."[61]

Wilson's early characterization of the underclass can be read as a racialized derivation of Myrdal's structural con-

---

[58] Wilson, *The Declining Significance of Race*, p. 2; see also pp. 19, 22. On page 154, Wilson lists the "basic structural changes in the modern American economy" involved in "underclass" formation: "uneven economic growth, increasing technology and automation, industry relocation, and labor market segmentation."

[59] Wilson, *The Declining Significance of Race*, p. 134. Compare with Myrdal, who bemoans "a vicious circle tending to create in America an underprivileged class of unemployed, unemployables, and under-employed who are more and more hopelessly set apart from the nation at large and do not share in its life, its ambitions, and its achievements" (Myrdal, *Challenge to Affluence*, p. 10).

[60] Wilson, *The Declining Significance of Race*, p. 22, also p. 120.

[61] Wilson, *The Declining Significance of Race*, p. 154.

The three faces of the "underclass" 95

ception that comes close to the neo-Weberian elaboration of Anthony Giddens. *Mais voilà*, Wilson was unaware of both Myrdal's and Giddens's books at the time. So from where did he get the term and his view of the underclass as precarious labor market position? The key endnote in *The Declining Significance of Race* refers to an article on "Race, Economics, and Public Policy" by the black economist Vivian Henderson, published in the periodical of the NAACP, *Crisis*, in 1975.[62] In this text, Henderson proposes that "the concept of working poor coupled with the concept of economic class makes up an 'underclass' which will not differentiate between those who work and those who assume roles of income dependency." This underclass "will become a protest force in the economic warfare for the benefits from the nation's products and services." And Henderson continues:

> What this all adds up to is two faces of the same coin: improvements in education, more blacks in middle-income groups, a strong and highly concentrated Negro market, all on one side, and on the other side, entrenched poverty, growing rigidity in class difference, unemployment and underemployment, and increasing welfare. The great question is *whether the masses of blacks will become a permanent underclass in America*. This is why it is so important to recognize the role of economic class in contrast to race, per se, as critical to the problem and as a primary target in race relations strategy today.[63]

Whether or not Henderson got his concept of "underclass" from Myrdal, whose work was well known among economists involved in civil rights circles, we do not know. But we do know that Wilson developed an early view of the

---

[62] Wilson, *The Declining Significance of Race*, pp. 163 and 213, and personal communication with William Julius Wilson, September 2017.

[63] Vivian Henderson, "Race, Economics, and Public Policy" (1975), p. 55, original italics. From communication with the staff of the Archives Research Center, Robert W. Woodruff Library, at the Atlanta University Center, I was able to establish that the Vivian Wilson Henderson Papers do not contain a draft of this article allowing us to establish whether or not Henderson had taken the notion of "underclass" from Gunnar Myrdal.

96   Part One: The Tale

"underclass" that defined it as a structural location in a polarizing class structure traversed by deep ethnoracial inequality.

A decade later, Wilson stakes out a new analytic position and deploys a new language that expresses the shift from a readership of fellow social scientists to a target audience centered on policy analysts and policy makers.[64] The intent to plug into the exploding public debate on the "underclass" is signaled by the late change in the title of his book: the working title was *The Hidden Agenda: Race, Social Dislocations, and Public Policy in America*; the final title is *The Truly Disadvantaged: The Inner City, the Underclass, and Public Policy*. Instead of a multi-ethnic "underclass" emerging at the bottom of the class structure across the nation, now Wilson is concerned with a black "ghetto underclass" trapped in the dilapidated urban core, in keeping with the racialized vision disseminated by journalists. He uses the term as short-hand for a cluster of interrelated "social dislocations" manifested by catastrophic rates of "joblessness, teenage pregnancies, out-of-wedlock births, female-headed families, welfare dependency, and serious crime,"[65] the same litany rolled out by think-tank proponents of the behavioral "underclass."

Wilson makes a point of forthrightly addressing these "unflattering and stigmatizing behaviors" – he even revives Moynihan's infamous expression (borrowed from Kenneth Clark) of the "tangle of pathology."[66] He chides liberal

---

[64] This is to be expected, as discursive products are always the result of the anticipated "censorship exercised by the linguistic market" on which they are offered. Pierre Bourdieu, *Langage et pouvoir symbolique* (2000), ch. 2. A telltale sign of this shift in audience is the fact that the three endorsements on the book's back cover are not by academics but by public figures (Michael Harrington, Eleanor Holmes Norton, and Daniel Patrick Moynihan) influential in policy debates. It is also evident from Wilson's choice of theme for the meetings of the American Sociological Association over which he presided in 1990: "Sociology and the Public Agenda," and his edited volume by the same title: William Julius Wilson (ed.). *Sociology and the Public Agenda* (1993b).

[65] William Julius Wilson, *The Truly Disadvantaged: The Inner City, the Underclass, and Public Policy* (1987, new exp. ed. 2012), p. 3.

[66] Wilson, *The Truly Disadvantaged*; it is the title of a section in chapter 2, pp. 21–9.

The three faces of the "underclass" 97

scholars for shying away from the increase in "inner city pathologies" and for leaving a policy vacuum eagerly filled by the newly dominant views of neo-conservative analysts, led by the Manhattan Institute's Charles Murray, according to whom ghetto dislocations result from the excessive munificence of the welfare state toward the dependent poor and the latter's stubborn cultural deviancy.[67]

Wilson is particularly critical of liberal scholars who "refuse even to use terms such as *underclass*" while their conservative opponents are busy elaborating a version of it "focused almost exclusively on individual behavior." In his view, it behooves them to adopt the term because "one cannot deny that there is a heterogeneous grouping of inner-city families and individuals *whose behavior contrasts sharply with that of mainstream America.*"[68] Beyond candidly describing it, the question is how to explain such behavior, and Wilson maintains that the concept of "underclass" is helpful in that endeavor.

While Wilson's position evolved after the publication of *The Truly Disadvantaged* in 1987 (leading to the sidelining of the concept of "underclass" discussed in the next chapter), it has remained anchored by two fundamental propositions and two concepts elaborated in the book. The first proposition is that the transition from an urban industrial economy to a suburban service economy eliminated the factory jobs on which unskilled blacks had relied into the 1960s. Wilson surveys five factors involved in the rise of inner-city dislocations: historic and contemporary discrimination; the continuing inflow of black migrants from the South; the high share of youths in the age distribution; the exodus of black middle-class households from the inner city; and the structural transformation of the economy. Of these, economic change, and especially the collapse of urban demand for low-skill manual labor, is far and away the most potent. It explains skyrocketing male joblessness which, in turn, accounts for the steady drop in marriage and the vertiginous increase in single-parent households and, by ricochet, the rise in out-of-wedlock births. The *vanishing*

[67] Murray, *Losing Ground*, who gets the term "underclass" from journalist Ken Auletta.

[68] Wilson, *The Truly Disadvantaged*, pp. 6 and 7–8, my italics.

98   Part One: The Tale

of industrial employment from the metropolis, and not the generosity or permissiveness of welfare programs (bewailed by Murray on the think-tank side and Mead on the academic side) or the sole persistence of racism (as asserted by some radical scholars and race advocates),[69] is the trigger for the spiraling ills afflicting the hyperghetto.

Wilson's second key proposition makes the *neighborhood the crucial sociospatial mediation* through which deindustrialization wields its destructive effects upon households and individuals. The exodus of the stable black working class and middle class from the historic core of the ghetto and the endemic joblessness prevailing in it converge to erode local institutions (churches, stores, schools, recreational facilities, etc.) and deprive residents of the "social buffer" liable to cushion the shock of economic restructuring. The *differentia specifica* of the "underclass" among the "underprivileged economic groups," then, resides in the fact that "their economically fragile position or weak labor market attachment is uniquely exacerbated by the neighborhood."[70] African Americans in the fin-de-siècle hyperghetto are indeed alone among urban denizens to be both dispossessed *and* trapped in devastated urban districts where the vast majority of residents are equally dispossessed: in 1980, 39% of poor blacks in the country's top five cities lived in census tracts with poverty rates exceeding 40%, compared to only 7% of poor whites.[71]

The class and institutional ecology of the neighborhood acts in the manner of a meso-level *prism* that intensifies hardships and accelerates the spatial accumulation of "social pathologies," in accordance with the causal chain charted by figure 2. The dissolution of the nuclear family and massive recourse to public assistance, for example, are explained by the drying up of the "pool of marriageable men" caused by astronomical rates of joblessness among men and by the

---

[69] Murray, *Losing Ground*; Mead, *The New Politics of Poverty*; Alphonso Pinkney, *The Myth of Black Progress* (1986); and Derrick Bell, *Faces at the Bottom of the Well: The Permanence of Racism* (1993).

[70] William Julius Wilson, "Public Policy Research and 'The Truly Disadvantaged'" (1991b), p. 474.

[71] Wilson, *The Truly Disadvantaged*, p 58.

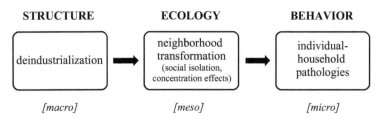

Figure 2 The causal chain articulated in Wilson's *The Truly Disadvantaged* (1987)

inability of the proximate milieu, depleted of resources, to furnish informal socioeconomic support.[72]

The two concepts through which Wilson purports to link macro-structural change to individual micro-behavior inside the hyperghetto are *social isolation* and *concentration effects*. Wilson puts forth the notion of "social isolation," defined as "the lack of repeated contacts or intercourse with individuals and institutions that represent mainstream society," to distance his reasoning from a culture-of-poverty claim.[73] He is concerned above all by the regressive policy implications of an argument that would grant full autonomy to "the basic values and attitudes of the ghetto culture"; so he insists that "culture is a response to social structural constraints and opportunities," and therefore that remedial policies must focus on institutions and not on subcultural traits.[74] According to Wilson, social isolation, springing from the out-migration of the black middle class and the reluctance of outsiders to come into the hyperghetto, deprives the black precariat of two key resources: at the social level, it cuts them

---

[72] Wilson, *The Truly Disadvantaged*, p. 133.

[73] Wilson, *The Truly Disadvantaged*, p. 60. In a workshop discussion with his research team (in which I participated) while he was finalizing his book in early 1987, Wilson grew worried that his ecological argument could be misconstrued as reviving the "culture of poverty," and he subsequently elaborated the concept of "social isolation."

[74] Wilson, *The Truly Disadvantaged*, p. 61. Wilson will later amend this position in *More than Just Race: Being Black and Poor in the Inner City* (2009), in which intense poverty results from the interplay of culture and social structure.

100   Part One: The Tale

off from "job networks"; at the cultural level, it removes conventional "role models."[75]

The kindred notion of "concentration effects" refers to the fact that the ecology of the deindustrialized inner city is different from the ecology of other poor districts and from that of the ghetto of yesteryear in that it harbors only "the most disadvantaged segments of the black urban population" and accumulates multiple forms of deprivation, creating a distinctive social milieu in which pathologies fester together and intensify one another.[76] In later work, Wilson adds a social-psychological plank to his model, borrowed from the writings of psychologist Albert Bandura: one of the concentration effects of persistent joblessness is to diffuse a low sense of "individual self-efficacy" by immersing individuals in an unresponsive economic environment in which internalized self-doubt is prevalent "among networks of kin, friends, and associates."[77]

Wilson deserves credit for putting forth a provocative *theory* of the transformation of the inner city – as distinct from a descriptive portrait or a moral jeremiad about its ills. This theory bridges the chasm between the structural and the behavioral constructs of the "underclass" by incorporating elements of both. It brings back to the analytic epicenter the structural economic factors spotted by Myrdal a generation earlier and adds to them the social and demographic makeup of the neighborhood that is the touchstone of the ecological approach originating with the first Chicago school.[78] In so

[75] These role models are the "old heads" mentioned by Elijah Anderson in his expert testimony to congress (see *supra*, p. 57). This aspect of Wilson's theory is developed at the microsociological level by Anderson in *Streetwise: Race, Class, and Change in an Urban Community* (1990). Anderson is careful to eschew the behavioral definition of the "underclass," but he does differentiate it from the working class, reporting that the latter treat the former as "convenient objects of scorn, fear, and embarrassment" (p. 66).

[76] Wilson, *The Truly Disadvantaged*, p. 58.

[77] William Julius Wilson, "Social Theory and the Concept Underclass" (2006), pp. 110–11.

[78] Robert E. Park, Ernest W. Burgess, and Roderick D. McKenzie, *The City* (1923), especially ch. 3 by McKenzie. Note that Wilson was neither versed in, nor influenced by, the early Chicago school, so this

The three faces of the "underclass"   *101*

doing, his model solidly links the labor market and urban poverty – a causal linkage which, in the United States, is hardly taken for granted, even among social scientists, owing to the prevalence of the individualistic mode of thinking and the prevalence of the moral(izing) vision of the poor.[79] And it invites closer scrutiny of the proximate social and symbolic world within which the urban black precariat evolves day to day.

The Truly Disadvantaged has had an incomparable impact on research on race, poverty, and policy. It has inspired inquiries from, and indeed changed the intellectual trajectory of, countless scholars in multiple disciplines. It is one of the most cited tomes of urban sociology of the past 50 years, garnering some 21,000 hits on Google Scholar; in his postface to the 25th anniversary edition of the book, Wilson reacts to hundreds of articles that engaged it (out of an estimated 3,500).[80] The book has also influenced federal housing policy aiming to reduce concentrated poverty and rebuild neighborhood institutions. It deserves a serious critique on a par with its impact. I will limit myself to three theoretical points about segregation, the state, and multiethnicity.

First, Wilson underestimates the combined weight of class *and caste* in his characterization of the prismatic power of the neighborhood. He does acknowledge historical and contemporary *discrimination* as a causative force but he overlooks *segregation* as a distinctive modality of ethnoracial domination. In *American Apartheid*, Massey and Denton show that the hypersegregation of blacks in the city is a powerful self-standing vector reinforcing the "concentration effects" that Wilson attributes *in toto* to the changing class composition of

---

is a case of *reinvention* of an ecological model. Regardless, *The Truly Disadvantaged* helped revive the lost tradition of "social area analysis" under the new name of "neighborhood effects."

[79] Edward Royce, *Poverty and Power: The Problem of Structural Inequality* (2018).

[80] William Julius Wilson, "Reflections on Responses to *The Truly Disadvantaged*" (2012); see also the panoramic review of Mario Luis Small and Katherine Newman, "Urban Poverty After *The Truly Disadvantaged*: The Rediscovery of the Family, the Neighborhood, and Culture" (2001).

102   Part One: The Tale

the inner city. A series of simulation exercises reveals that elevating racial segregation in a neighborhood struck by rising poverty mechanically increases the crime rate, the share of single-parent households, and the incidence of welfare receipt, and lowers average household income and educational attainment. The argument here is that "segregation *and* rising poverty *interact* to deliver an exogenous shock to black neighborhoods that pushes them beyond the point where physical decay and disinvestment become self-perpetuating."[81] Interestingly, Massey's causal argument has the same formal structure as Wilson's (outlined by figure 2): a structural variable at the macro level, hypersegregation, combines with economic restructuring to impact the neighborhood at the meso level, and thence shapes individual and group behavior at the micro level through the creation of an oppositional "culture of segregation."[82] This suggests that, far from being antagonistic, Wilson's and Massey's theories are logically germane and indeed empirically complementary.[83]

Second, Wilson vastly underestimates the causal role of *state structures, interests, and policies* in the (re)production of urban inequality and marginality. Nowhere in the capitalist West is the fate of the urban poor decided by economy and demography alone. Historical and cross-national variations in the prevalence, intensity, and sociospatial dispersion of poverty are the product of differences between states, especially the degree to which they have institutionalized social and economic rights and deliver on those rights.[84] National

---

[81] Douglas Massey and Nancy A. Denton, *American Apartheid: Segregation and the Making of the Underclass* (1993), p. 132, my italics.

[82] Massey and Denton, *American Apartheid*, p. 167.

[83] This is acknowledged by Massey: "Wilson and I agree that the core issue is not whether urban poverty is caused by factors associated with class *or* race, but how race *and* class factors *interact* to render urban poverty such an intractable social problem. The political economy *has* been transformed by the wealthy in ways that have increased inequality and deepened poverty; but racism also remains a potent and corrosive force in US society, especially in its housing market." Douglas Massey, "Race, Class, and Markets: Social Policy in the 21st Century" (2006), p. 130.

[84] Brady, *Rich Democracies, Poor People*.

The three faces of the "underclass" 103

states shape symbolic space by inculcating shared categories of perception (such as conceptions of poverty and beliefs about ethnicity); social space by setting the broader parameters of social disparity and mobility, through such mechanisms as taxation, the provision of public goods, and the allocation of school credentials; and physical space by laying down the material infrastructure molding the geographic distribution and (im)mobility of objects, people, and activities. Local states, including county and municipal governments, filter and redirect these national forces across the expanse of the metropolis.[85] The *condition* of a neighborhood, its *position* in the hierarchy of places that make up the city, and its *trajectory* over time are the products of collective *struggles over appropriated physical space* whose weapons and stakes are city policies spanning the gamut from infrastructure and housing to education and welfare to health, policing, and criminal justice.[86]

Nothing demonstrates that there is a *politics of place*, waged in the national and local fields of power, irreducible to the economics of space better than the persistence of caste division in the layout of the American metropolis in the second half of the twentieth century. After World War II, a triangular alliance of white ethnic homeowners, downtown corporations, and city officials arose to remake the built environment and erect America's "second ghetto" from above through policies such as redlining, slum clearance, urban renewal, infrastructural projects, and the building of public housing.[87] The "skills mismatch" said to contribute to high joblessness is caused by the planned incapacity of public schools to prepare hyperghetto residents for the new jobs; the "spatial mismatch" of jobs

[85] "The parts played by the national and local state in shaping cities have become so substantial and well institutionalized in all Western societies that it is no longer plausible to argue that economic forces are or can be primarily responsible for urban growth and decline." Ted Robert Gurr and Desmond S. King, *The State and the City* (1987), p. 3.

[86] Loïc Wacquant, *Urban Outcasts: A Comparative Sociology of Advanced Marginality* (2008), pp. 11–12, 75–91, 286–7.

[87] Arnold R. Hirsch, *Making the Second Ghetto: Race and Housing in Chicago 1940–1960* (1983, new exp. ed. 1998).

104   Part One: The Tale

and people is due to the deficiencies of the public transport grid, the failure to enforce anti-discrimination statutes on the housing market, and the political refusal to locate multi-unit lodging and public housing in suburban municipalities. Similarly, the family dissolution, school failure, and neighborhood crime described by Wilson as by-products of male joblessness can also be traced back to the destabilizing effects of the deep penetration of the penal state into the hyperghetto.[88] Indeed, I would venture that the *local state is a more potent prism* of exogenous structural forces than the neighborhood when one considers how its social welfare and punishment strategies join to impact the life chances of the urban poor.[89]

Third, whereas the early Wilson of *The Declining Significance of Race* spotted the *multiethnic* character of the underclass,[90] the late Wilson of *The Truly Disadvantaged* zeroes in on the black poor in the hyperghetto. Why this narrowed focus? I submit that the answer is twofold: first, this is the one population that is both exoticized and feared by middle-class whites and blacks (urban analysts and members of the media included), and for this reason stands at the center of scholarly and policy debates; second, Wilson's actual *theoretical object* is not the "underclass" but the *fate of the ghetto after the crash of the 1960s* – the novel sociospatial formation I call the *hyperghetto*. For it is not as if the pincer of "class subordination under advanced capitalism" (as Wilson phrased it in 1978) suddenly released white and Hispanic subproletarians.

Ethnic comparison with the situation of Native Americans is instructive here. If one defines the "ghetto" by a rate of

---

[88] Todd R. Clear, *Imprisoning Communities: How Mass Incarceration Makes Disadvantaged Neighborhoods Worse* (2009); Reuben Jonathan Miller, *Halfway Home: Race, Punishment, and the Afterlife of Mass Incarceration* (2021).

[89] The omission of public policy as a *cause* of urban marginality upstream (rather than just a remedy for it downstream) is partially corrected in Wilson's *More than Just Race*, "The Role of Political Actions" (pp. 28–39). But Wilson continues to underplay the role of the state (it does not figure in that book's detailed index).

[90] "The situation of marginality and redundancy created by the modern industrial society deleteriously affects all the poor, regardless of race" (*The Declining Significance of Race*, p. 154).

The three faces of the "underclass"

poverty exceeding 40%, as Wilson does, then most Indian reservations are ghettos; if one defines the "underclass" by weak labor attachment reinforced by the proximate social milieu, then American Indians in reservations form a second "ghetto underclass," and have done so for a century. They suffer from "economic, social, and physical isolation from the majority society" and "this isolation has produced extreme poverty, high unemployment, unstable families, low rates of high school graduation, and high rates of alcoholism and/or drug abuse and crime on reservations."[91] This empirical anomaly – that Indian reservations spawned a "ghetto underclass" long before the implosion of the black ghetto in the postindustrial metropolis – reveals the conceptual incoherence of "ghetto" and "underclass" according to Wilson. In other words, the considerable empirical and theoretical advances of Wilson in *The Truly Disadvantaged* were achieved *in spite* of the concept of "underclass" and not thanks to it. Final proof is that he did not need the category to produce the lucid observations and rich analyses contained in *When Work Disappears* (1996).

---

[91] Gary D. Sandefur, "American Indian Reservations: The First Underclass Areas?" (1989), p. 41. In 1990, one-quarter of 2.4 million native Americans resided in reservations located in rural areas mostly devoid of economic opportunities. The per capita income of that population was one-third of the US average and had decreased during the previous decade. Over 42% of households and 53% of children on reservations lived under the poverty line, four times and twice the figures for the country, respectively. The rate of "deep poverty" (less than 75% of the poverty line) was thrice the US rate at 30%. One household in five received welfare, compared to 8% nationally; the unemployment rate was 25% compared to 6% for the country; 52% of all adults were not gainfully employed and a mere 11% were college graduates. Jonathan B. Taylor and Joseph P. Kalt, *American Indians on Reservations: A Databook of Socioeconomic Change between the 1990 and 2000 Censuses* (2005).

4

The strange career of a racialized folk devil

~

The stunning triumph of the "underclass" at the intersection of the academic, journalistic, and political-policy-philanthropic field was as swift as it proved fleeting: no sooner had the notion reached its peak of popularity around 1992 that it underwent a vertiginous fall. By the close of the decade, the "underclass" had all but *vanished from the national conversation on race and poverty* in the metropolis. Figure 3 shows that mentions of "underclass" in US newspapers jumped ninefold between 1976 and 1988 and then plummeted until 1997. The category continued to circulate in the social sciences, mostly in its structural and ecological guises, but think tanks, politicians, and journalists jettisoned it, and it no longer framed the scholarly and policy debate.[1] Aside from the relentless critique of its detractors pointing to the epistemological flaws, analytic ambiguities, and moral baggage of the notion, three developments conspired to produce this sudden reversal of fortune.

A first chink in the armor of the "underclass" appeared when its most influential advocate among social scientists, William Julius Wilson, publicly distanced himself from the

---

[1] Michael B. Katz, "From Underclass to Entrepreneur: New Technologies of Poverty Work in Urban America" (2012). See the Appendix on "The nine lives of the 'underclass'," *infra*, pp. 189–94.

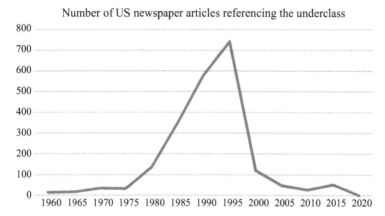

Figure 3 The rise and fall of the "underclass" in public debate, 1960–2017 (source: Proquest historical newspapers)

term. In 1988, in his Godkin Lecture at Harvard's Kennedy School of Government, Wilson had expressed consternation at the sensationalistic invocations of the "underclass" by journalists playing on well-worn racial stereotypes.[2] Soon this consternation was redoubled by alarm at the dominance of the behavioral conception pushed by the Urban Institute economists, which sidelined considerations of social and economic structure. In the summer of 1990, in his presidential address to the Annual Meetings of the American Sociological Association, Wilson relayed the warning of Herbert Gans that the "newest buzzword for the undeserving poor" was "hopelessly polluted in meaning."[3] He announced that, to skirt the "contentious and acrimonious" controversy coalescing over the (mis)uses of the "underclass" and "to keep us focused on research issues, I will substitute the term 'ghetto poor' for the term 'underclass'."[4]

---

[2] William Julius Wilson, "The American Underclass: Inner-City Ghettos and the Norms of Citizenship" (1988).
[3] Herbert J. Gans, "Deconstructing the Underclass: The Term's Danger as a Planning Concept" (1990), p. 272.
[4] William Julius Wilson, "Studying Inner-City Social Dislocations: The Challenge of Public Agenda Research: 1990 Presidential Address" (1991a), p. 6.

108   Part One: The Tale

Wilson's courageous if cautious decision to put the "under-class" on pause reverberated far and wide, including in the national press. Jason Deparle alerted the readers of the *New York Times* that, "two weeks ago, Prof. William Julius Wilson stood up before 1,500 colleagues and called into question the usefulness of a term that has become a fixture of the American political vocabulary and one that he, more than anyone, helped legitimize: 'the underclass'." In the *Washington Post*, Thomas Edsall reported that the concept's surprising "fall from favor" was causing concern among some of its exponents, such as the economist Sheldon Danziger (the former director of the Institute for Research on Poverty), for whom the term "ha[d] served as a valuable bridge between conservatives and liberals."[5]

Wilson was quite ambivalent at this stage: he insisted in the lecture that "the controversy over the underclass concept [had] been productive," stimulating new research on race and poverty in the metropolis; he warned that "any crusade to abandon the concept underclass, however defined, could result in premature closure of ideas"; and he confessed in a later interview with Edsall that he had not decided whether to give up the term permanently. But he quietly abandoned it as the organizing theoretical category of his work. By 1996, Wilson had openly shifted from "underclass" to the designator "ghetto poor" or "new poor" (borrowed from research colleagues in Western Europe, where the term was in vogue a decade earlier). Instead of being called *The American Underclass* (as stipulated in the book contract with his publisher Knopf), the 1996 sequel to *The Truly Disadvantaged* was entitled *When Work Disappears* and subtitled: *The World of the New Urban Poor*.[6]

---

[5] Jason Deparle, "What to Call the Poorest Poor?" (*New York Times*, 1990); Thomas B. Edsall, "'Underclass' Term Falls from Favor: Leading Poverty Researcher May Abandon Politically Charged Word" (*Washington Post*, 1990). See also "The Game of the Name" (*Time Magazine*, August 27, 1990).

[6] William Julius Wilson, *When Work Disappears: The World of the New Urban Poor* (1996); Graham Room, Roger Lawson, and Frank Laczko, "'New Poverty' in the European Community" (1989). Ironically, Wilson borrowed "new poverty" from European scholars just as the latter were forsaking it in favor of "exclusion."

Buoyed by the proliferation of critiques of the category from varied historical and theoretical perspectives, Wilson's change of heart was no doubt fortified by a second major defection from the ranks of the "underclass" sponsors: the Rockefeller Foundation. In 1987, the foundation had intended to bankroll the Research Committee on the Urban Underclass at the Social Science Research Council for a full decade, but it abruptly pulled the plug on it after five years in response to two unforeseen adverse developments. First, the foundation was dismayed by the "underlying, ongoing tension within the Committee over whether the 'underclass' existed at all."[7] The various working groups it sponsored recurrently, if inadvertently, raised the issue and even those participating scholars who believed there was such an urban animal "out there" in the city could not come to a consensus over its characterization; and all silently worried about validating the hoary visions of the undeserving and dangerous poor gleefully projected by neo-conservative commentators on the "underclass." As for the SSRC officers and staff associates, they kept dancing around the issue: remarkably, the foundation's initial proposal for the creation of the Committee submitted to the Rockefeller Foundation in 1988 used the term 127 times (in 71 single-spaced pages of text) but carefully avoided defining it; and the periodic reports on the committee's work employed a variety of circumlocutions, the favorite being "persistent and concentrated urban poverty," rather than endorse one or another definition.[8]

---

[7] Alice O'Connor, *Poverty Knowledge: Social Science, Social Policy, and the Poor in Twentieth-Century US History* (2001), p. 278.

[8] Social Science Research Council, *A Proposal for the Establishment of a Program of Research on the Urban Underclass* (1988); Martha A. Gephart and Robert W. Pearson, "Contemporary Research on the Urban Underclass. A Selected Review of the Research that Underlies a New Council Program" (1988); Robert W. Pearson, "Economy, Culture, Public Policy, and the Urban Underclass" (1989); and Martha A. Gephart, "Neighborhoods and Communities in Concentrated Poverty" (1989). The roundabout of "persistent and concentrated poverty" only introduced more confusion: sometimes the expression was used as a stand-in *for* the "underclass," sometimes as a property *of* the "underclass," and sometimes as an independent phenomenon *related to*, a *cause* or a *consequence of* the rise of the "underclass."

110   Part One: The Tale

The second issue that motivated the Rockefeller Foundation to prematurely pull back from its "underclass" venture was the inability of academic researchers to connect their inquiries to the concerns of policy makers and to speak to the agenda of community activists in poor segregated neighborhoods. The foundation had hoped that the SSRC Research Committee on the Urban Underclass would serve as a vehicle to bridge the gap between pure and applied knowledge. Accordingly, it instructed the SSRC to liaise with the Community Planning and Action Program (CPAP) that the foundation was funding in six cities to tackle problems in the derelict territories believed to harbor the "underclass." But the junction between researchers and practitioners was never made due to "a clash of culture and political priority." Worse yet, all of the grass-roots advocates participating in the CPAP "rejected 'underclass' as a label" and "discarded the census-based designation of neighborhood that quantitative social scientists used."[9] The fact that "the committee did not directly address the day-to-day struggles of poor people in inner cities" or "the needs of activists responding to the effects of public and private disinvestment" was dramatized by the eruption of the Rodney King riots in Los Angeles in April of 1992, about which the Research Committee on the Urban Underclass had precious little to say.[10] The retreat of the Rockefeller Foundation from the "underclass" enterprise not only deprived academics and think tankers of a major source of funding; it also sent the signal, to other foundations as well as to the university, that it no longer signposted the fabled "cutting edge" of research and advocacy.

But the *coup de grâce* for the "underclass" came from the social microcosm whose struggles had driven its rise to national eminence in the first place, that is, the field of policy-politics, in the form of the "welfare reform" voted by the Republican congress and signed into law by the Democractic President Bill Clinton in summer of 1996. Against the backdrop of a booming economy and a palpable decline in street crime, this controversial reform, which replaced the right to

---

[9] O'Connor, *Poverty Knowledge*, pp. 281 and 282.
[10] Michael B. Katz, *Improving Poor People: The Welfare State, the "Underclass," and Urban Schools as History* (1997), p. 63.

minimal public assistance for poor single mothers with the obligation of low-wage employment, overhauled the social policy problematic from top to bottom.[11] Overnight, the meta-question of the "underclass," lumping together welfare mothers, absent fathers, derelict districts, joblessness, and street crime, was *pulverized into a scattershot of separate issues*, each with its own research audience and bureaucratic constituency: for poor urban women, the policy priority shifted from fighting "welfare dependency" to moving recipients "from welfare to work"; on the side of hyperghetto men, "zero-tolerance policing," "mass incarceration," and "prisoner reentry" became the newest investigative frontier and policy puzzles; and the spatial fixation on the hyperghetto found its expression in the thriving cottage industry of research on "neighborhood effects."[12]

The linked relationship between the "underclass" and "welfare reform" was not lost on savvy observers of the political scene, such as the editors of the liberal magazine *The New Republic*, who urged President Clinton to sign the contentious legislation in a punchy editorial published on the morrow of the law's passage: "The continuing agony of the underclass is destroying our cities, our race relations, our sense of civility, our faith in the possibilities of government. It's worth taking

---

[11] R. Kent Weaver, *Ending Welfare As We Know It* (2000); Sharon Hays, *Flat Broke with Children: Women in the Age of Welfare Reform* (2004); Ellen Reese, *Backlash Against Welfare Mothers: Past and Present* (2005); and Loïc Wacquant, *Punishing the Poor: The Neoliberal Government of Social Insecurity* (2009b), ch. 3, "Welfare 'Reform' as Poor Discipline and Statecraft."

[12] Revealingly, the *Annual Review of Sociology* published the following articles in close succession, which together attest to the intellectual obsolescence of the "underclass": Alice O'Connor, "Poverty Research and Policy for the Post-Welfare Era" (2000); Mario Luis Small and Katherine Newman, "Urban Poverty After *The Truly Disadvantaged*: The Rediscovery of the Family, the Neighborhood, and Culture" (2001); Robert J. Sampson, Jeffrey D. Morenoff, and Thomas Gannon-Rowley, "Assessing 'Neighborhood Effects': Social Processes and New Directions in Research" (2002); and Christy A. Visher and Jeremy Travis, "Transitions from Prison to Community: Understanding Individual Pathways" (2003).

112 Part One: The Tale

some risks to end it."[13] Indeed, the new welfare legislation instantly shrank the public aid rolls and combined with a steep drop in crime and full employment to allay the country's urban anxieties, so that public agitation about the "underclass" quickly dissipated in the second half of what historian James Patterson calls the "amazing 1990s."[14]

The vanishing act of the "underclass" *preceded* by a decade the empirical realization that the number of "underclass neighborhoods" had declined significantly by century's close (as a result of the booming economy and tight labor market), which confirms the disconnect between discourse and reality.[15] It retroactively reveals its chief *raison d'être* during the two decades of its bloom from 1977 to 1997: it functioned as an *urban esperanto* – spoken among academics, journalists, and think tankers – suited to expressing the collective reaction of fear and disgust at the *material and symbolic intrusion of the black precariat* into the mental and physical spaces of the middle class. Charles Murray, ideologue-in-chief of the Manhattan Institute (which rose during the same period to wage a campaign aiming to shrink welfare and boost policing as the dual means of class cleansing in the city),[16] has the merit of giving this emotive and cognitive response a frank formulation based on a revealing opposition between "us" and "them": "It wasn't the existence of an underclass that bothered us, but the fact that the underclass was in our face." It "directly affected the lives of mainstream America, or simply 'us'," in four ways: "busing sent children of the black underclass into our schools"; "the homeless physically invaded our public spaces"; "public order deteriorated," as attested by the spread of graffiti and the ubiquitousness of "squeegee men"

---

[13] Editorial bluntly entitled, "Sign it," *The New Republic*, August 11, 1996.

[14] James T. Patterson, *America's Struggle Against Poverty in the Twentieth Century* (2000), title of the last chapter.

[15] Paul A. Jargowsky and Rebecca Yang, "The 'Underclass' Revisited: A Social Problem in Decline" (2006). The research for this article was funded by the Brookings Institution and prepublished as a Brookings Working Paper. See also John F. McDonald, "The Deconcentration of Poverty in Chicago: 1990–2000" (2004).

[16] Loïc Wacquant, *Prisons of Poverty* (2009c), pp. 10–19.

Career of a racialized folk devil   *113*

at stoplights, not to mention "knots of menacing teenagers and prostitutes working the streets in what were supposed to be nice parts of town"; and "crime made fear a chronic part of urban life,"[17] such that the law-abiding, deserving citizenry felt beleaguered inside and endangered outside.

In our face, invasion, deterioration, fear: this vocabulary vividly articulates the acute *sense of siege* felt by "mainstream society" at the thought and sight of the advanced marginality it had forcibly secluded in its desolate urban core. Crucially, it is not the hyperghetto itself, as *terra damnata* harboring the picture negative and the living negation of the "American dream," that was the source of alarm, but the *spillover* of dangerous and defiling black bodies out of control beyond its boundaries, whether in the form of riots, crime, sexual promiscuity, and civic immorality run rampant. The vituperation of the "underclass," overt and abrasive in the writings of think tankers and subtly euphemized in the works of academics, is a form of rhetorical *desecration* of that accursed population that simultaneously effects the *purification* of the imagined middle class forming the mythical "mainstream" of American society.[18]

This case study in the political sociology of knowledge suggests the fruitfulness of Bourdieu's field theory as an analytic framework to dissect intellectual-political controversies. As with every domain of cultural production, to transcend the opposition between an internalist interpretation of texts and an externalist causal analysis of their making, one must *relate* the space of discursive *position-takings* on the "underclass" (structural, behavioral, ecological) to the space of *positions* occupied by their producers and consumers in the web of pertinent institutions.[19] In the case at hand, it has meant locating

---

[17] Charles Murray, *The Underclass Revisited* (1999), pp. 29, 30, 31.

[18] The symbolic dialectic of desecration and cleansing is elaborated by Mary Douglas, *Purity and Danger: An Analysis of Concepts of Pollution and Taboo* (1966).

[19] Pierre Bourdieu, *Fields of Cultural Production* (1993c), chs. 1 and 6. "Fields of cultural production propose to those who are involved in them a *space of possibles* that tends to orient their research, even without them knowing it, by defining the universe of problems, references, intellectual benchmarks (often constituted by the names of its leading figures), concepts in *–ism*, in short, all that one must have in the

114   Part One: The Tale

the various contributors to the debate in one of the *three intersecting fields* engaged in the collective fabrication of the "urban underclass" as classificatory schema: the academic field, wielding scientific authority; the field of policy-politics, philanthropy, and think tanks, obeying a political reason disguised as civic goodwill; and the field of journalism, following a media logic of priority, novelty, and sensationalism.[20] By way of recapitulation, figure 4 presents the main stages in the tribulations of the "underclass" and traces the flows of transactions across the three fields.

Forged by economist Gunnar Myrdal in 1963, the structural concept of "underclass" influenced Glasgow (1980) and was echoed by the Wilson of *The Declining Significance of Race* (1978). But in the mid-1970s, the notion migrated to the world of philanthropic policy (arrow 1), where it mutated into a behavioral and moral construct endorsed and disseminated by Sviridoff and other Ford Foundation officials, notably via work programs run by the Manpower Development and Research Corporation (MDRC). This construct was then picked up, amplified and racialized by the media (arrow 2), starting with the post-riots 1977 article by *Time Magazine*, which triggered Ken Auletta's 1982 account, both of which motivated the Chicago Tribune's 1986 book, *The American Millstone*, and the 1986 articles by Nicolas Lemann on "The Origins of the Underclass" in *The Atlantic Monthly*.

Journalistic accounts and media interest activated and slanted inquiries by academic researchers and think-tank experts (arrow 3), such as the Underclass Project at the Urban Institute, funded by the Rockefeller Foundation. This project

---

back of one's mind in order to be in the game" (p. 176). Furthermore, every position-taking "receives its distinctive *value* from its negative relationship with the co-existing position-takings to which it is objectively related and which determine it by delimiting it" (p. 30).

[20] For exemplary studies of these three universes, see Pierre Bourdieu, *Homo Academicus* (1984) on the scholarly field; Thomas Medvetz, *Think Tanks in America* (2012), on the microcosm of policy institutes; and Jan Fredrik Hovden, *Profane and Sacred: A Study of the Norwegian Journalistic Field* (2008), on the logics of the media.

eventuated in a series of articles by the economists Mincy, Ricketts, and Sawhill in the mid-1980s that codified the behavioral conception of the "underclass" and (arrow 4) came to dominate research on the topic despite Wilson's (1987) and Massey and Denton's (1992) neo-ecological theories.

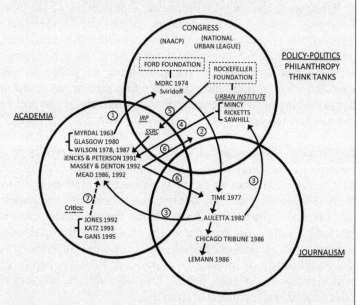

Figure 4 The peregrinations of the "underclass" across the academic, policy-political-philanthropic, and journalistic fields (1963–1996)

This research rocketed (arrow 5) when the Rockefeller Foundation financed the Committee of Research on the Underclass at the Social Science Research Council (SSRC) in 1988–93 and germane activities of the Institute for Research on Poverty (IRP), and in turn (arrow 6) stimulated further production by both policy-philanthropic institutes and journalists. By the early 1990s, dissent and resistance coalesced inside the academic field (arrow 7), led by the historical and analytic critiques of Jones (1992), Katz (1993a), and Gans (1995). Congress gave its stamp of approval to the moral-behavioral notion through official hearings and publications, while civil rights organizations such as the NAACP and the National Urban League were ambivalent about the sudden

116   Part One: The Tale

> rise of the "underclass": they used the term sparingly and
> gingerly, due to concern over its pejorative denotations and
> blame-the-victim implications.

What were the social conditions of possibility of the rise,
flowering, and fall of the demonic tale of the "underclass"
beyond the *structural complicity* between the academic,
journalistic and policy-political fields and the active pros-
elytizing and booming financial backing of philanthropic
foundations?[21] Much like the pseudo-scientific association
between blackness and criminality crystallizing at the end of
the nineteenth century was solidified by what historian Khalil
Muhammad calls the "racial data revolution,"[22] the debate on
the "underclass" coalescing in the 1980s was powerfully propelled and decisively shaped by the *poverty data revolution*,
that is, the exponentially rising availability of statistical information measuring income deprivation along with the gamut
of correlated properties drawn from the decennial census
(including public-use microsamples), the Current Population
Survey (and its Annual Social and Economic Supplement),
the Panel Study of Income Dynamics, and the profusion of
national reports on vital, health, housing, welfare, economic,
educational, and criminal statistics.

This data revolution was a delayed offshoot of Lyndon
Johnson's War on Poverty. The latter fostered the stupendous
growth of a "poverty research industry" that canonized the
official "poverty line" created in 1969 for bureaucratic purposes and soon remade the visage of American social science:
it elevated the topic of poverty in the hierarchy of scientific
objects (its share of federal research funding exploded from
under 1% in 1965 to over 30% in 1980); it granted priority to economic models based on human capital theory and

---

[21] "The interests inherent in belonging to a field are the foundation of
complicities that are, in part at least, hidden from the participants
themselves by the conflicts of which they are the principle." Pierre
Bourdieu, "Champ politique, champ des sciences sociales, champ
journalistique" (1996), p. 26.

[22] Khalil Gibran Muhammad, *The Condemnation of Blackness: Race,
Crime, and the Making of Modern Urban America* (2010), ch. 1.

Career of a racialized folk devil 117

boosted large-scale controlled experiments, microdata simulation and program evaluation; and it furthered the founding of public policy schools at leading universities.[23]

Locating perennial data sources, building robust information systems, and diffusing databases are central to the development of a *positivist problematic*, since good empiricist common sense teaches that, if there is data about it, then it must be real – and if there is lots of data, it must also be important (to wit, data science). In point of fact, one of the major achievements of the SSRC Committee on the Urban Underclass – and a special point of pride of the Rockefeller Foundation which funded it – was the creation of the Underclass Database under the direction of the quantitative sociologist John Kasarda. The Underclass Database was a panel design containing some "7,300 economic, social, demographic, and health indicators for the 100 largest metropolitan central cities and their underclass and poverty subareas," with items drawn from 32 sources in multiyear machine-readable files and variables chosen for being "central to underclass research."[24] The SSRC database was vast and rich enough to outshine the Under Class Data Base (containing 1,098 variables for 43,221 tracts for the year 1980) developed at about the same time at the Urban Institute, also with funding from the Rockefeller Foundation.[25]

Among the bureaucratic indicators undergirding "underclass" research, none was more vital than the geo-coded

[23] Michael B. Katz, *The Undeserving Poor: From the War on Poverty to the War on Welfare* (1989), pp. 115–22; Robert H. Haveman, *Poverty Policy and Poverty Research: The Great Society and the Social Sciences* (1987), esp. ch. 3; and O'Connor, *Poverty Knowledge*, ch. 9, "The Poverty Research Industry."

[24] John D. Kasarda, *Urban Underclass Database: An Overview and Machine-Readable File Documentation* (1992). At about the same moment, Pearson, the staff associate in charge of the SSRC Committee on the Urban Underclass, pitched the need for *more* statistical data on the animal to the American Statistical Association: Robert W. Pearson, "Social Statistics and an American Urban Underclass: Improving the Knowledge Base for Social Policy in the 1990s" (1991, in *Journal of the American Statistical Association*).

[25] A short description is available from the National Bureau of Economic Research at data.nbr.org/udbdesc.pdf (accessed October 26, 2020).

118 Part One: The Tale

measurement of poverty, that is, the identification of census tracts by aggregate level of poverty (containing 20%, 30%, and over 40% households falling below the government "poverty line").[26] These thresholds set by the Census Bureau made it possible to measure and track the spatial diffusion and concentration of poverty; this measurement stimulated the income-based redefinition of the ghetto eliding caste, the policy designation of "underclass areas," and the neo-ecological conception of the "underclass" of William Julius Wilson.[27] As for time frame, analysts of the "underclass" focused narrowly on the decade from 1970 to 1980 for the simple reason that these were the only two years for which the Bureau of the Census provided poverty figures by census tract. Administrative constrictions thus defined the contours of the object of study and explain the utter lack of historical depth of the debate.

Historical inquiry shows indeed that the combination of urbanization and (post)industrialization has everywhere generated social marginality, often acute and enduring, and spaces of disorder, real or perceived; the question here is how to characterize and name them, and with what scientific and political consequences. "Underclass" is the latest entry in a long and tumultuous roster of labels specifically aiming to designate and incriminate the problem populations of the city's underbelly. But it differs in three crucial ways from previous derogatory markers such as "paupers," "scum," "residuum," "rabble," "mob," "underworld," "tramps," "submerged tenth," "ragged classes," "dangerous classes," and "lumpenproletariat."[28]

[26] Chris Herring, "Concentrated Poverty" (2019).

[27] I can speak to this point with confidence: as Wilson's lead research assistant, in 1986–9, I carried out the data collection and computation of the distribution of black and white residents by poverty area in large US cities that was the basis for his thesis of the "concentration effects" propelling the rise of the "underclass." Back then, this involved long days and nights of labor in the bowels of Regenstein library, combing through the massive physical tomes of the census reports for each city and each decade, and tabulating aggregate totals and rates by hand.

[28] For germane dissections of salient concepts pertaining to urban marginality, see Louis Chevalier, *Classes laborieuses et classes dangereuses*

Career of a racialized folk devil   *119*

First, at the hands of its American users, the "underclass" morphed from an ethnically neutral structural concept into a *cryptoracial moral category* that flags deprived and depraved African Americans in the corroding "inner city" under cover of pointing to a "class." This semantic legerdemain was particularly valuable in a period during which overt mention of race was considered in bad taste in philanthropic circles and ineffectual on the policy front. Racial imagery was thus paradoxically deployed to advocate race-neutral disciplinary policies, such as restrictive "workfare" on the social front and expansive "prisonfare" on the penal front, effectively targeting the hyperghetto population.[29] Next, the idiom of the "underclass" was supported, not just by ordinary and political common sense: it was powerfully backed by a new sprawling "poverty research industry" formed by a plethora of interlinked think tanks, policy institutes, and specialized academic centers,[30] plugged into government institutions,

---

à Paris pendant la première moitié du XIXe siècle (1958); Hyman Rodman, "Culture of Poverty: The Rise and Fall of a Concept" (1977); Gertrude Himmelfarb, *The Idea of Poverty: England in the Early Industrial Age* (1983), on the "residuum" and the "ragged classes"; Robert L. Bussard, "The 'Dangerous Class' of Marx and Engels: The Rise of the Idea of the Lumpenproletariat" (1987); Peter Stallybrass, "Marx and Heterogeneity: Thinking the Lumpenproletariat" (1990); Ann M. Woodall, *What Price the Poor? William Booth, Karl Marx and the London Residuum* (2005); Jeffrey S. Adler, "The Dynamite, Wreckage, and Scum in our Cities: The Social Construction of Deviance in Industrial America" (1994); Erik H. Monkkonen, *Walking to Work: Tramps in America, 1790–1935* (1984); Nancy Fraser and Linda Gordon, "A Genealogy of Dependency: Tracing a Keyword of the US Welfare State" (1994); Didier Fassin, "Exclusion, 'underclass', 'marginalidad': Figures contemporaines de la pauvreté urbaine en France, aux États-Unis et en Amérique latine" (1996); Alan Gilbert, "The Return of the Slum: Does Language Matter?" (2007); Mary Daly and Hilary Silver, "Social Exclusion and Social Capital: A Comparison and Critique" (2008); Dominique Kalifa, *Les Bas-fonds. Histoire d'un imaginaire* (2013), on the "underworld"; and Tom Slater, "The Invention of the 'Sink Estate': Consequential Categorisation and the UK Housing Crisis" (2018).

[29] Loïc Wacquant, "The Wedding of Workfare and Prisonfare Revisited" (2011).

[30] The stupendous growth of that industry in the three decades after the

120   Part One: The Tale

animated by criss-crossing debates that gave it an impeccable certificate of apparent scientificity and the imprimatur of public officials that none of the previous labels enjoyed. The symbolic powers of science and state were thus mobilized to *authorize and sanitize* the policy doxa of the day.

A third distinctive feature of the "underclass" is that it designates, not just a problem population, but also a *place* of fear and loathing: a redoubt of social villainy, vice, and violence that corrupts its residents and threatens to contaminate the city like a virus. The invention of the "underclass area," quantitatively delimited by seemingly neutral and objective indicators, marks out a new locus in the imaginative geography of urban horror and terror. So much to say that the "underclass" was not just the latest in a long list of synonyms for the undeserving poor, as argued by Michael Katz and Herbert Gans.[31] Rather, members of the "underclass" are *triply disreputable*: they carry the stigma of idle poverty; they are tainted by low-caste membership; and they dwell in a blemished district perceived as an urban inferno, the hyperghetto. It is this *treble stigma*, flagging the "group" simultaneously in symbolic, social, and physical space that makes the "underclass" label unprecedented.

Like its historical predecessors and cognates, the "underclass" turns out to be a *specular concept*: it reflects the moral obsessions and social fantasies of those who employ it in the manner of a mirror. This is why, far from being an obstacle to its diffusion, the fuzziness and malleability of the "underclass" was key to its short-lived success. This is why it was exclusively deployed from afar and from above by alarmed observers of the dreaded "inner city."

A brief contrast of the opposed provenance, uses, and semantic charge of the vocabularies of "soul" and "underclass" is instructive here. The notion of *soul*, which gained wide appeal during the racial turmoil of the 1960s, was a

---

declaration of the "War on Poverty" is charted by Alice O'Connor in *Poverty Knowledge*, ch. 9.

[31] Michael B. Katz, "The Urban Underclass as a Metaphor of Social Transformation" (1993b); Herbert J. Gans, "Positive Functions of the Undeserving Poor: Uses of the Underclass in America" (1994). This position was defended earlier by Leslie Innis and Joe R. Feagin, "The Black Underclass Ideology in Race Relations Analysis" (1989).

"folk conception of the lower-class urban Negro's own 'national character'."[32] Produced from within for in-group consumption, it not only designated black speech, music, food, and style; it served as a symbol of solidarity and a badge of group endurance and honor. By contrast, "underclass" status is established wholly from the outside (and from above) and forced upon its putative members by specialists in symbolic production – journalists, politicians, academics, and governmental experts – for purposes of cultural sense-making and bureaucratic disciplining, and this without the slightest concern for the self-understanding of those who are arbitrarily dumped into this paper fiction. Whereas the folk concept of soul, as part of an "internal ghetto dialogue" toward an indigenous reassessment of black identity,[33] was appraisive, the idiom of "underclass" is derogatory, an identity that nobody invokes except to pin it onto a denigrated other. That even black oppositional intellectuals such as Cornell West should have embraced the terminology of "underclass," and separated the latter from the "black working poor," is revealing of the degree to which the hyperghetto has become an *alien object* on the landscape of American society.[34]

---

[32] Ulf Hannerz, *Soulside: Inquiries into Ghetto Culture and Community* (1969), p. 54, and idem, "The Rhetoric of Soul: Identification in Negro Society" (1968); also John Horton, "Time and Cool People" (1967).

[33] Charles Keil, *Urban Blues* (1966); for an extension of this argument, see Monique Guillory and Richard C. Green (eds.), *Soul: Black Power, Politics, and Pleasure* (1998).

[34] Cornell West, *Keeping Faith: Philosophy and Race in America* (1993).

5

Implications for the social epistemology of urban marginality

~

After two decades of heated debate and the expenditure of millions of research dollars in its chase, the greatest confusion continued to surround the American "underclass." The notion rose, spread, and crashed with equal alacrity. While it continues to be used in contemporary social research as a *rhetorical* placeholder (signifying exclusion from, or location at the bottom of, a variety of ranked orders, to which I return in the Appendix, pp. 189–94) or in quotation marks (signaling the unease of the user), it has lost its scientific aura and fallen out of fashion in public debate.[1] One can draw several enduring lessons from the strange career of the "underclass" in post-civil rights America as soon as one recognizes that this confusion does not stem from deficiencies in its analysis but is one of its constitutive properties.

First, the invention of the "underclass" bespeaks the national ideological turnaround of the 1970s, a *sea change in the collective perception and attitude of the middle and upper classes toward marginal categories*, incarnated by the double threat

---

[1] Contemporary rhetorical extensions include the global underclass, rainbow underclass, adjunct underclass, financial underclass, creative underclass, nursing underclass, information underclass, constitutional underclass, energy underclass, internet underclass, digital underclass, math underclass, and viral underclass.

Social epistemology of urban marginality   *123*

of the dissolute teenage "welfare mother" on the feminine side and the dangerous street "thug" on the masculine side, and toward the welfare and penal state believed to mollycoddle them. The spiking middle-class fear of the imploding ghetto fueled revanchist conservatism and punitive poverty policies, and it recharged the Malthusian stereotype according to which deprivation results from the psychological defects, moral misconduct, and improvidence of the poor. Charles Murray expresses this lucidly when he defines "underclass ethics" as follows: "Take what you want, respond violently to anyone who antagonizes you; despise courtesy as weakness; take pride in cheating (stealing, lying, exploiting) successfully."[2]

Indeed, the contents of the category "underclass" reflects the perennial concerns of urban elites for those segments of the dispossessed that escape the yoke of official disciplines: to demarcate the deserving from the undeserving poor, to detect and prevent the supposed perverse effects of public aid, to identify and neutralize the disruptive poor, and, lastly, to minimize the financial and administrative burden they impose on the city and nation. Uniquely, the deployment of the racialized trope of the "underclass" also betrays the concern to separate "good Negros" from "bad Niggers,"[3] stemming from the white trauma caused by the racial uprising of the 1960s and a *double class tension, between* the black middle and working class and, *within* the black working class itself, between its stable fraction, oriented toward "respectability" as permitted by steady employment and home-ownership, and its precarious fraction, drawn to the "street," relying on a mix of insecure jobs, public aid, informal trades, and the criminal economy.[4]

[2] Charles Murray, *The Underclass Revisited* (1999), p. 33. On the return of moralism in the perception of poverty, see Stephen Pimpare, *The New Victorians: Poverty, Politics, and Propaganda in Two Gilded Ages* (2004).

[3] This historical and folkloric opposition is recounted by Randall Kennedy, *Nigger: The Strange Career of a Troublesome Word* (2008); Leon F. Litwack, *Trouble in Mind: Black Southerners in the Age of Jim Crow* (1999), pp. 437–57; and Roger D. Abrahams, *Deep Down in the Jungle: Negro Narrative Folklore from the Streets of Philadelphia* (1970).

[4] The first battle is chronicled by Mary Pattillo, *Black on the Block:*

124   Part One: The Tale

Second, despite repeated attempts at codification, the criteria for membership in the urban "underclass" remained multiple, woolly, and heterogeneous. Some pertain to the labor market (employment, income) and to kinship (marriage, household type), others to the state in its function of education (lack of credentials), occupational training (lack of skills), and management of derelict and dangerous populations (welfare provision and criminal justice), and still others to the divisions of urban space ("no-go areas" or "poverty census tracks"). Defining a group by the frequency of certain behaviors among its members presumes resolved the question of its boundary and *undermines the very notion of group*, which presupposes a constancy and coherence that behavior does not possess. Moreover, the concept conflates dependent and independent variables to the point of definitional tautology. In one variant, the existence of the group explains the onslaught of "social pathologies"; in another, it is the prolixity of "antisocial behaviors" that causes the rise of the group and serves as proof for its reality.[5] Such *logical circularity* and *semantic indeterminacy* should have quickly disqualified the "underclass" as instrument for social inquiry. The very opposite turns out to be the case: tautology and indeterminacy were the surest source of the notion's attractiveness, for it allowed those who invoked it to redraw its perimeter at will in accordance with their intellectual or ideological interests.

A third failing of the thematics of the "underclass" is its utter *lack of historical depth and sensibility*, in two different senses. To start with, history is *constitutive* of the sociospatial constellation observed at the fin de siècle: the hyperghetto cannot be understood in its specificity but replaced in the full trajectory of black urbanization over a century. The transition from segregation to ghettoization to hyperghettoization marks a transformation of the form and function of African-American seclusion in the metropolis, parallel to the tran-

---

The Politics of Race and Class in the City (2007), and the second by Elijah Anderson, *Code of the Street: Decency, Violence, and the Moral Life of the Inner City* (1999).

[5] This circularity is pointed out by Herbert J. Gans, *People, Plans, and Policies: Essays on Poverty, Racism, and Other National Urban Problems* (1991), p. 279.

Social epistemology of urban marginality 125

sition from competitive capitalism to Fordism to neoliberal postindustrialism against the backdrop of anti-urbanism.

The physical dilapidation of the hyperghetto is the layered materialization of these two historical shifts; its double segregation by caste and class results from the machinations of real estate boards, banks, and city officials over the whole stretch of a century; changes in family strategies and gender relations in the early twentieth century paved the way for the rise of single-parent households among the poor in the postwar period; the accelerating deproletarianization of urban blacks in the 1980s is partly the delayed offshoot of the fragility of black working-class formation in the interwar years; the catastrophic educational profile of hyperghetto children is a product of the establishment of a separate and inferior public education system doubly segregated by caste and class with roots in the politics of housing and public bureaucracy of the 1940s; the exodus of the African-American middle class from the metropolitan core comes as the culmination of black collective mobilization against white exclusion in the Northern city going back to the 1920s.[6] So much to say that the narrow focus of the "underclass" debate on the 1970s, because geocoded poverty data covered only that decade, truncates the very object to be constructed and ignores the *sedimentation of historical forms inside contemporary constellations*.

The "underclass" discourse fails the test of historicity in a second sense: it does not take stock of *comparable* concerns documented earlier and elsewhere by the historical record. It claims to have ensnared in its net an unprecedented American reality born in the 1970s when many of the trends, diagnoses, and policy strategies it encompasses have come up time and

---

[6] See, respectively, Camilo José Vergara, *The New American Ghetto* (1995); Arnold R. Hirsch, *Making the Second Ghetto: Race and Housing in Chicago 1940–1960* (1983, new exp. ed. 1998); Kathryn M. Neckerman, "The Emergence of 'Underclass' Family Patterns, 1900–1940" (1993); Harvey Kantor and Barbara Brenzel, "Urban Education and the 'Truly Disadvantaged': The Historical Roots of the Contemporary Crisis, 1945–1990" (1993); Joe William Trotter, Jr., *Black Milwaukee: The Making of an Industrial Proletariat, 1915–45* (1985); and Thomas J. Sugrue, *Sweet Land of Liberty: The Forgotten Struggle for Civil Rights in the North* (2008).

126   Part One: The Tale

again at the intersection of urbanization, capitalist industrialization, and class inequality. Thus the notion that the *concentration* of the poor in dilapidated districts undermines their
family life, morality, and morale, and prevents them from
escaping their condition was a staple of social commentary
on the big cities of the nineteenth century in both England
and America, as was the idea that these districts threaten to
infect the respectable poor and, left unchecked, contaminate
the whole city.[7] The belief that slum residents *lack contact*
with the broader society and are cut off from the wholesome
cultural influence of the middle class was a common trope in
the mid-nineteenth century. So much so that "social policies
designed to reduce the social isolation of the poor became
a dominant component of philanthropic thought on both
sides of the Atlantic."[8] The *neighborhood* was portrayed as
an incubator of marginality and immorality in the recurring
debate on the slums and it supplied the central practical construct orienting the work of the settlement movement a full
century before the advent of the "underclass."[9]

In other words, the focus on the neighborhood, concentration effects and social isolation are not innovations of "underclass" scholars in the 1980s so much as perennial concerns of
students of the city's underbelly across a long century. Lastly,
the urge to categorize, measure, and quantify the "underclass,"
in order to displace the sensationalist account of journalists
and to lay the neutral knowledge foundation for enlightened

[7] Michael B. Katz, "From Underclass to Entrepreneur" (2012),
pp. 103–5. The classic English studies on this topic are Friedrich
Engels, *The Condition of the Working Class in England* (1993
[1845]), and Charles Booth's mammoth sociography of the London
poor in the 1890s: Christian Topalov, "The City as *Terra Incognita*:
Charles Booth's Poverty Survey and the People of London, 1886–
1891" (1993 [1991]). The best account on the United States is Paul
S. Boyer, *Urban Masses and Moral Order in America, 1820–1920*
(1978).

[8] David Ward, *Poverty, Ethnicity, and the American City, 1840–1925:
Changing Conceptions of the Slum and the Ghetto* (1989), p. 22.

[9] Christopher Silver, "Neighborhood Planning in Historical
Perspective" (1985); Thomas Lee Philpott, *The Slum and the Ghetto:
Neighborhood Deterioration and Middle-Class Reform* (1978), part
IV.

Social epistemology of urban marginality   *127*

policy, merely updates the rationale and practice of the "social survey" innovated by Charles Booth in the 1890s and encapsulated by the triad "observe, classify, reform."[10]

What is more, the monomaniacal focus on the "ghetto underclass" hides the proliferation of precarized populations of all hues caused by the restructuring of American capitalism after the dissolution of the Fordist–Keynesian social compact. And the exclusive attention bestowed upon the urban poor reinforces the erroneous notion that "rural poverty [is] somehow more wholesome, healthy, and less degrading than its urban counterpart."[11] In fact, in absolute terms, the most crushing, tenacious, and isolated poverty in America is found, not at the heart of big cities, but in the Native American reservations of the Great Plains, the small towns of the Rio Grande region, the Mississippi delta, Appalachian Kentucky, and assorted agrarian hinterlands across the country. Whether defined in structural, behavioral or neo-ecological terms, the rural "underclass" outclasses its urban cousin in size, intensity, and persistence.[12] In addition to sheer material deprivation, the rural poor in small towns and sparsely populated territories suffer from lack of access to the core public institutions that buttress the life strategies of the urban poor, such as postsecondary education, hospitals, social welfare, public transport, and the courts.[13]

"Car-window sociology"* en route for the Mississippi delta

"Rural areas often have dreadful conditions. Tunica, Mississippi, is an example. [Footnote: We visited Tunica in

---

[10] Topalov, "The City as *Terra Incognita*," p. 420.

[11] Jacqueline Jones, *The Dispossessed: America's Underclasses from the Civil War to the Present* (1992), p. 270.

[12] Cynthia M. Duncan, *Worlds Apart: Why Poverty Persists in Rural America* (1999); Kathleen Ann Pickering, Mark H. Harvey, and David Mushinsky, *Welfare Reform in Persistent Rural Poverty: Dreams, Disenchantments, and Diversity* (2006).

[13] David Showalter, "Steps Toward a Theory of Place Effects on Drug Use: Risk, Marginality, and Opportunity in Small and Remote California Towns" (2020).

128   Part One: The Tale

> May 1989 as part of a trip that took us from Memphis down through the Mississippi delta area to Jackson and then up through the Arkansas side of the delta to Little Rock.] The houses are little more than run-down shacks, without plumbing or sewage fixtures in many cases. The streets are unpaved and social problems are rampant. Clearly, these conditions are in some ways the equal of, if not worse than, conditions in urban ghettos. We know very little about rural pockets of poverty and the subject deserves much greater attention. Nevertheless, Tunica, Mississippi, and Harlem, New York, are very different places. In the remainder of this chapter, we talk about ghetto poverty in metropolitan areas only."
>
> > Paul A. Jargowsky and Mary-Jo Bane, "Ghetto Poverty: Basic Questions" (1990), in a report on *Inner-City Poverty in the United States* published by the National Academy of Sciences, p. 34
>
> * "Car-window sociology" is the expression by which W.E.B. Du Bois denotes the studies of black life by white scholars in the Jim-Crow South, based on cursory and blurry observation from afar (such as can be carried out while riding a Pullman car).

How then, given these brute facts, can one justify circumscribing the scholarly and policy focus to the sole metropolitan centers and account for the curious *disappearance of the white "underclass,"* despite Charles Murray's valiant efforts to thrust it onto the collective radar?[14] Ken Auletta provides an answer to these two questions that has the merit of candor: if "the races all behave in the same manner," he observes, "defiant antisocial behaviors" are notably less "prevalent" in the rural South and black "misfits" in the cities are "notably more dangerous and visible" than their white counterparts from the countryside. Lawrence Mead confirms this diagnosis when he avers in testimony to congress that, "although there is a white underclass, the white

[14] Charles Murray, "The Coming White Underclass" (*Wall Street Journal*, 1993a), and "The Emerging White Underclass and How to Save It" (*Philadelphia Inquirer*, 1993b).

Social epistemology of urban marginality

> ### "The white underclass will show its face"
>
> "The white underclass will begin to show its face in isolated ways. Look for certain schools in the white neighborhoods to get a reputation as being unteachable, with large numbers of disruptive students and indifferent parents. Talk to the police; listen for stories about white neighborhoods where the incidence of domestic disputes and casual violence has been shooting up. Look for white neighborhoods with high concentrations of drug activity and large numbers of men who have dropped out of the labor force."
>
> Charles Murray, *The Coming White Underclass*
> (American Enterprise Institute, 1993c)

people *don't make special claims. They don't resist social authority.*"[15]

Finally, from the spectacular bursting of the *speculative conceptual bubble* of the "underclass," one can derive several recommendations for the social epistemology of urban marginality and pointers on the politics of theory. The first is to beware of the *Christopher Columbus complex*, that is, the urge to periodically announce the discovery of a new "group" – all too often characterized by dysfunction and disrepute – in the nether regions and remote corners of urban space.[16] The mission of the sociologist here is to report on the classification struggles to differentiate, organize, and name problem populations, not to enter these struggles to designate winners and losers by putting social science in the position of performative symbolic power. A second recommendation is to eschew *turnkey problematics* offered on a silver platter by current journalistic and policy debates or surging academic fashion:

---

[15] Ken Auletta, *The Underclass* (1982), p. 200; Lawrence Mead in Joint Economic Committee, *The Underclass, Hearing Before the Joint Economic Committee of the 101st Congress of the United States* (1989), p. 71, my italics. A full analysis of this hearing appears *supra*, pp. 54–8.

[16] The built-in logic of this periodic (re)discovery is explored in the classic essay by David Matza, "The Disreputable Poor" (1966).

130 Part One: The Tale

they are wont to inscribe the sociopolitical prejudices of the moment and the practical preoccupations of city managers and state elites into the research enterprise, and to skew it accordingly. (I return to this point in the conclusion.) This is especially true when venturing into territories of relegation in a society steeped in anti-urbanism and puritanism such as the United States, which means approaching an object *preconstructed in reality as dirty and dangerous*, and therefore liable to pollute the analysis with degrading denotations and sulfurous connotations.

Third and relatedly, resist the *pull of heteronomy inside* the social scientific field, where philanthropic foundations and think tanks shape knowledge production by cultivating envoys, proxies, and allies, not just through funding streams and directives, but also by subtly altering the hierarchy of research questions and the terms of inquiry. In the case of the "underclass," one would need a fulsome sociology of "Rockefeller sociology" to fully elucidate how that foundation, along with the Ford Foundation and the Russell Sage Foundation, breathed life into the "underclass" and influenced its academic students by crowding out other possible problematics[17] – such as deproletarianization and the casualization of labor, the role of neoliberal state restructuring in the making of the black precariat, the continued spatial seclusion of urban African Americans, or the abysmal failure of government institutions to distribute essential public goods at the bottom of the class structure. Extra-scientific agencies hold sway inside the scientific field, not just by *cognitive colonization*, but also by *analytic preemption*. By advancing "neutral" agendas accepting the institutional order as a given, they actively contribute to the collective ignorance of the political roots of urban marginality by social science.[18]

---

[17] A first contribution to such as sociology is David L. Seim, *Rockefeller Philanthropy and Modern Social Science* (2013).

[18] For an exemplary study of how think tanks exert influence by altering categories, launching intellectual flares, and buffering policy makers from autonomous academics, see Thomas Medvetz, *Think Tanks in America* (2012), ch. 5, "From Deprivation to Dependency: Expert Discourse and the American Welfare Debate." On collective ignorance as the outcome of cultural and political struggles, more

Social epistemology of urban marginality 131

A fourth recommendation growing out of this case study of the rise and fall of the "underclass" is to be alert to the *semantic lability and echoes of keywords*, how the same term takes on different meanings and resonances as it circulates across fields of cultural production or across sectors of the same field (e.g., different disciplines in the academic universe or different theoretical traditions inside the same discipline). Explicate these shifting meanings, check their coherence and compatibility, and disclose the social properties and vested interests of those who give them weight. In the case at hand, because the "underclass" was a *racialized* pseudo-scientific folk devil, its validation depended critically on the endorsement of *black* scholars and on their intellectual authority, much like controversial research on children and the family gains from being vetted by *women* scholars or, better yet, by *feminist* scholars.[19]

Finally, make sure that your analytic categories do not presuppose that which needs to be demonstrated. Deplorably, the logical fallacy of *petitio principii* (begging the question) is all too common in social science – none other than Émile Durkheim was a known repeat offender.[20] Thus, characterizing the "underclass" as social disorganization incarnate and urban exoticism personified prevents us from identifying the principles of its organization and the properties its putative

---

generally, see Robert N. Proctor and Londa Schiebinger (eds.), *Agnotology: The Making and Unmaking of Ignorance* (2008).

[19] As a progressive black scholar renowned for his writings on controversial racial issues and a forceful advocate of social democratic policies, William Julius Wilson played a disproportionate role in both legitimating and delegitimating the "underclass." Wilson's politics are disclosed in *The Bridge over the Racial Divide: Rising Inequality and Coalition Politics* (1999). Black researchers also provided *racial cover* for think-tank studies and official testimony before government bodies. According to Herbert Gans, moreover, "an internal ethnic class conflict" was at play between Caribbean-born professionals and the African-American poor, as evidenced by the fact that most black "advocates of a behavioral definition [of the underclass] [were] of West Indian origin." Herbert J. Gans, *The War Against the Poor: The Underclass and Anti-Poverty Policy* (1995), p. 53.

[20] Steven Lukes, *Émile Durkheim, his Life and Work: A Historical and Critical Study* (1973), p. 31.

132 Part One: The Tale

members share with other urban denizens; defining it as a walking and breathing concentrate of immorality makes it impossible to specify the social conditions under which residents of the hyperghetto cling to, diverge from, or creatively reshape conventional norms.

All of this is not to say that one cannot *construct* robust analytic concepts to investigate a novel social reality, as I endeavored to do elsewhere with the notions of ghetto, hyperghetto, and advanced marginality, and as I will essay later with "precariat" (*infra*, pp. 162–8) and with "race" in the conclusion to this book. On the contrary. It is to insist, as I will in the epilogue to this intellectual and social journey through the underside of the American metropolis, that such concepts be historicized, clearly differentiated from folk constructs, and forged out in the open with a clear-eyed view of their purpose, limitations, and virtues, which should minimally include semantic coherence, logical consistency, and cognitive productivity. Only by practicing what Pierre Bourdieu calls "reformist reflexivity," combining epistemological vigilance and prudence, can one hope to advance the sociology of dangerous categories and mysterious territories.[21]

[21] Pierre Bourdieu, *Science de la science et réflexivité* (2001), p. 179.

Exit

In his commanding dissection of "The Denial of Slavery in American Sociology," Orlando Patterson identifies three causes for the stunning "silence of the sociological clan" on the question: "disciplinary parochialism," "pervasive presentism," and subservience to "ideological fads and fashions."[1] These same three causes lie behind the sudden rise, garrulous spread, and quick demise of the "underclass." Studying urban marginality through that conceptual prism was a way of *denying the changing yet enduring nexus of caste, class, and state* in the postindustrial metropolis by focusing investigative attention and remedial action on individual behavior, family, and neighborhood.

With the benefit of hindsight, it emerges that the "underclass" proliferated at the intersection of two urgent public debates over urban marginality that ignited the media, obsessed policy makers, and sucked scholarly energy during the period opened by the 1977 New York City blackout riots and closed by the passage of the 1996 welfare reform bill eliminating the legal right to poor support. Set against the backdrop of entrenched anti-urbanism and stirred by the profound white trauma from the 1960s black uprising, these two debates were overtly racialized as well as bifurcated by gender and inflected by age.

On the *feminine side*, public concern fastened onto the alleged *welfare dependency* of poor black women, and particularly on pregnancy among black teenage girls ("babies having babies") – even though field research showed conclusively that welfare payments were too meager for poor households to rely on them without supplements from off-the-book jobs, kin networks, and street commerce.[2] On the *masculine*

---

[1] Orlando Patterson, "The Denial of Slavery in Contemporary American Sociology" (2019), pp. 908–9.

[2] Michael B. Katz, *The Undeserving Poor* (1989); Leon Dash, *When Children Want Children* (1989); Kristin Luker, *Dubious Conceptions: The Politics of Teenage Pregnancy* (1996); Kathryn Edin and Laura Lein, *Making Ends Meet: How Single Mothers Survive Welfare and Low-Wage Work* (1997), chs. 2 and 6.

134   Part One: The Tale

side, public apprehension focused on perceived *rampant criminality* on the street, nourished by a lenient "revolving-door" system of justice, and especially on the spread of gang violence and its lurid effluents, crack dealing, drive-by shootings, and car-jackings committed, it was believed, by ever younger offenders – even though violent victimization rates were stable and incarceration rates more than tripled between 1975 and 1995.[3]

The "welfare mother" and the "gang banger" (and his cousin the "super-predator") thus stepped forth into the public limelight as the two iconic figureheads of the urban hydra of the "underclass," embodying, the one a moral threat in the domestic sphere, and the other a physical threat in public space.[4] These two avatars of hypermarginality furthermore presented a fiscal paradox: while black women on welfare were deemed to put an intolerable burden on the nation's coffers, necessitating steep budget cutbacks, no expense was deemed excessive when it came to building jails and prisons to corral black street criminals. Thence a bifurcated policy stream: welfare contraction and penal expansion, the shredding of the social safety net and the knitting of the criminal dragnet, discipline and neutralization, workfare and prisonfare, the two planks in the building of the neoliberal state, converging on the deprived and stigmatized populations trapped in the hyperghetto.

To capture the novelty of the "underclass" of the fin de siècle as *redoubled public dishonor,*[5] marked by the taint of

---

[3] Michael Tonry (ed.), *Youth Violence* (1998); John M. Hagedorn, *People and Folks: Gangs, Crime and the Underclass in a Rustbelt City* (1988); Katherine Beckett, *Making Crime Pay: Law and Order in Contemporary American Politics* (1999); Loïc Wacquant, *Prisons of Poverty* (2009), pp. 144–50, on the stability of criminal victimization and the boom in prison resulting in a growing crime–incarceration disconnect over time.

[4] This double-headed monster is all the more arresting when one realizes that the vast majority of the "underclass" – by any definition – was and is composed of children.

[5] On the workings of "social estimation of honor," positive or negative, see Max Weber, *Economy and Society* (1978 [1918–22]), vol. 2, pp. 932–6; on race as a form of state dishonor, Loïc Wacquant, "Race as Civic Felony" (2005).

pauperism and race on the (feminine) social front and by the stain of criminality and race on the (masculine) penal front, it is crucial to recall that the association between blackness, welfare, and the prison in the national mind was then a recent and novel one. Until the 1960s, welfare was not identified with parasitic black mothers but with hardy white widows. It is only after the rise of the welfare rights movement, led by the black activists of the National Welfare Rights Organization, and the subsequent expansion of the public aid rolls that blackness and assistance became fused, activating white resistance to the further extension of the social safety net for poor mothers and cementing the view that welfare recipients were undeserving freeloaders.[6]

Similarly, in the 1950s, the dominant public image of the prisoner was of a "humorous, patriotic, Caucasian, and hapless" male who was "infinitely redeemable" and hungered for social integration. By the 1970s, this "altruistic Caucasian" had been supplanted by the fearsome figure of a virulent black convict issued from the racial strife of the 1960s, deemed "violent for the sake of violence alone," and who, because he was obeying his intrinsically criminal nature, behaved in ways defying rehabilitation and thus demanding brute restraint.[7] The racialization of the image of the convict, caused by the wave of *street riots* of the 1960s and the turning of prisoners into symbols of black oppression, was both accelerated and solidified by the wave of *prison riots* that followed the uprising and massacre at the Attica penitentiary in 1971, triggered by the migration of the Civil Rights Movement behind bars.[8]

---

[6] Jill S. Quadagno, *The Color of Welfare: How Racism Undermined the War on Poverty* (1994); Premilla Nadasen, *Welfare Warriors: The Welfare Rights Movement in the United States* (2004); Martin Gilens, *Why Americans Hate Welfare: Race, Media, and the Politics of Antipoverty Policy* (2009).

[7] John Sloop, *The Cultural Prison: Discourse, Prisoners, and Punishment* (2001), p. 15 and pp. 16–17.

[8] Heather Ann Thompson, *Blood in the Water: The Attica Prison Uprising of 1971 and its Legacy* (2016); Bert Useem and Peter Kimball, *States of Siege: US Prison Riots, 1971–1986* (1991); Dan Berger, *Captive Nation: Black Prison Organizing in the Civil Rights Era* (2014).

136   Part One: The Tale

The joint blackening of the female welfare recipient and of the male street criminal and soon-to-be convict made *workfare and the prison two core institutions in the government of urban blackness*. It tilled the symbolic ground for the planting of the demonic tale of the "underclass," whose growth and blooming in turn reinforced those very associations, cementing them in a garrulous and monotonous discourse endowed with the authority of science, journalism, and the state. Liberal scholars, think-tank experts, officials of philanthropies and research foundations, and journalists thus collaborated in a gigantic paper bonfire fueled by class disgust and racial fear. Deployed from the right, the thesis of the growth of the "underclass" in the inner city also fit snugly with the ambient anti-statism of the period in that it spotlighted the scandalous profligacy and culpable leniency of government in its treatment of urban marginality. Every time they invoked the concept to call the state to the rescue, scholars from the left inadvertently but inevitably gave credence to this indictment of big-city liberalism.[9]

The "underclass" personified: the welfare queen and the rapist – and the "subway vigilante" to the rescue

The two symbolic figureheads of the "underclass" – the dissolute "welfare mother" and the unregenerate "street thug" – were personified by two real individuals. The first is the Cadillac-driving "welfare queen" Linda Taylor, lambasted by Ronald Reagan for a decade starting in the 1976 presidential campaign. The second is the murderer-rapist Willie Horton, vilified by George Bush the father in his own race for the White House in 1988. Both of them were African American and emblems of big-city government gone haywire. Both stereotypes were successfully mobilized to cut social welfare and expand criminal punishment, the two main planks of the policy response to the urban "underclass."

Linda Taylor was a 47-year-old itinerant and psychotic con artist who served time in prison for welfare fraud (she had

---

[9] Jonathan Rieder, *Canarsie: The Jews and Italians of Brooklyn Against Liberalism* (1985).

used four aliases to illegally collect $3,000) when she was profiled by the *Chicago Tribune* in a story on the incompetence of public bureaucracy. Suitably embellished, she became a highlight of the stump speeches of Ronald Reagan, and the figure of the "welfare queen" endured in the national conscience long enough to help Clinton "end welfare as we know it" in 1996 (1). To the outraged gasps of his audience, Reagan claimed that "she has 80 names, 30 addresses, 12 Social Security cards and is collecting veterans' benefits on four non-existing deceased husbands. And she's collecting Social Security on her cards. She's got Medicaid, getting food stamps, and she is collecting welfare under each of her names. Her tax-free cash income alone is over $150,000" (2). The story was proof positive that welfare chiselers were bankrupting the country's budget and morals. It tapped into the racialized resentment of the white working- and middle-class voters toward public aid recipients and African Americans getting ahead of the social queue thanks to profligate government programs of affirmative action. It merged seamlessly into the tale of the "underclass."

William Horton was a 37-year-old convicted murderer in Massachusetts who went on the lam while on a week-end furlough program. He kidnapped a white couple, stabbed the man and repeatedly raped his wife. Bush made him the centerpiece of his aggressive campaign plank on crime, lambasting his Democratic rival, Massachusetts governor Michael Dukakis, for "allowing murderers to have week-end passes." In the lugubrious campaign video featuring his mug shot, William Horton was renamed "Willie" and pictured as the emblematic member of the criminal "underclass" writing the "New American crime story: random violence against innocent middle-class victims, committed by criminals the system might have controlled better" (3).

A third public character *completes the symbolic triangle of the urban "underclass": the white victim of its physical and mental abuses.* Days before Christmas of 1984, the 47-year-old white nuclear engineer Bernhard "Bernie" Goetz gained instant national fame – and hero status – as "the subway vigilante" when he shot four black teenagers on a Manhattan subway car, after one of them had approached him and intoned, "Give me five dollars." Goetz, who turned

138 Part One: The Tale

himself in to the police after a frenetic nine-day manhunt, was initially charged with attempted murder, assault, and a raft of related charges. He claimed to have fired in self-defense, out of fear that the boys were about to rob him (he had been "mugged" by three black teenagers a few years back and had taken to carrying a pistol loaded with hollow-point bullets inside his waist-strap).

The incident sparked a nationwide debate on race, crime, and guns, fueled by lurid images of an "underclass" rampaging through the city. The dominant public reaction was "a sense of pleasure, even gratitude"; Goetz was "the embodiment of everyone's fantasies. He's the one who acts instead of talks, the guy who's mad as hell and isn't going to take it any more." A New York City supermarket manager expounded: "If you ask me, the man's a saint. We should give him extra bullets, extra guns, and a year's supply of tokens and turn him loose on the subways." The head of the Congress for Racial Equality lauded the shooter as "the avenger for all of us. Some black man ought to have done it long before . . . I wish it had been me" (4).

The media painted an empathetic, full-color picture of Goetz whereas the four victims (one of whom was brain damaged and paralyzed for life as a result of the shooting) were lumped together, alien creatures issued out of female-headed families living off public aid in some derelict housing project in the Bronx. "Uneducated, with criminal records, on the prowl for a few dollars, they exemplified the underclass of teenage criminals feared by both blacks and whites" (5). A Bernard Goetz Legal Defense Fund was quickly set up; admiration for the man turned into a cult. A *New York Times* columnist quoted from his readers' mail (running five to one in favor of the shooter) a letter that exulted: "Bernhard Hugo Goetz makes me proud, P-R-O-U-D, to be a white, male American!" A graffito on the subway explicated, "Goetz rules niggers" (6). Goetz's defense attorney announced that his client would put the criminal justice system on trial and focus on the dire need for public safety in the city.

Two full years and three grand juries after the shooting, a trial jury acquitted Goetz of all twelve charges on grounds of self-defense, save for a single count of illegal weapons possession, for which he served eight months in jail, even though he had made this confession to the police, which was read into evidence during the trial: "My intention was to do anything I could to hurt them ... My intention was to murder them, to hurt them, to make them suffer as much as possible ... If I had had more bullets, I would have shot them again and again and again" (7).

1. Ange-Marie Hancock, *The Politics of Disgust: The Public Identity of the Welfare Queen* (2004). The role of the stereotype is proudly acknowledged by Ron Haskins, a Senior Fellow at the Brookings Institution and early advocate of the 1996 welfare reform, which he summarized by the punchy formula: "Goodbye Welfare Queens, Hello Working Moms" (cited in Carly Hayden Foster, "The Welfare Queen: Race, Gender, Class, and Public Opinion" [2008], p. 163).

2. Josh Levin, *The Queen: The Forgotten Life behind an American Myth* (2019), p. 26; Jeremy Lybarger, "The Price You Pay: On the Life and Times of the Woman Known as the Welfare Queen" (2019).

3. David C. Anderson, *Crime and the Politics of Hysteria: How the Willie Horton Story Changed American Justice* (1995), p. 55. Bush's campaign manager boasted that they would broadcast the advertisement with such frequency that "voters [will] think Horton had become Dukakis's running mate" (p. 223).

4. Cited in Lillian B. Rubin, *Quiet Rage: Bernie Goetz in a Time of Madness* (1988), pp. 42–3, 55 and 10.

5. George P. Fletcher, *A Crime of Self-Defense: Bernhard Goetz and the Law On Trial* (1990), p. 2.

6. Rubin, *Quiet Rage*, p. 104.

7. Rubin, *Quiet Rage*, p. 38. An insider account by the judge who tried the case is Stephen G. Crane, "The Trial of Bernhard Goetz" (1990). Eleven years later, Goetz was ordered by a civil court to pay $43 million in damages to one of his victims. A second infamous New York crime triggered the same collective emotions around "underclass" violence run amuk: the beating and rape of the "Central Park jogger" leading to the false conviction of five black and Hispanic youths: Sarah Burns, *The Central Park Five: The Untold Story behind One of New York City's Most Infamous Crimes* (2012), and the Netflix miniseries by Ava Du Vernay, *When They See Us* (2020).

140   Part One: The Tale

To borrow the language of Reinhart Koselleck, the "under-class" turns out to be a keyword (*Stichwort*) of the post-civil-rights conjuncture of American history characterized by intense class disgust and suffusive racial fear, rooted in the functional obsolescence and structural implosion of the dark ghetto, but not a basic concept (*Grundbegriff*) of the sociology of caste and class in the city. It *animated* a debate crossing the boundaries of the scientific, journalistic, and politics-policy-philanthropic fields, but it did not *illuminate* it. On the contrary, it instilled conceptual ambiguity and empirical opacity where clarity and transparency were sorely needed given the volatile nature of the question, and it harnessed heated emotion where cold ratiocination was in order. In the end, the tale of the "underclass," as the illegitimate daughter of the ghetto uprising of the 1960s, exacerbated racialized representations of urban destitution and perpetuated the poverty of a classless sociology of poverty.

PART TWO

LESSONS FROM
THE TALE

"Truth is nothing but the rectification of a long string of errors."

Gaston Bachelard, *Le Nouvel esprit scientifique*, 1934

"Terminology does matter. It often swings the thoughts; when illogical and false, it reveals a disposition toward biases; and it indicates the direction of that disposition. To keep concepts and terms clean, disinfected, logical and adequate to reality is a primary behest to the scientist. In this slippery field only the utmost purism can be accepted."

Gunnar Myrdal, *Against the Stream: Critical Essays on Economics*, 1973

PART TWO

LESSONS FROM
THE TALE

In the manner of a conceptual coroner, I have documented the life and death of the "underclass" in the American debate on race and poverty. I have traced how the notion was coined, diffused and employed in three distinct but overlapping institutional arenas: the fields of academic research, journalism, and politics-policy-philanthropy in the United States.[1] I have shown how the paramount symbolic agencies of science, media, and politics now converged, now clashed, in the drive to articulate and legitimate the rival structural, behavioral, and neo-ecological conceptions of the "underclass," and to act upon urban marginality thus defined through public policies of welfare, housing, and criminal justice devised accordingly. I have found that, as a result of these symbolic struggles, in which social scientists were entangled *nolens volens*, the notion grew chaotic, became overloaded with moral baggage, and remained impregnated with social fears and racial fantasies – and, for these reasons, lost scientific value, even as it continued (and continues) to circulate under the pen of social researchers unaware of, or unperturbed by, its convoluted genealogy and confounding anatomy.

Quandaries and consequences of naming

It bears stressing that this is not inherent to the term "underclass" (although the prefix "under" has a ring of inferiority) and that this epistemic fiasco was not a preordained outcome. The linguistic ruminations of the later Wittgenstein remind us that the meaning of a word is decided by the array of uses to which it is put.[2] The trajectory of the "underclass" could have been otherwise. The British excursus discussed in chapter 1 suggests that there once was a viable path toward a fruitful neo-Weberian concept in the late 1970s in the works

---

[1] On the dynamics of fields as spaces of forces and spaces of struggles, see Pierre Bourdieu and Loïc Wacquant, *An Invitation to Reflexive Sociology* (1992), pp. 15–19, 94–115.

[2] "For a *large* class of cases of the employment of the word 'meaning' – though not for all – this word can be explained in this way: the meaning of a word is its use in the language." Ludwig Wittgenstein, *Philosophical Investigations* (2009 [1953]), p. 43.

144 Part Two: Lessons from the Tale

of Anthony Giddens and John Rex, one that was consistent with Myrdal and converged with the tacit Weberianism of the early William Julius Wilson of *The Declining Significance of Race*.

This opportunity to extend class theory "downward" and across the Atlantic while taking ethnicity and space into account was foreclosed by the national parochialism and heteronomy of the American debate on the "underclass"; by the swift subsumption of the term under the national obsession with race as blackness; by the interest of philanthropies in relegitimating their programs in reference to a new target "group"; and by Wilson's later turn toward a policy problematic and audience that undermined his dogged, but ultimately unsuccessful, effort to re-embed the notion into a robust theory of urban inequality and marginality.[3] By then, the demonic horse of the behavioral "underclass" was out of the scientific barn and the concept could not be salvaged.

The tale of the "underclass" reminds us of a sociological truism that is worth unpacking: social realities, starting with the words used to label them and the discourses deployed to know and shape them, on paper and in objectivity, are the result of a *historical work of collective fabrication* – in the double etymological sense of manufacturing and forgery, for social reality is always to some degree both recognized and misrecognized. In this joint effort, symbolic producers vie for what Pierre Bourdieu calls the *power of legitimate naming*, involving the capacity to "make and unmake groups" by cutting up social space in a particular way, and imposing that way as the "dominant principle of vision and division."[4] Whether they realize it or not, like it or not, social scientists

---

[3] See, in particular, William Julius Wilson, "Social Theory and the Concept Underclass" (2006).

[4] Pierre Bourdieu, "The Social Space and the Genesis of Groups" (1985 [1984]); "Esprits d'État. Genèse et structure du champ bureaucratique" (1993a); and *Sociologie générale. Cours du Collège de France, 1981–1983*, Vol. 1 (2015), esp. pp. 121–72. Classification struggles are "struggles over the monopoly of the power to make people see and believe, to make them know and recognize, to impose the legitimate definition of the divisions of the social world, and thereby to *make and unmake groups*" (*Langage et pouvoir symbolique* [2000], p. 183, original italics).

Quandaries of naming *145*

are caught up in this classification struggle and must grapple with the continual *blending and bleeding of meaning* it entails.

On the one side, scientific categories escape the academic field to circulate in the media, policy circles, and even everyday life where they glean new senses: thus the sociological notions of individualism, charisma, upper-middle class, role model, cultural capital, and others that have entered into common parlance. On the other side, folk constructs validated by the state, journalism, think tanks, and business or ordinary common sense seep into the scientific field and contaminate analytic thinking, as with the notions of "neighborhood," "governance," "exclusion," and "diversity." The most delicate and dangerous notions are those *hybrid epistemic constructs* that can be read alternately or simultaneously as ordinary, policy, and scholarly, such as the terms "race," "urban," "ghetto," "crime," or "community" when it comes to marginality in the city. These words thrive on the ongoing misunderstanding that their users mean the same thing because they use the same terms, when in fact they are talking past one another about different realities.[5]

There is a *special difficulty and danger in naming dispossessed and dishonored categories* residing in the city's districts of relegation, for three reasons. First, these categories are generally deprived of the symbolic means of producing their own representation such that their name and images are crafted by outsiders – until they can be collectively contested, rejected, or reappropriated, according to the paradigm "Black is beautiful."[6] From the mid-nineteenth century onwards, it is social reformers, police officials, social scientists, novelists, and journalists who have forged the public idiom of urban marginality, anchored by the trinity of misery, immorality, and criminality. Second, the denizens of the city's underbelly

---

[5] The dangers of the "illusion of agreement" caused by the mixing of everyday and sociological definitions are spotlighted by Richard Swedberg, "On the Use of Definitions in Sociology" (2020).

[6] A recent example of a strategy of symbolic inversion is the organization of an annual "Roma pride" march by Romani (Gypsy, Sinti, Tsingani, Manouches) activists in a dozen cities across Europe to denounce discrimination, counter negative stereotypes, and foster collective identification with the diaspora.

146 Part Two: Lessons from the Tale

have historically evoked strong emotions, long stamped by fascination and titillation, among the educated bourgeoisie, as exemplified by the joint invention of "slumming" and "undercover" journalism centered on the underbelly of the industrial metropolis in the late nineteenth century.[7] The same is true of political and cultural elites – academics included – in the postindustrial metropolis of the late twentieth century, except that then fascination turned into revulsion and titillation into terror, as illustrated by the wide circulation of a new vocabulary of urban horror and degeneration attached to the "underclass," "dependency," "illegitimacy," "welfare mother," "gang banger," "mugging," "wilding," and "super-predator."

A third difficulty is that categories situated at the bottom of social and physical space are the carriers of what Norbert Elias (building on Max Weber) calls "group disgrace," which elicits contempt and ostracism, and threatens to contaminate and debase those who come in contact with them, speak about them or, worse, speak in their name.[8] Elias stresses that group charisma and group disgrace are "twin phenomena" that exist in and through contraposition. This raises the question of who is the charismatic counterpart to the disgraced "underclass," deserving of praise and admiration. The answer is the fabled "middle class" of the (white) American "mainstream," destabilized by the precarization of work and family under the press of neoliberal state policies and fearful of downward mobility – as brilliantly shown by anthropologist Katherine Newman in *Falling from Grace: Downward Mobility in the Age of Affluence*, which is the essential companion volume and political complement to Wilson's *The Truly Disadvantaged*

---

[7] Dominique Kalifa, *Les Bas-fonds. Histoire d'un imaginaire* (2013). The closing chapter of this book on the chronicle of the urban underworld in the Western social imaginary deals with the "underclass" as the latest avatar in a long line of incarnations of social squalor, vice, and crime.

[8] "Weber himself conceptualized a variant of group charisma [*Gentilcharisma*, the charisma of a clan] without conceptualizing to the same extent the reverse side of group charismatic claims such as group contempt, group ostracism, group disgrace and group abuse." Norbert Elias, "Group Charisma and Group Disgrace" (1998 [1964]), p. 107.

Quandaries of naming

(the two books were published one year apart).[9] And so we come to realize that the ritual degradation of the "underclass" in public discourse between 1977 and 1997, unrestrained in journalism and subdued but stubborn in scholarship, served the symbolic revalorization of the anxious middle class, unmoored from its sense of safety and identity by the seeping of social insecurity up the social and spatial structure of the metropolis. This confirms that the equally mythical "underclass" and "middle class" are two components of a single "asymmetric counter-concept" à la Koselleck.

Symbolic categories inform our perception of the world and thereby orient our action in the world and our efforts to shape it, individual and collective. The split between the three constructs of the "underclass" – structural, behavioral, and neo-ecological – matters because these point in three different public policy directions, with or without the express support of their advocates. The structural concept of Myrdal favors ensuring full employment through Keynesian-style measures of social and economic support, education and training, and the eventual provision of public jobs at living wages (such as variants of a "federal jobs guarantee"), designed to blunt the marginalizing effect of postindustrialism. Building the social and economic state is the path *not* taken by the United States and other advanced societies afflicted with persistent urban dispossession. This is attested, among other trends, by the international rise of homelessness, generalization of working poverty, and the diffusion of social insecurity, objective for the working class and subjective for the middle class. An alternative path suggested by the Myrdalian diagnosis of the *coming* of marginality rooted in the most *advanced* sectors of the economy is to disconnect work from subsistence by means of a universal basic income (with or without a concurrent jobs guarantee).[10]

---

[9] Katherine S. Newman, *Falling from Grace: Downward Mobility in the Age of Affluence* (1988).

[10] Loïc Wacquant, *Urban Outcast: A Comparative Sociology of Advanced Marginality* (2008), pp. 252–6. For a fulsome civic and economic defense of such policy, read Philippe Van Parijs and Yannick Vanderborght, *Basic Income: A Radical Proposal for a Free Society and a Sane Economy* (2017).

148   Part Two: Lessons from the Tale

The behavioral conception of think-tank economists and their followers suggests a campaign of cultural inculcation to restore norms of work and family and increased punishment to reduce the incidence of anti-social conduct such as crime. This is the policy track traveled by the United States at century's end: the wedding of disciplinary social policy (workfare, instituted by the 1996 Personal Responsibility and Work Opportunity Act) and neutralizing criminal justice (prisonfare, propelled by the Violent Crime Control and Law Enforcement Act of 1994), trained onto the black precariat of the hyperghetto according to a gendered division of the labor of control, workfare handling the women (and their children) and prisonfare their men.[11] This approach is theorized by the conservative political scientist Lawrence Mead, with the diligent support of the liberal think tank the Brookings Institution, under the label of *new paternalism*, that is, "supervisory programs" whereby the government enforces behavioral requirements on "dependent" populations – welfare recipients, wayward high-schoolers, the homeless, drug addicts, and criminals – as a condition of public support.[12]

The neo-ecological perspective developed by Wilson, Massey, and students of "neighborhood effects" designates the residential neighborhood as prime site of state interven-

---

[11] Loïc Wacquant, *Punishing the Poor: The Neoliberal Government of Poverty* (2009), and idem, "The Wedding of Workfare and Prisonfare Revisited" (2011).

[12] Lawrence M. Mead (ed.), *The New Paternalism: Supervisory Approaches to Poverty* (1997). The president of the Brookings Institution, which supported the research and published the book on the topic, notes in his preface: "Recently government has sought to supervise the lives of poor people who become dependent on it, either *through welfare or the criminal justice system* . . . This policy is highly controversial, because some people think it implies 'blaming the victim' for social problems or signals an abandonment of government's commitment to the needy. However, directive programs have advanced *because the public is alarmed about welfare and crime.*" Michael H. Armacost, "Preface" (1997), pp. vii–viii, my italics. Remarkably, the requirement of behavioral supervision does not extend to the middle and upper classes, even though they are heavily "dependent" on the state via tax deductions for higher education, home-ownership, health care, and retirement.

Quandaries of naming   *149*

tion. It has fostered programs intended to reduce "concentrated poverty" by demolishing large public housing projects, promoting mixed-income housing, and scattering residents of the inner city through the expanded use of rent subsidies (as instituted by the Quality Housing and Work Responsibility Act of 1998).[13] But the main effects of these programs have been to dramatically reduce the stock of public housing, over and against the resistance of poor black tenants; to cream the more stable households out of the hyperghetto, leaving behind the more precarious ones; to exacerbate class tensions within the African-American population between homeowners and renters battling for the same enclaves in transition; and to create new opportunities for the gentrification of the razed wastelands thus created.[14] They have obscured the gross insufficiency of the stock of viable low-income housing in the major cities. Most crucially, these programs have fostered the misbegotten perception, among scholars, state officials, and city elites, that space is an autogenic causal variable that generates intense economic destitution and social dereliction of its own logic, rather than the physical agglomeration of capitals over time, reducing the question of the formation and fate of a racialized precariat to a simple geographic equation.

There was another, more direct, neo-ecological route to deflating the "underclass," advocated by Douglas Massey and Nancy Denton in *American Apartheid*: a frontal and multiscalar attack on residential segregation, animated by

---

[13] It should be noted that focusing on housing alone is not the policy direction advocated by Wilson, who favors across-the-board state efforts on the economic and fiscal, educational, family and child support, health, and jobs training and provision fronts. This positions him closer to Myrdal than to the advocates of housing reform inspired by "neighborhood effects." William Julius Wilson, *The Truly Disadvantaged: The Inner City, the Underclass, and Public Policy* (1987), pp. 150–7; *When Work Disappears: The World of the New Urban Poor* (1996), ch. 8; and "Responses to *The Truly Disadvantaged*," pp. 285–8.

[14] Edward G. Goetz, *Clearing the Way: Deconcentrating the Poor in Urban America* (2003); Lawrence J. Vale, *Purging the Poorest: Public Housing and the Design Politics of Twice-Cleared Communities* (2013).

150 Part Two: Lessons from the Tale

"a moral commitment and a bipartisan leadership."[15] The political will for such an attack never materialized. Moreover, concerted national action on this front is rendered difficult and unlikely by the disjointed and fragmented structure of the American bureaucratic field. The hyper-localism of decision-making regarding housing and the provision of public services, from schools to public safety to clean water, also weighs heavily in favor of the spatial status quo characterized by the conjugation of high class and ethnoracial segregation.[16]

The combination of workfare, prisonfare, and forced spatial dispersion has shrunk the territory and population of the hyperghetto and intensified marginality in its midst. But its main virtue from the standpoint of state officials and city managers holds: it has rendered nearly *invisible* the predicament of the black poor in the urban core, thus allaying the fear of the "inner city" by middle-class households, black and white, and making possible the "urban renaissance" of the early twenty-first century.[17]

Forging robust concepts

Sociologists rarely stop to think about the tools with which they think, other than methodological ones. By default, they leave issues of concept formation and validation to philosophers of science, who themselves rarely investigate the actual conceptual practices of working social scientists, preferring instead to engage in metatheoretical reflection and normative stipulation.[18] But failing to turn the instruments

[15] Douglas Massey and Nancy A. Denton, *American Apartheid: Segregation and the Making of the Underclass* (1993), p. 235.

[16] Jessica Trounstine, *Segregation by Design: Local Politics and Inequality in American Cities* (2018).

[17] Derek S. Hyra, *The New Urban Renewal: The Economic Transformation of Harlem and Bronzeville* (2008); Mary Pattillo, *Black on the Block: The Politics of Race and Class in the City* (2007).

[18] Four exceptions are Robert Merton and Rogers Brubaker in sociology and Giovanni Sartori and David Collier in political science. For illustrations, see Robert K. Merton, "Socio-Economic Duration: A Case Study of Concept Formation in Sociology" (1984), and Robert K. Merton and Elinor Barber, *The Travels and Adventures of*

Forging robust concepts 151

of their science onto these very instruments comes at considerable sociological cost. When it concerns the naming of social groups – arguably one of the most delicate of intellectual operations, since it engages a whole political ontology and it is in dispute in reality itself – it permits the proliferation and circulation of *hybrid constructs* that mix ordinary and scholarly meanings, sentiment and reason, moral judgment and empirical ascertainment, accusation (or celebration) and elucidation. The solution to this quandary is found in the teachings of historical epistemology as developed by Gaston Bachelard (for physics and chemistry) and Georges Canguilhem (for biology and medicine), and extended into social science by Pierre Bourdieu:[19] to make a clear and clean *demarcation between folk concepts and analytic concepts*, notions developed as pragmatic cognitive recipes to orient

---

Serendipity: A Study in Sociological Semantics and the Sociology of Science (2004); Rogers Brubaker, *Ethnicity Without Groups* (2004), and *Grounds for Difference* (2015); Giovanni Sartori, "Concept Misformation in Comparative Politics" (1970), and idem (ed.), *Social Science Concepts: A Systematic Analysis* (1984); David Collier and James E. Mahon Jr., "Conceptual 'Stretching' Revisited: Adapting Categories in Comparative Analysis" (1993); and David Collier and Robert Adcock, "Democracy and Dichotomies: A Pragmatic Approach to Choices about Concepts" (1999).

Note that issues of conceptual critique and articulation were central to the works of sociology's founders: Karl Marx, *A Contribution to the Critique of Political Economy* (2020 [1859]); Émile Durkheim, *Les Règles de la méthode sociologique* (2017 [1895]); and Max Weber, *Economy and Society* (1978 [1918–22]), ch. 1, and *The Methodology of the Social Sciences* (1947). For two recent elaborations in sociology and political science, respectively, see Richard Swedberg, *The Art of Social Theory* (2014), ch. 3, "Naming, Concept, and Typology," and Gary Goertz, *Social Science Concepts and Measurements* (2020), ch. 9, "Intension-Extension: Concept Structure and Empirical Description."

[19] Gaston Bachelard, *Le Nouvel esprit scientifique* (1934); Georges Canguilhem, *La Connaissance de la vie* (1952); Pierre Bourdieu, Jean-Claude Chamboredon, and Jean-Claude Passeron, *Le Métier de sociologue. Préalables épistémologiques* (1968, 2nd ed. 1973). On the French discontinuist school in the philosophy of science, see Gary Gutting (ed.), *Continental Philosophy of Science* (2008), chs. 11, 13, and 15.

152 Part Two: Lessons from the Tale

oneself in social life versus notions geared to producing descriptions, interpretations, and explanations of social phenomena. Émile Durkheim puts it best when he writes in *The Rules of the Sociological Method*:

> It is not simply a question of discovering the means to retrieve with fair accuracy the facts to which the words of common parlance refer and the ideas that they convey. What is needed is to formulate fresh concepts, appropriate to the needs of science and expressed by means of a special terminology.[20]

But realizing that, like all scientists, sociologists must elaborate their own concepts, rather than accept them ready-made and prepackaged by common sense – ordinary, policy or scholarly – does not tell us how to construct *good ones*. Based on the trials and tribulations of the "underclass" as keyword of the debate on race and urban poverty at century's end, let me suggest three pairs of criteria that make for a robust analytic concept, aiming to strike a balance between comprehensiveness and compactness.

(1) Semantics – clarity and neutrality: the meaning of the concept is clear, distinct, and stable. It minimizes the possibility of discrepant interpretations. It does not play on emotions, ride on political belief, or imply a moral verdict (what Max Weber puts under "*Werturteilsfreiheit*").

(2) Logics – coherence and type specificity: the attributes of the concept "stick together" and do not contradict one another. The concept identifies a distinctive configuration and separates it from neighboring configurations, preventing the lumping of related but different objects.

(3) Heuristics – empirical adequacy and theoretical productivity: the concept serves well to generate rich and varied observations. It suggests hypotheses and fosters theorizing extending across cases and linking up with other theories (to validate, develop, or challenge them).

The "underclass" turns out to be a poor concept on all three counts. *Semantically*, it is blurry and open to multiple,

---

[20] Durkheim, *Les Règles de la méthode sociologique*, p. 130.

Forging robust concepts   *153*

conflictive readings. It is unstable over time and across discursive domains. The suffix "class" suggests that it partakes of a theory of stratification when it does not.[21] It is overburdened with ideological and moral baggage (hitched to the prefix "under"); and, instead of fostering what Durkheim calls "cold and dry analysis," it activates strong emotions and carries a negative moral judgment. Indeed, its emotive resonance is what made the "underclass" attractive to many of its users. And collective emotions are epicentral to the prompting of the racial habitus and the patrolling of racial boundaries, and thereby to the racialization of the category.[22]

The "underclass" is also wanting *logically*: it lumps together disparate social categories redounding to different social relations: labor market, family, neighborhood, school, welfare, housing, policing, etc. It refers by turns to a population, a set of behaviors, a place in the metropolis, a position in social space, or a discourse on race and poverty, failing to achieve what Carl Hempel calls "intersubjective certifiability." The "underclass" provides no rationale for why the predicament of African Americans in the "inner city" should be carved out and isolated from the broader continent of hypermarginality, black, white, and Hispanic, urban and rural. And, if the focus is on racialized dispossession, why not refer to an "undercaste" instead to make that clear?[23]

Did the "underclass" prove *heuristic*? It certainly energized empirical research on the intersection of race, space, and poverty in the metropolis, and it offered a lexicological springboard for scholars to enter into the whirling policy

---

[21] Erik Wright's proposal to insert the "so-called 'underclass'" into a neo-Marxist theory of class, as "a category of social agents who are economically oppressed but not consistently exploited," did not catch on. Erik Olin Wright, *Interrogating Inequality: Essays on Class Analysis, Socialism and Marxism* (1994), p. 48.

[22] On the centrality and materiality of collective emotions in the construction and maintenance of racial division, see Mustafa Emirbayer and Matthew Desmond, *The Racial Order* (2015), pp. 117–26, and Eduardo Bonilla-Silva, "Feeling Race: Theorizing the Racial Economy of Emotions" (2019).

[23] Herbert J. Gans, "From 'Underclass' to 'Undercaste': Some Observations about the Future of the Post-Industrial Economy and its Major Victims" (1996).

154 Part Two: Lessons from the Tale

debate on welfare, albeit on terms they did not set.[24] But did it produce any empirical discovery one would not have made without it? The spatial concentration of urban poverty is one candidate but, after increasing slightly in the 1980s, it decreased dramatically in the 1990s, before rising again rapidly in the 2000s, without the concept suggesting how or why.[25] The idea of neighborhood effects is another candidate but, despite its technical sophistication and quantitative profusion, that line of research is dogged by continuing issues of selection bias and has yet to weigh the specific impact of the neighborhood against, say, the effects of changing state policies or labor market shocks. This is not to say that place does not matter, but that its influence is modest according to the more favorable studies and gets easily washed out by the exogenous forces spotlighted by Wilson's own model.[26]

Did the "underclass" produce rich and nuanced data giving new insights into social life in the urban core? On the contrary, it has encouraged the rote accumulation of aggregate data based on administrative categories (the poverty line, the census tract, the black/white dichotomy, welfare versus work, etc.) that are ill-suited to capturing the social morphology and strategies of marginalized populations in the metropolis.[27]

---

[24] Mario Luis Small and Katherine Newman, "Urban Poverty After *The Truly Disadvantaged*: The Rediscovery of the Family, the Neighborhood, and Culture" (2001); Alice O'Connor, "Poverty Research and Policy for the Post-Welfare Era" (2000). See also the array of studies reviewed by William Julius Wilson, "Responses to *The Truly Disadvantaged*" (2012).

[25] Paul A. Jargowsky, *Concentration of Poverty in the New Millennium* (2013), and John Iceland and Erik Hernandez, "Understanding Trends in Concentrated Poverty: 1980–2014" (2017).

[26] In a recent paper, Sampson seems to rebalance the theoretical claim of this research program when he positions the neighborhood as "an important driver *and mediator* of urban transformation" (my italics) produced in part by "higher-order structures" (including "state, economy, law, racism, mobility networks"). What part exactly remains to be determined. Robert J. Sampson, "Neighbourhood Effects and Beyond: Explaining the Paradoxes of Inequality in the Changing American Metropolis" (2019).

[27] Contrast the poverty of the picture of poverty provided by the "underclass" research program with the lush and nuanced field studies

Forging robust concepts

More crucially still, research on the "underclass" has *effaced the institutions that govern their lives* and trapped them in a bureaucratic maze perpetuating their marginality.

It is revealing in this regard that the best field studies of the period, Martín Sánchez-Jankowski's *Islands in the Street: Gangs in Urban American Society*, Philippe Bourgois's *In Search of Respect: Selling Crack in El Barrio*, and Kathryn Edin and Laura Lein's *Making Ends Meet: How Single Mothers Survive Welfare and Low-Wage Work*, studiously eschew the notion of "underclass" and associated ideas (such as "disorganization," "social isolation," and "welfare mother"). These studies effectively undermine the vision from afar of macro-analysts of poverty by showing how people at ground level continually contradict and overrun their categories (such as the fictitious opposition between the "working poor" and the "non-working poor").[28]

One methodological implication of this disjuncture is the necessity to combine indirect measurements at a distance with *direct observation from near* and to *adapt macro-categories* (say, household composition, employment status, or criminal involvement) to the fluidity and porousness of life situations, lest the statistical study of aggregates gravely distort or miss entirely the specificity of the social relations and experiences of the urban poor. Another implication is that macro-sociologists of marginality should rediscover the scientific

---

surveyed by Faith M. Deckard and Javier Auyero, "Poor People's Survival Strategies: Two Decades of Research in the Americas" (2022).

[28] Martín Sánchez-Jankowski, *Islands in the Street: Gangs in Urban American Society* (1991); Philippe Bourgois, *In Search of Respect: Selling Crack in El Barrio* (1995); Kathryn Edin and Laura Lein, *Making Ends Meet: How Single Mothers Survive Welfare and Low-Wage Work* (1997); Sudhir Alladi Venkatesh, *American Project: The Rise and Fall of a Modern Ghetto* (2000). A later wave of ethnographies reinforces that argument, among them Mario Luis Small, *Villa Victoria: The Transformation of Social Capital in a Boston Barrio* (2004); Alford A. Young Jr., *The Minds of Marginalized Black Men: Making Sense of Mobility, Opportunity, and Future Life Chances* (2011); Nikki Jones, *Between Good and Ghetto: African American Girls and Inner-City Violence* (2010); Randol Contreras, *The Stickup Kids: Race, Drugs, Violence, and the American Dream* (2012).

156 Part Two: Lessons from the Tale

value of close-up, multilayered depiction of the social world in which depth, granularity, and carnality are prioritized over representativeness and replicability, and reassess the pertinence of the statistical models they build accordingly. Matthew Desmond and Bruce Western put it thus:

> Where disadvantages are highly correlated and mutually determining, a fixation on causal inference may be misplaced. The thought experiment of manipulating a single condition lacks realism. Social scientists cannot and should not control away that which society has stitched together. The challenge is to develop new methods for describing the very nature of poverty, avoiding the discipline's reductionist tendencies that sanitize a messy social problem. Where disadvantages cluster together, the causal priority of one over another may be less important (and impossible to determine) than the qualitatively distinct type of hardship that emerges from their assemblage.[29]

Finally, the "underclass" has failed to generate new social theory or to connect with existing theories of class, race, or place. In point of fact, the notion has reinforced the *unvarnished empiricism and aggressive anti-structuralism* that have dominated research on poverty since the 1960s, as it substitutes rates for relations, populations for institutions, and administrative constructs for sociological categories. The "underclass" has also accentuated the national parochialism of inquiries into urban dispossession, centered as they are "solely on the United States, and often just on a few Northern cities," and it has entrenched the disregard of academic and policy scholars of urban poverty for power relations.[30]

[29] Matthew Desmond and Bruce Western, "Poverty in America: New Directions and Debates" (2018), p. 309.
[30] David Brady, "Theories of the Causes of Poverty" (2019), p. 156. Brady notes that, three decades after the acme of the "underclass," "poverty research continues to lack clear theory. There are few explicitly named theories and little explicit theoretical debate. If a theory of the causes of poverty is articulated, it is usually only compared against the null hypothesis of no effect. Studies rarely compare two or more theories against each other. Even more than in other fields, poverty researchers often focus on descriptive or normative claims without explaining poverty's causes." Revealingly, the term "underclass" does not appear once in this panoramic article.

Forging robust concepts

In point of fact, the word "power" does not appear even once (except in the expression "purchasing power") in the canonical volume edited by Jencks and Peterson, *The Urban Underclass* (1991). The words exploitation, domination, and subordination are also conspicuous by their absence. Scholarship on the "underclass" reduces poverty to a *state*, as opposed to an *asymmetric relation* binding agents located in the higher and lower regions of social space through the mediation of the bureaucratic field (where front-line state functionaries implement the policies decided by state managers). It erases the organizational sites where these agents, endowed with contradictory interests and faced with chronic resource penury, meet face-to-face: the welfare and housing office, the public school, the county hospital, the street and the police station, the jail, and the criminal, housing, and family courts. More crucially still, it scotomizes the commanding institutions that produce and shape urban marginality *from above and from afar* by determining the social and spatial distribution of forms of capital in the metropolis: the local and central state, corporations, the real estate and financial industries, and the ethnoracial division of everything.[31]

The silences of the normal sociology of poverty and the budding science of affluence

"When Americans talk about poverty, some things remain unsaid. Mainstream discourse about poverty, whether liberal

---

[31] A close dissection of encounters across the "multi-institutional maze" of public bureaucracies supervising the poor is Leslie Paik, *Trapped in a Maze: How Social Control Institutions Drive Family Poverty and Inequality* (2021). An analysis of the dilemmas faced by street-level agents is Bernardo Zacka, *When the State Meets the Street: Public Service and Moral Agency* (2017). A deft discussion of the macrosocial institutions, by turns allies and adversaries, that shape the metropolis as physical and social form is John R. Logan and Harvey L. Molotch, *Urban Fortunes: The Political Economy of Place* (2007 [1987]), chs. 1, 3 and 5 ("How Government Matters"). A sharp treatment of the manifold sources of racial division and dispossession in the city is Douglas Massey, *Categorically Unequal: The American Stratification System* (2007), chs. 3 and 4.

158   Part Two: Lessons from the Tale

or conservative, largely stays silent about politics, power, and equality. But poverty, after all, is about distribution; it results because some people receive a great deal less than others. Descriptions of the demography, behavior, or beliefs of subpopulations cannot explain the patterned inequalities evident in every era of American history. These result from styles of dominance, the way power is exercised, and the politics of distribution . . . For over a century, American political discourse has redefined issues of power and distribution as questions of identity, morality, and patronage. This is what happened to poverty, which slipped easily, unreflectively, into a language of family, race, and culture rather than inequality, power, and exploitation. The silence is therefore no anomaly."

Michael B. Katz, *The Undeserving Poor: From the War on Poverty to the War on Welfare* (1989), p. 8

In the 2010s, a new generation of activists versed in digital communication mobilized to put the issue of inequality of both income and wealth on the public agenda in the United States, from Occupy to the presidential campaigns of Bernie Sanders to Black Lives Matters to the election of hundreds of progressive representatives at the local level. Sociologists have responded to this sociopolitical thrust by providing intellectual clarification and ammunition for these movements (1). The normal social science of poverty, dominated by economists, demographers, and public policy scholars, has yet to notice them and absorb the challenge they pose for their common-sense framework that extracts dispossession from the class structure in which it is embedded.

Social scientists should think long and hard collectively about this question: why is there virtually no sociology of wealth, regular college courses and graduate seminars on the topic, professional networks and meetings, and journals devoted to it, the way there is for poverty (2)? Do the social seclusion and rapacity of the superwealthy not represent a major "social problem" for the society, as they destabilize the economy, pervert educational institutions, and capture political institutions (3)? Do the pejorative and anxious views that the wealthy have of the poor not shape the structure of urban inequality through the mediation of spatial strategies and city policy (4)? Is the "culture of wealth" and its deterritorialization not damaging to the social and moral fabric of the country (5)? Is wealth not pivotal to the reproduction of ethnoracial inequality and thus the perpetuation of black poverty across generations in the United States (6)? When will funding from scientific and philanthropic foundations for research on wealth accumulation and disparities amount to more than an infinitesimal fraction of support for poverty research?

As it grows, the nascent social science of affluence must beware not to develop into an isolated, self-enclosed domain bogged down in technicalities and separated from the study of poverty, corporate control, elite education, and public policy. Indeed, the challenge before this generation of scholars of poverty and wealth is to *link up* and become a joint scientific and civic enterprise shining a bright light on the *state as both producer and reducer of inequality* and paramount distributor of asymmetric life chances at the bottom and at the top (7).

1. Michael A. Gould-Wartofsky, *The Occupiers: The Making of the 99 Percent Movement* (2015); David Graeber, *The Democracy Project: A History, a Crisis, a Movement* (2013); Manuel Castells, *Networks of Outrage and Hope: Social Movements in the Internet Age* (2015); Keeanga-Yamahtta Taylor, *From #BlackLivesMatter to Black Liberation* (2016); and Jonathan Smucker, *Hegemony How-To: A Roadmap for Radicals* (2017). A cogent analysis of the generational component of these movements is Ruth Milkman, "A New Political Generation: Millennials and the Post-2008 Wave of Protest" (2017).

2. For a panorama of the timid beginnings of such a research area, see Lisa A. Keister, "The One Percent" (2014), and Alexandra Killewald, Fabian T. Pfeffer, and Jared N. Schachner, "Wealth Inequality and Accumulation" (2017), who proffer, generously, that the field has moved "from infancy to adolescence." A rare pairing of the dual political economy of poverty and wealth is Douglas S. Massey, *Categorically Unequal: The American Stratification System* (2007), ch. 5. A major exception to this pattern of collective cecity is the pioneering work of French sociologists on the upper bourgeoisie, nobility, traders, and wealth managers (Michel and Monique Pinçon, who have co-authored a half-dozen monographs on the topic in the wake of Pierre Bourdieu's work, Sébastien Chauvin, Bruno Cousin, Olivier Godechot, Grégory Salle, Isabelle Hugo, Céline Bessière, Sibylle Gollac, and Camille Herlin-Giret), and the extensive historical

160   Part Two: Lessons from the Tale

and multi-country research carried out and inspired by economists Thomas Piketty, Emmanuel Saez, and Gabriel Zucman at the global level; see the works surveyed in Gabriel Zucman, "Global Wealth Inequality" (2019). Read also the fascinating study by Cristobal Young, *The Myth of Millionaire Tax Flight: How Place Still Matters for the Rich* (2017), on what one might call "neighborhood effects" of the wealthy.

3. Kevin Phillips, *Wealth and Democracy: A Political History of the American Rich* (2003); Jacob Rowbottom, *Democracy Distorted: Wealth, Influence and Democratic Politics* (2010); Michel Pinçon and Monique Pinçon-Charlot, *Le Président des riches* (2011); Martin Gilens, *Affluence and Influence: Economic Inequality and Political Power in America* (2012); Benjamin I. Page, Jason Seawright, and Matthew J. Lacombe, *Billionaires and Stealth Politics* (2018). Richard D. Kahlenberg (ed.), *Affirmative Action for the Rich: Legacy Preferences in College Admissions* (2010). See also the research surveyed by Kenneth Scheve and David Stasavage, "Wealth Inequality and Democracy" (2017).

4. Serge Paugam, Bruno Cousin, Camila Giorgetti, and Jules Naudet, *Ce que les riches pensent des pauvres* (2017).

5. Brooke Harrington, *Capital without Borders: Wealth Managers and the One Percent* (2017); Rachel Sherman, *Uneasy Street: The Anxieties of Affluence* (2017); Ashley Mears, *Very Important People: Status and Beauty in the Global Party Circuit* (2020); and the thematic issues of *Actes de la recherche en sciences sociales* on "Servants of the Rich" (no. 230, December 2019), and *Cultural Politics* on "Questioning the Super-Rich: Representations, Structures, Experiences" (vol. 15, no. 1, March 2019).

6. Dalton Conley, *Being Black, Living in the Red: Race, Wealth, and Social Policy in America* (2000, new ed. 2010); Thomas M. Shapiro, *The Hidden Cost of Being African American: How Wealth Perpetuates Inequality* (2004); Melvin L. Oliver and Thomas M. Shapiro, *Black Wealth, White Wealth: A New Perspective on Racial Inequality* (2006); Keeanga-Yamahtta Taylor, *Race for Profit: How Banks and the Real Estate Industry Undermined Black Homeownership* (2019).

7. The state is the *structural hinge* through which the fate of rich and poor are linked, even as their social worlds grow more disjoint. In the main, poverty and wealth are not connected through interactional mechanisms (as with the illusory pair of landlord and tenant, cf. Matthew Desmond, *Evicted: Poverty and Profit in the American City* [2016]). The wealthy need not encounter any poor person in their daily round to affect the latter's life chances (think of a hedge fund owner and an undocumented fruit picker).

> Indeed, in the present polarized class and spatial structure, the only institutions where members of the cultural bourgeoisie (say, doctors, lawyers, university professors) and subproletarians come face-to-face are commercial establishments, the public hospital, the college campus, and the family and criminal courts. These are sites not of economic extraction but of social domestication.

In his extended "Reflections on Responses to *The Truly Disadvantaged*" that conclude the second edition of the book, Wilson discusses mountains of empirical studies stimulated by that tome, but these invariably disaggregate the concept of "underclass" and trace the role of one or another of its components (weak labor market attachment, spatial mismatch, social isolation, concentration effect), rather than the cluster of properties that defines it. When it comes to theory proper, Wilson sketches an alluring "theory of the social transformation of the inner city" (pp. 255–9), *a different object than the birth and growth of a "group."* Far from being an asset, the "underclass" turns out to be an epistemological burden, a "terministic screen" à la Kenneth Burke that masked reality and prevented him from fully deploying that theory.

Indeed, to explain why he shifted from "underclass" to "ghetto poor" as his organizing category, Wilson concedes: "I have made this nominal change because of a concern that even a theoretically derived concept of underclass will be overcrowded in the long run by *nonsystematic, arbitrary, and atheoretical usages* that often end up as ideological slogans or code words."[32] Likewise, the most ambitious and successful extension of the neo-ecological dimension of Wilson's work, Robert Sampson's *Great American City: Chicago and the Enduring Neighborhood Effect*, does not use the concept of "underclass," and it diplomatically acknowledges that "its design might be read as an implicit criticism of the underclass 'poverty paradigm' in urban sociology."[33]

---

[32] William Julius Wilson, "Responses to *The Truly Disadvantaged*" (2012), p. 259, my emphasis.

[33] Robert J. Sampson, *Great American City: Chicago and the Enduring Neighborhood Effect* (2012), p. 87.

162   Part Two: Lessons from the Tale

The cautious case for precariat

The reader is entitled to ask of this author: if not "under-class," what term are we to use to designate the inhabitants of the American hyperghetto at century's end and, more gener-ally, the dispossessed and dishonored populations residing in the neighborhoods of urban relegation across advanced socie-ties after deindustrialization? The value of a concept, it should by now be clear, is always *historical, even conjunctural,* that is, relative to a particular social moment, intellectual constel-lation, and epistemic purpose. Its choice hinges on the over-arching theory that, tacitly or explicitly, informs it and shapes its analytic contours as well as sets its empirical mission. As proposed in my 2008 book *Urban Outcasts* and mentioned in the introduction to this book, I favor the cautious use of the term *precariat,* born of the portmanteau merging of *precari-ous* (meaning insecure, unreliable, unstable, intermittent) and *proletariat* (in the Marxian sense of sellers of labor power) (1).

A brief genealogy is in order here. The word was coined in the 1980s by Italian trade unionists (*precariato*) influenced by the Bologna-based anarcho-communist collective *Precari nati* ("born precarious") to designate the spread of contin-gent employment in the lower tiers of the job market. The theme of *précarité,* tying labor insecurity to life insecurity, was then developed in the 1990s and 2000s by French social scientists, among them Robert Castel, Serge Paugam, Évelyne Perrin, and Patrick Cingolani, to highlight the proliferation of nonstandard, short-term, part-time, benefit-reduced, and episodic work arrangements as well as enduring joblessness and their corrosive effects on the social psychology, existential possibilities, and strategies of reproduction of the postindus-trial working class (2). From there, the word precariat diffused into the English-language debate on the neoliberal transfor-mation of labor and politics in the early twenty-first century, animated in particular by the British economist Guy Standing. It has come into scholarly usage in numerous countries, from Sweden to Japan and Germany to Canada. Lately, this includes the United States where, to take but three salient instances, the President of the American Political Science Association gave her 2018 presidential address on "The American Precariat:

US Capitalism in Comparative Perspective"; a leading student of the postindustrial working class proposed to rethink immigrant labor through the prism of the precariat; and the preeminent theorist of class thought it necessary to tackle the question, with a touch of worry, "Is the Precariat a Class?" (3).

By this definition, the precariat comprises those social categories, shorn of economic or cultural capital, that are stuck in, or circulating between, insecure low-pay employment, chronic underemployment, and durable unemployment pursuant to the generalized degradation of labor, not to mention the gamut of job-readiness programs, subsidized jobs, training schemes, and other liminal statuses between employment and inactivity. Their social strategies of persistence – rather than survival – typically combine resources spanning what I call *the four economic corners of marginality*: unstable wage work (the market), stopgap or perennial informal activities (the street), restrictive welfare support (the state), and the reciprocal economy of kin, friends, and neighbors (social ties). In Weberian terms, one may say that their "class situation" is stamped by abiding insecurity, material and statutory, and their "life chances" truncated accordingly. The cultural and administrative construct that best encapsulates the institutionalization of precarity is the notion of "employability" and the distinct subjectivity it produces (4).

Ethnoracial division enters into the picture as a *multiplier of precarity*, through three mediations: the labor market, the neighborhood, and the state. First, it accentuates marginality on the labor front via job discrimination, especially for black men with a street habitus who are perceived by employers as threatening, unruly, and liable to bring criminal mischief into the workplace. Second, it concentrates the black precariat in the most deteriorated districts of the city, with the more chaotic housing situations, thereby aggravating their living conditions and prompting exclusion based on territorial stigma (as with address discrimination). Third, race as negative symbolic capital facilitates the rolling out of the paired public policies of disciplinary workfare and neutralizing prisonfare insofar as welfare recipients and judicial convicts are perceived to be dissolute black women and dangerous black men, respectively. The discourse of the "underclass" crystallizes this negative association between race, class, and state in the neoliberal metropolis through a classic self-fulfilling prophecy: it exacerbates social insecurity in the hyperghetto by designating its residents as the prime target of punitive social and penal government programs (5).

Precariat presents the advantage of being a relatively novel term, which means that it stops the reader and invites them to check up on its meaning. It is semantically clear and compact as well as free of moral connotations and political overtones – of the kind that burden *Lumpenproletariat*, for instance. It refers both to an objective condition, rooted in the fragmentation of wage labor and the retraction of the social state, and to the subjective experience of living in a world without guarantees, protections, and safe tomorrows. Precarity is a condition that afflicts other providers of desocialized labor, gig workers, artists, college lecturers, consultants, but we should not conflate the positive precarity chosen by credentialed operators, at one end, with the negative precarity imposed on dispossessed populations, at the other, which reaches a crescendo in the lower regions of social and physical space, and therefore inside the hyperghetto. As it intensifies, precarization morphs into outright deproletarianization and entrapment in long-term or permanent joblessness.

Needless to say, there exists different approaches and claims to the study of the precariat, so let me clarify where I stand on four key issues. First, periodization: the precariat arises from the *dissolution of the Fordist-Keynesian social compact* that anchored the life of the working class (sellers of labor power devoid of credentials) roughly from World War I to the mid-1970s and created the collective expectation of economic support and social protection from the state. This political-economic regime came unglued in the last three decades of the twentieth century due to (i) the accelerating mobility of capital, technological innovation, and the attendant rise of flexible labor and structural un(der)employment; (ii) the feminist revolution eroding masculine domination in the domestic sphere and inadvertently helping to generate a new pool of vulnerable workers; (iii) the universalization of secondary schooling and the consequent devaluation of manual labor and culture; (iv) the morphing of the protective welfare state into a neoliberal Centaur state practicing laissez faire at the top of the class structure, toward holders of economic and cultural capital, and punitive paternalism at the bottom in the form of restrictive social policy and expansive penal policy (6).

In the polarizing city, wage labor fragmentation and territorial stigmatization (closely correlated with class and ethnicity, meaning blackness in the United States and postcolonial immigration in Western Europe) combine to constitute a new regime of urban poverty that I christen *advanced marginality*, because it is neither residual nor transitional but fed by the forward march of neoliberal postindustrialism. In the American metropolis specifically, precarization mates with the implosion of the communal ghetto of the Fordist era to spawn hypermarginality on the triple basis of class, caste, and place (7).

It follows, second, that use of the concept of precariat is best confined geographically to the *advanced societies of the capitalist West* and not extended to cover the insecure (would-be) workers of the entire planet. To speak of a global precariat, as Guy Standing insists on doing, lumps together political-economic legacies and structural dynamics that are too disparate to be encompassed by the same notion. In the postcolonial South, "super-exploitation, accumulation by dispossession, and 'permanent primitive accumulation'" have been the norm, such that the notion of precarity, defined by contraposition with the economic stability and social succor afforded by Fordism and the Keynesian welfare state, is of little relevance (8).

Thirdly, I differ fundamentally with the leading theorist of the precariat Guy Standing in holding that, far from being a "class in formation," a class-in-itself on the road to becoming a class-for-itself evolving a shared consciousness and identity, the precariat is a *still-born group*, a fissiparous aggregate devoid of the minimal cohesion needed to accede to collective existence and engage in sustained coordinated action – notwithstanding valiant activist efforts to organize the three major categories of the *sans*, the job-less, home-less, and paper-less migrants on both sides of the Atlantic. Unlike members of the industrial proletariat, who, endowed with a positive occupational identity, banded together to defend a shared position and improve their collective condition,

166 Part Two: Lessons from the Tale

when members of the precariat mobilize, it is to find a job, get housing, or join legal residents, and thereby *escape the category* and deflate its numbers, not to unify it, defend its boundaries, and ameliorate its common fate. In the language of Albert Hirschman, the proletariat favors *voice* whereas the very makeup of the precariat inclines it toward *exit* (9).

For this very reason, and this is my fourth point, the precariat is best thought of as a *vulnerable fraction of the working class*, spawned by the attrition of the wage labor contract and socioeconomic citizenship, and not a new class of its own (10). The majority of its members issue from the working class, aspire to join it, and merge into it when they experience upward mobility. Conversely, members of the established working class are always at risk of sinking into the precariat, gradually or suddenly, with the erosion of their work status, pay, and social protections. Precarity is a matter of degree and not kind. Here it is not just a matter of avoiding the epistemic trap of "groupism," defined as "the tendency to take discrete, sharply differentiated, internally homogeneous and externally bounded groups as basic constituents of social life, chief protagonists of social conflicts, and fundamental units of social analysis" (11). It is to recognize that the analytic construct of the precariat is a *category that cannot be realized* as such in practice.

So much to say that my argument in favor of precariat as a heuristic concept for the study of racialized (de)proletarianization in the polarized city is premised on a radically *historicist social ontology* that treats *groupness as a historical variable* – ranging from a mere category on paper to a collective fully organized for joint action on the political stage – and a contingent product of the "making and unmaking of groups" through the symbolic labor of naming, delegating, and mobilizing across social space (12). The question here is not, *pace* exponents of critical realism and doxic empiricism, whether a new "group" exists "out there" in society but whether the category of precariat is a fruitful guide for describing, interpreting, and explaining the changing social structure, strategies, and experience of advanced marginality in the hyperghetto.

1. Loïc Wacquant, *Urban Outcasts: A Comparative Sociology of Advanced Marginality* (2008), pp. 244–7, and *supra*, p. 7.

According to the *Oxford English Dictionary*, precarious derives from the classical Latin *precārius* meaning "depending on the favour of another, uncertain, doubtful, suppliant."

2. Robert Castel, *Les Métamorphoses de la question sociale* (1995), and idem, "Au-delà du salariat ou en deçà de l'emploi? L'institutionnalisation du précariat?" (2007); Serge Paugam, *Le Salarié de la précarité* (2000); Évelyne Perrin, *Chômeurs et précaires au coeur de la question sociale* (2004); Patrick Cingolani, *La Précarité* (2006).

3. Guy Standing, *The Precariat: The New Dangerous Class* (2011), and idem, *A Precariat Charter: From Denizens to Citizens* (2014). This debate is sampled by Matthew Johnson (ed.), *Precariat: Labour, Work and Politics* (2016). On recent American usages, see Kathleen Thelen, "The American Precariat: US Capitalism in Comparative Perspective" (2019); Ruth Milkman, *Immigrant Labor and the New Precariat* (2020); Erik Olin Wright, "Is the Precariat a Class?" (2016).

4. Gretchen Purser and Brian Hennigan, "Disciples and Dreamers: Job Readiness and the Making of the US Working Class" (2018).

5. These three mechanisms of marginalization are elaborated in Loïc Wacquant, "Marginality, Ethnicity and Penality in the Neo-liberal City: An Analytic Cartography" (2014).

6. Loïc Wacquant, *Punishing the Poor: The Neoliberal Government of Social Insecurity* (2009b), and idem, "Three Steps to a Historical Anthropology of Actually Existing Neoliberalism" (2012b).

7. Wacquant, *Urban Outcasts*, ch. 8, especially pp. 233–47, and idem, *The Zone: Making Do in the Hyperghetto* (2022).

8. Ronaldo Munck, "The Precariat: A View from the South" (2013), p. 752.

9. Albert O. Hirschman, *Exit, Voice, and Loyalty: Responses to Decline in Firms, Organizations, and States* (1970).

10. A modicum of theoretical prudence is advised: sociologists trumpeting the birth of a new class have been burned before, as recounted by Bill Martin and Iván Szélényi, "Three Waves of New Class Theory" (1988). Curiously, Standing separates the precariat from both the working class, the unemployed, and the "under-class": "It is below the proletariat where the *precariat* is growing. It is not an under-class. That is the *lumpen-precariat*, victims eking out an existence in the streets, sad souls going to an early death" (Standing, *The Precariat*, p. 26). With the "salariat" and the "proficians," Standing invents no fewer than four new classes in a seven-class schema with no coherent classificatory basis.

11. Rogers Brubaker, *Ethnicity Without Groups* (2004), p. 8.

168   Part Two: Lessons from the Tale

> 12. Pierre Bourdieu, "What Makes a Social Class? On the Theoretical and Practical Existence of Groups" (1987).

Epistemic opportunity costs

In *The Formation of the Scientific Mind*, Gaston Bachelard stresses that "knowledge of reality is a light that always casts shadows somewhere."[34] This means that we must always query a concept (theory, problematic, paradigm) for what it obfuscates, occludes, or omits – assess what we may call its *epistemic opportunity cost*. The obsession of students of the "underclass" with income deprivation, neighborhood, welfare, family, illegitimacy, and antisocial behavior inside the hyperghetto has caused them to miss four major developments that have redrawn the landscape of urban marginality in the closing decades of the twentieth century and since.

1. The generalized destabilization and degradation of labor, caused by the fragmentation of wage work, leading to the prevalence of flexible, contingent and underpaid employment in the lower tier of the occupational structure – which is not, *pace* Wilson, reducible to deindustrialization and the simple vanishing of jobs. The inexorable propagation of expendable employment, epitomized by "McJobs" in the United States, *petits boulots* in France, *Billig-Jobs* in Germany, "zero-hour contracts" in the United Kingdom, and *lavoretti* in Italy, attests that this is a structural tendency of advanced capitalism.[35] Labor

---

[34] Gaston Bachelard, *La Formation de l'esprit scientifique. Contribution à une psychanalyse de la connaissance objective* (1938), p. 13.

[35] Loïc Wacquant, *Urban Outcasts: A Comparative Sociology of Advanced Marginality* (2008), ch. 8; Serge Paugam, *Le Salarié de la précarité* (2000); Robert Castel and Klaus Dörre (eds.), *Prekarität, Abstieg, Ausgrenzung: Die soziale Frage am Beginn des 21. Jahrhunderts* (2009); Arne L. Kalleberg, *Good Jobs, Bad Jobs: The Rise of Polarized and Precarious Employment Systems in the United States, 1970s to 2000s* (2011); Guy Standing, *The Precariat: The New Dangerous Class* (2011); Marc Doussard, *Degraded Work: The Struggle at the Bottom of the Labor Market* (2013).

Epistemic opportunity costs
169

precarity, and with it, suffusive social insecurity impacting all strategies of household reproduction, has become the new normal for the postindustrial working class. Even in its most economistic version, the tale of the "underclass" ignores the *rise of the precariat*.

2. The massive *influx of new immigrants* into the United States has altered the functioning of *both labor and housing markets* at the bottom of the metropolitan order, and not just in gateway cities. The foreign-born population of the country boomed from 9.7 million in 1970 to 31.1 million in 2000, nearly equal the total black population (it is now over 40 million, one-third undocumented). New migrants have flooded the low-wage sector, providing employers with a pliable workforce suited to accelerating the casualization of labor.[36] They have also settled in the least desirable neighborhoods of the city, oftentimes at the margins of the historic ghettos, as well as in mixed "ethnoburbs" that have brought both demographic dynamism and poverty to the metropolitan periphery. Together with the catastrophic rise of the rent burden among low-income households, the increase of immigrant demand for rental housing between 1970 and 2000 (when foreign-born households accounted for fully 17% of the sector) and the high susceptibility of immigrants to eviction and forced displacement have profoundly altered the spatial structure of poverty in ways entirely missed by the "underclass."[37]

3. *The explosive growth and deep reach of the penal state*: one searches in vain for an analysis of the "underclass" that takes account of the stupendous expansion of criminal

---

[36] Roger Waldinger and Michael I. Lichter, *How the Other Half Works: Immigration and the Social Organization of Labor* (2003); Ruth Milkman, *Immigrant Labor and the New Precariat* (2020).

[37] Dowell Myers and Cathy Yang Liu, "The Emerging Dominance of Immigrants in the US Housing Market 1970–2000" (2005); Matthew Desmond, "Heavy is the House: Rent Burden among the American Urban Poor" (2018); Matthew Desmond and Tracy Shollenberger, "Forced Displacement from Rental Housing: Prevalence and Neighborhood Consequences" (2015).

170 Part Two: Lessons from the Tale

justice that directly targeted residents of the hyperghetto through differential policing, derailed their life trajectories, corroded their families and networks, and helped capsize their neighborhoods.[38] To get a sense of the penetration of the penal state into this territory, consider the case of North Lawndale, a district of Chicago's West Side: in 1999, the police made 17,059 arrests for a total population of 47,000 (99% black, 44% living under the poverty line, 60% in single-parent households, 3% with a college degree), one-third of them for narcotics offenses; nearly 3,000 men were remanded in the custody of the Illinois Department of Corrections that year, following which the total number of North Lawndale males over 18 serving time in prison (9,800) almost equaled the number still present in the neighborhood (10,600), over 80% of whom were on parole/probation, had a criminal record, or cycled through the county jail.

The building of a gargantuan and voracious penal apparatus, unprecedented in world history in its scope and reach, *during the very reign of the "underclass,"* is part and parcel of the supplanting of the Keynesian welfare state of the 1960s by the neoliberal Centaur state of the 1990s, practicing laissez-faire liberalism at the top and punitive paternalism at the bottom.[39] This puts the state – not the market, the family, culture, or the neighborhood – at the epicenter of the production and distribution of hypermarginality in the polarized metropolis. The "underclass" is stridently silent when it comes to punishment and state transformation.

[38] Loïc Wacquant, "Deadly Symbiosis: When Ghetto and Prison Meet and Mesh" (2001); Bruce Western, *Punishment and Inequality* (2006); Megan L. Comfort, "Punishment Beyond the Legal Offender" (2007); Todd Clear, *Imprisoning Communities: How Mass Incarceration Makes Disadvantaged Neighborhoods Worse* (2009); Sara Wakefield and Christopher Wildeman, *Children of the Prison Boom: Mass Incarceration and the Future of American Inequality* (2013); Reuben Jonathan Miller, *Halfway Home: Race, Punishment, and the Afterlife of Mass Incarceration* (2021).

[39] Wacquant, *Punishing the Poor*, and idem, "Three Steps to a Historical Anthropology of Actually Existing Neoliberalism" (2012b).

Epistemic opportunity costs   *171*

4. Behind the different incarnations of the "underclass" lurks a historical rupture that went unnoticed and a sociological object that was never named: the *crash of the dark ghetto*, announced by the wave of riots of the 1960s, and its *replacement by a new dual sociospatial structure of ethnoracial closure*. This dual sociospatial formation is composed, on one side, of the segregated black middle-class districts and, on the other, of the hyperghetto, doubly segregated by race and class, stripped of economic function, in which the framework of life is supplied by the social control institutions of the state (police, courts, jail and prison, probation and parole, social welfare and child protective services, county hospital, public housing, and public schooling). Because scholars of the "underclass" did not have a robust sociological concept of the ghetto, relying instead on the current folk notion (as poor segregated district), they could not realize that the ghetto was dead and buried, and that the territory of dereliction and despair left in its wake was a different urban animal altogether.[40]

The birth of the postindustrial precariat, surging immigration and scarce housing, the penalization of poverty, and the death of the ghetto: these four profound *institutional transformations of hypermarginality* in the dual metropolis are the product of a shift in the balance of class power in the economy and the state that caused both to erode social citizenship in the lower regions of social and physical space. No statistical parsing of the rate of neighborhood poverty, female-headed households, teenage pregnancy or violent crime gives us a grip on these transformations. Only a theory of the evolving nexus of class fragmentation, ethnoracial division and state restructuring in the neoliberal city can help us capture and explicate these changes and the resulting consolidation of a *punitive politics of poverty* at century's end.[41]

[40] Loïc Wacquant, "Designing Urban Seclusion in the 21st Century" (2010), pp. 169–70, and idem, *The Zone: Making Do in the Hyperghetto* (2022), ch. 2.

[41] Loïc Wacquant, "Marginality, Ethnicity and Penality in the Neoliberal City: An Analytic Cartography" (2014).

172   Part Two: Lessons from the Tale

Bandwagons, speculation, and turnkeys

Three notions broached in the present book to scrutinize the travails of the "underclass" as phantom group may help us parse the use and abuse of other social science terms and collectively practice better conceptual hygiene. Lemming effects, conceptual speculative bubble, and turnkey problematic are intended as *sensitizing concepts* to assess the value of analytic constructs in circulation.[42] Admittedly, they overlap, hybridize, and morph into one another; and they can be confounded with the normal life-cycle of a concept or research program (e.g., the fall of structural functionalism in the 1960s was not retroactively indicative of a conceptual bubble, but a result of the exhaustion of a paradigm in the Kuhnian sense). But, used pragmatically, they can alert us to the misapplication, maltreatment, or defects of concepts.

The *lemming effect* denotes a bandwagon of enthusiastic scholars rushing en masse to invoke a notion because everyone around them is invoking it, only to fall into a scientific precipice because that notion was flawed or impertinent to the phenomenon at hand. (For the zoological record, let it be noted that, in reality, lemmings do not blindly follow their leaders into danger and commit collective suicide by jumping off cliffs). The formula here is given by Christopher Jencks's candid admission that "since almost everyone else now talks about the underclass rather than the lower class, I will do the same," even though no social change warranted that shift (see the full citation *supra*, p. 91).

This is an apt characterization of the proliferating deployment of Carl Schmitt's "state of exception" in political science and Giorgio Agamben's "bare life" in anthropology – Gilles Deleuze's "assemblage" and Homi Bhabha's "hybridity" also come to mind. States of exception have multiplied at such rapid pace in the most varied settings that they threaten to become the rule, which impoverishes the very notion of the political

---

[42] On the opposition between "sensitizing" and "definitive" concepts, see Herbert Blumer, "What is Wrong with Social Theory?" (1954), pp. 7–8.

that Schmitt was supposed to enrich.[43] Anthropologists, of all people, should know that life is never "bare": their richly textured ethnographic inquiries show time and again that, even under the most stripped down of circumstances, such as famine, war, or the radical destitution and disorientation of migrants crossing a deadly border desert, the sheer biological fact of life (*zoë*) is never completely dislodged from a way of life (*bios*), as Agamben would have it.[44] Lemming effects are especially strong when the author of the concept(s) entailed is freshly (re)discovered or suddenly canonized (as is happening at this writing with W.E.B. Du Bois), or when a novel phenomenon is believed to have appeared on the social horizon. Disciplines that borrow their theories from their neighbors are particularly susceptible to these effects. Dedicated funding streams, media attention, and political currency reinforce their force and frequency.

A *conceptual speculative bubble* develops when an inchoate, unbounded, or unfinished notion, often borrowed from political discourse and action, is invoked to capture an ever wider range of historical realities before its semantics have solidified – in the language of Giovanni Sartori, its "extension" (the universe of cases to which it is applied) grows out of proportion with its "intension" (the meaning it evokes).[45] Epistemic speculation differs from epistemic bandwagon

---

[43] Jef Huysmans, "The Jargon of Exception – On Schmitt, Agamben and the Absence of Political Society" (2008); Benno Gerhard Teschke, "Fatal Attraction: A Critique of Carl Schmitt's International Political and Legal Theory" (2011).

[44] Kristin Phillips shows this by developing the concept of "subsistence citizenship" in *An Ethnography of Hunger: Politics, Subsistence, and the Unpredictable Grace of the Sun* (2018). Jason De León's fascinating journey through *The Land of Open Graves: Living and Dying on the Migrant Trail* (2015) is paradoxical in that its granular data undermine the analytic of "bare life" it invokes. Similarly, Mariane C. Ferme's rich observations in *Out of War: Violence, Trauma, and the Political Imagination in Sierra Leone* (2018), overrun her invocations of Agamben.

[45] This distinction is introduced by Giovanni Sartori in his classic article "Concept Misformation in Comparative Politics" (1970), and elaborated by Collier and Mahon in "Conceptual 'Stretching' Revisited: Adapting Categories in Comparative Analysis" (1993).

174   Part Two: Lessons from the Tale

in that its mechanism is cognitive, whereas lemming effects are activated by networks of scholars who watch, read, and imitate one another, but admittedly in many cases the two dynamics blur into one another.

The anticipation of future cognitive profits, empirical or theoretical, that fail to materialize helps us understand the extraordinary diffusion and dispersion of the notion of "diaspora" since the 1980s. In his lucid dissection of the "'diaspora' diaspora" inside and outside of the academy, Rogers Brubaker refutes the view that the concept spread because it encapsulated a novel analytic perspective and/or captured a fundamentally new phase in historical development. Its astounding success – if one may call it that – comes from the headlong rush toward new usages promoted by the continual confusion between analytic and folk understandings of the term and by activist mobilization invoking it.[46]

Similarly, Julian Go has pointed out that invocations of "racial capitalism" have recently boomed across disciplines even as definitions of the same remain murky, incomplete and inconsistent across authors. Its users have failed to specify the fundamental constituents of the concept, including what is meant by race (and whether such a construct can be universalized), what is meant by capitalism, and why race, rather than some other social criterion (religion, citizenship, gender, etc.) must be harnessed to grease the wheels of capitalist exploitation. Yet, surprisingly, Go ends up further inflating the speculative bubble when he recommends that we "embrace rather than overthrow the racial capitalism concept," in spite of its current glaring deficiencies, presumably as a political bet on its future cognitive payoffs. Should we rather not pause and submit the concept to further scrutiny and elaboration, rather than run with it as is?[47]

---

[46] Rogers Brubaker, "The 'Diaspora' Diaspora" (2005). I agree with Brubaker when he suggests that his double deflation of the notion would apply to a whole family of kindred concepts such as "transnationalism, postnationalism, globalization, deterritorialization, postcolonialism, creolization, and postmodernity."

[47] Julian Go, "Three Tensions in the Theory of Racial Capitalism" (2021), p. 44; see also the critique of Michael Ralph and Maya Singhal, "Racial Capitalism" (2019), drawing on the historical sociology of Orlando Patterson.

Bandwagons, speculation, turnkeys 175

Four factors exacerbate the anticipative valuation of concepts: the academic or policy success of intellectual leaders, the creation of dedicated scholarly journals and professional networks, novel lines of research funding, and the push of social movements or the pull of political actors with a vested interest in the scientific legitimation of a particular notion (as with the recent saturation of academic and public debate with the term "structural racism"). I will not speculate here on the range of factors that trigger the bursting of conceptual bubbles, other than to note that it can be sudden and translate in the instant bankruptcy of a research program in which a generation of scholars may have invested their entire scientific savings. Think of the sudden discrediting and sometimes outright disappearance of such influential concepts as "mass society," "role," and "reference groups" in the 1960s; "culture of poverty" and "articulation of modes of production" in the 1970s; "structuration theory" and "new class," in the 1980s; "postmodernity" and "globalism" in the 2000s; and "creolization" in the 2010s. And there are telltale signs that the bubble of "cosmopolitanism" may burst this decade.

Finally, social scientists are always in danger of falling for a *turnkey problematic*, that is, a set of prepackaged categories, questions, methodological moves, and data banks encapsulated by a term, often promulgated by research agencies, public bureaucracies, political officials, and private philanthropies to suit their own agendas, or propelled by the mere routine of professorial reproduction. A turnkey differs from the disciplined application of paradigmatic principles in that it invites the *routinized and unthinking* implementation of a rhetorical and technical formula whose social parameters are taken for granted by scholars and officials alike. Two salient cases in the twenty-first century are the thematics of "urban resilience" and the "creative city," two of the many visages of the brave new neoliberal metropolis.[48]

In his bold book, *Shaking Up the City: Ignorance, Inequality and the Urban Question*, geographer Tom Slater recounts how

---

[48] See the panoramic critique of Tali Hatuka et al. "The Political Premises of Contemporary Urban Concepts: The Global City, the Sustainable City, the Resilient City, the Creative City, and the Smart City" (2018).

176   Part Two: Lessons from the Tale

the notion of "resilience," borrowed from ecology and engineering, was promoted around the world by the Rockefeller Foundation through the "100 Resilient Cities" competition funding cities to "build their own capacities to prepare for, withstand, and bounce back rapidly from shocks and stresses."[49] Scholars rushing to work in that policy stream, on such topics as shrinking cities, green infrastructure, energy systems and disaster response, have accepted the terminology, boundaries, indicators, and purpose of "resilience," a construct that naturalizes the social consequences of market rule, exculpates the state by devolving responsibility to the municipal, neighborhood, and even individual level, and endorses the generalized downsizing of city government after the financial crash of 2008. Buying lock, stock and barrel into a planning practice guided by the notion, researchers have failed to stop and ask the elementary question: "resilience for whom and against what?"[50] Answering this question highlights the fundamentally conservative, if not reactionary, cast of "resilience" as applied to historical reality: it assumes that returning to an established urban pattern, rather than overturning it, is necessarily a social good.

The turn to catering to the city's upper class is blindly endorsed by urban scholars working in the stream of Richard Florida's international best-seller, *The Rise of the Creative Class* (2002), which has spawned a cottage industry of research and policy advocacy. In this model, "creative cities" compete to attract the mobile "talent" of the "creative class" (knowledge- and form-producing occupations) by valorizing the arts, culture, and heritage, and fostering a climate of tolerance, diversity, and hipness. The notion has informed a blizzard of studies documenting the antecedents, dimensions, and consequences of the urban clustering of culture professionals, complete with myriad rank correlations between the "Talent Index," the "Melting Pot Index" the "Bohemian Index,"

---

[49] Tom Slater, *Shaking Up the City: Ignorance, Inequality and the Urban Question* (2021), ch. 4, p. 24. A representative sample of this research area is Michael A. Burayidi et al. (eds.), *The Routledge Handbook of Urban Resilience* (2019).

[50] Lawrence J. Vale, "The Politics of Resilient Cities: Whose Resilience and Whose City?" (2014), p. 191.

Bandwagons, speculation, turnkeys   *177*

and the "Gay Index."[51] These studies leave unexamined the dubious assumption that we have moved into a "post-scarcity, post-material" stage of capitalism, where the "creatives" are a benevolent dominant class; mobility, an intrinsic value; inter-city competition and gentrification, public goods; and the free market and self-actualization, reconciled. Not to mention that much of the research conducted under this label reads like a garrulous tautology: cool cities attract the creatives because they harbor high densities of creatives – and the uncreative two-thirds of the city be damned.[52] Ironically, the very success of the creative-city model has brought about its denunciation as it deepens class bifurcation and escalates the costs of collective consumption and social reproduction.[53]

Turnkey problematics are particularly profuse in the applied sectors of social science, such as public policy, urban planning, and management, where scholarship meets professional action, and opportunities for outside lecturing and consultancy arise. But they also develop in the more autonomous sectors of sociology where methodological normalization, the use of large-scale administrative data sets, and a panoply of plug-and-play analytic moves offer a safe formula for rote research replication (as with "prisoner reentry"). Turnkeys also find a fertile terrain in the regions of social science interfacing with civic mobilization, as attested by the recent diffusion of "intersectionality" (itself challenged by "post-intersectionality") across and beyond the academy.

The political scientist John Gerring is right to stress that concept formation always entails trade-offs between desirable

---

[51] A compact presentation is Richard Florida, "Cities and the Creative Class" (2003); a sample of uses of the concept is David E. Andersson, Åke E. Andersson and Charlotta Mellander (eds.), *Handbook of Creative Cities* (2011).

[52] Jamie Peck, "Struggling with the Creative Class" (2005), p. 758.

[53] Thus the dramatic shift in Richard Florida's tone over a short decade: the 2002 celebration of *The Rise of the Creative Class: And How It's Transforming Work, Leisure, Community and Everyday Life* morphs into the 2012 deploration of *The New Urban Crisis: How our Cities are Increasing Inequality, Deepening Segregation, and Failing the Middle Class – And What we Can Do about It*. Both accounts, euphoric and dysphoric, are framed by one and the same concept: heads I win, tails you lose.

178   Part Two: Lessons from the Tale

properties.[54] This implies that we should give up the search for the "one perfect concept" and seek instead to craft *good-enough concepts*, or better concepts than the ones we inherit and find at hand. For analytic constructs should be evaluated, not just abstractly by a set of formal criteria, but also pragmatically, *relative to their purpose and compared with rival concepts* serving to generate insights, data, and theory about the same sector of historical reality. The epistemic abacus proposed here should be employed in this spirit. For concepts are living and breathing semantic-logical-heuristic creatures; they gestate and are birthed; they grow and change; they gain new usages, mate with other notions, and spawn offspring.[55] Some concepts, like good wine, grow better as they age and endure – thus Marx's capitalism, Durkheim's division of labor, and Weber's bureaucracy. Others get worn out, produce quickly diminishing returns, and even become obstacles to knowledge. Some can be "sent for cleaning" and "put back into circulation";[56] others need to be retired and buried. Such is the case of the "underclass": *requiescat in pace.*

[54] For Gerring, the trade-offs involve eight criteria he calls familiarity, resonance, parsimony, coherence, differentiation, depth, theoretical utility, and field utility. John Gerring, "What Makes a Concept Good? A Criterial Framework for Understanding Concept Formation in the Social Sciences" (1999).

[55] Georges Canguilhem, *Idéologie et rationalité dans l'histoire des sciences de la vie. Nouvelles études d'histoire et de philosophie des sciences* (1981).

[56] "Sometimes an expression has to be withdrawn from language and sent for cleaning – then it can be put back into circulation." Ludwig Wittgenstein, *Culture and Value* (1977), p. 39.

Coda: Resolving the trouble with "race" in the twenty-first century

~

"With race theories, you can prove and disprove anything you want."

Max Weber, 2nd Meeting of the Deutsche Gesellschaft für Soziologie (1909)

Race is arguably the single most troublesome and volatile category of the social sciences in the early twenty-first century – as Zora Neale Hurston put it, it is "like fire on the tongues of men." Do you put it in scare quotes or not? Do you pair it with ethnicity to specify its scope or extend its reach? Do you use it as a substantive (as if it were a "thing" out there in the world) or as an adjective (racial, racialized, racialist, or the accusatory racist) attached to a perception, belief, action, or institution? Is race premised on descent, phenotype, or skin tone, but what of such varied social properties as legal status, region, language, migration, and religion that have served as vectors of racialization?[1] What is the relationship between

[1] The luminous but little-known essay by Charles Wagley, "On the Concept of Social Race in the Americas" (1965 [1958]), suffices to demonstrate the variability of ethnoracial foundations. For recent empirical support from diverse countries, Marisol De La Cadena, *Indigenous Mestizos: The Politics of Race and Culture in Cuzco, Peru, 1919–1991* (2000); Gi-Wook Shin, *Ethnic Nationalism in Korea: Genealogy, Politics, and Legacy* (2006); John Lie, *Multiethnic*

180   Coda: Resolving the trouble with "race"

the social understanding of race and its genetic and neuro-
logical designation? Is race a self-propelled social force or
does it derive from other causal powers (for instance, class or
nationality)? A historical construct of utility in certain societies, such as imperial powers and their colonies, or an abstract
construct of universal reach? Most urgently still, is it a "sin
of the West" (linked to chattel slavery), as loudly proclaimed
by many race scholars and activists, or does it operate across
civilizations? The principles guiding the conceptual autopsy
of the "underclass" as racialized category may help us gain
some clarity and traction on these issues.

First, *historicize*. The trouble with race in the West did
not start this or the previous century. It is coextensive with
the life of the notion, which, from its coalescence in the mid-
eighteenth century, has constantly trafficked in the *complicity
between common sense and science*. The naturalists of that
era who concocted the idea that humanity could be divided
into biophysical categories (Carolus Linnaeus's four races,
white, black, yellow, red, corresponding to the four humors
of the body and to the four continents of the earth, which
survive to this day) that would later be decreed inherently
unequal were both codifying an extensive array of ordinary
premodern perceptions and partaking of a scientific revolution that, for the first time, was posing the question of how to
fit together human diversity and hierarchy.[2]

This originary confusion has continued to this day and is
embedded in the conventional coupling of "race and ethnicity." Whenever social scientists deploy this doxic duet, *they
endorse and amplify the defining symbolic effect of race* which
is, precisely, the ideological belief that it is fundamentally dif-

---

Japan (2009); Edward Telles, *Pigmentocracies: Ethnicity, Race, and
Color in Latin America* (2014).

[2] Ivan Hannaford, *Race: The History of an Idea in the West* (1996);
Anthony Pagden, *The Burdens of Empire: 1539 to the Present*
(2015), esp. ch. 3. A precursor of the modern notion of race as divid-
ing practice, East and West, is found in the Shinto and Christian reli-
gions, respectively: Frank Dikötter, *The Discourse of Race in Modern
China* (1992); George M. Fredrickson, *Racism: A Short History*
(2002). Religion, not race, was the criterion that initially justified the
enslavement of Africans for the transatlantic trade.

Coda: Resolving the trouble with "race" 181

ferent from ethnicity. The same applies to the pairing of "race and racism": what is race if not a figment of the collective belief in its autonomous existence, that is, racism, so why the duplication? This dubious commerce between common sense and science has gone on uninterrupted for three centuries so that countless presociological tenets about "race" survive, indeed thrive, in contemporary social science. Inside too many racial constructivists, there is a racial essentialist struggling to get out.[3]

Second, expand the *geographic scope* to decenter the discussion. This entails three moves. The first is to *bring West and East together* to escape continental parochialism. It is a curiously Eurocentric vision of history to believe that race as an essentialist principle of classification and stratification is a monopoly of Western nations and empires. The Japanese, to take but one example, did not wait for Commodore Perry's arrival in 1853 to racialize the medieval caste of the Eta (meaning "filth abundant") and the criminal class of the Hinin ("non-human") into the "invisible race" of the Burakumin ("hamlet people"), believed to be innately different, inferior, and defiling, and to treat them as such across the centuries, including after their emancipation in 1871, even as no phenotypical property marked them out.[4] The second move consists

---

[3] A vivid illustration is Howard Winant, *The World is a Ghetto. Race and Democracy since World War II* (2001), for whom race is "a flexible dimension of human variety that is valuable and permanent"; "race is present everywhere ... Race has shaped the modern economy and nation-state. It has permeated all available social identities, cultural forms, and systems of signification"; it is "infinitely incarnated in institution and personality"; "it is the foundation of every dream of liberation ... It is a fundamental social fact! To say that race endures is to say that the modern world endures" (pp. xiv, 1, 6).

[4] Hiroshi Wagatsuma and George DeVos, *Japan's Invisible Race: Caste in Culture and Personality* (2021 [1966]). For accounts of the Eastern, Middle-Eastern, and African histories and realities of ethnoracial division in these regions, see Frank Dikötter (ed.), *The Construction of Racial Identities in China and Japan: Historical and Contemporary Perspectives* (1997); Peter Duus, *The Abacus and the Sword: The Japanese Penetration of Korea, 1895–1910* (1998); Gyanendra Pandey, *A History of Prejudice: Race, Caste,*

182   Coda: Resolving the trouble with "race"

in *linking the colonial and the metropolitan domains* to track down the similarities and differences in the treatment of the subaltern of the interior (peasants, working class, ethnic minorities) and the subaltern of the exterior (colonial subjects), as well as the two-way transfer of racialized representations, subjectivities, and techniques of government between the imperial center and its periphery. This is the task of a new generation of scholars promising to produce a colonial and postcolonial sociology whose work bears directly on theories of race (and group-making) in the Global North of the contemporary era.[5]

The third spatial move is to *dislodge the United States from its Archimedean position.* Just as the tripartite tale of the "underclass" was a uniquely American story nourished by virulent anti-urbanism and suffusive racial fear activated by the black revolt of the 1960s, academic and civic debates on race globally are dominated by American categories, assumptions, and claims – as illustrated recently by the international diffusion of intersectionality in the academy and Black Lives Matter on the streets. But the American definition of race as civic felony and of blackness as public dishonor transmitted through strict hypodescent are historical outliers.[6] No other ethnic group in the United States is bounded on that basis and no other society on the planet defines blackness thus. The limitations of the best theorizing on race in American social science can be traced directly to the reliance of its progenitors

---

   and Difference in India and the United States (2013); Bernard Lewis, *Race and Slavery in the Middle East: An Historical Enquiry* (1990); and Bruce S. Hall, *A History of Race in Muslim West Africa, 1600–1960* (2011).

[5] The broad parameters of this research program are set out by George Steinmetz, "The Sociology of Empires, Colonies, and Postcolonialism" (2014). On racial division specifically, see the literature scanned by Julian Go, "Postcolonial Possibilities for the Sociology of Race" (2018), most of which is still programmatic or declamatory.

[6] Loïc Wacquant, "Race as Civic Felony" (2005), and F. James Davis, *Who Is Black? One Nation's Definition* (1990). A masterful geographic decentering of the race question is Mara Loveman, *National Colors: Racial Classification and the State in Latin America* (2014).

Coda: Resolving the trouble with "race" 183

upon the *oddities* of the national historical experience.[7] For instance, the idea that race equals "color" leaves out cases of ethnoracial domination where other phenotypical markers (such as hair, height, or eye color as in China, Central Africa, and the Andes) are used; situations where no phenotypical difference exists (the Burakumin of Japan, the Dalits of India); instances where the racializer is a "colored" population (the empires of Africa and Asia); and, final irony, it does not comprise the "canonical race," African Americans, who are defined by strict hypodescent regardless of physical appearance (what we might call the Walter White paradox), nor does it recognize the pervasiveness of color discrimination among people of color.[8]

Third, *avoid the logic of the trial*, which truncates inquiry by seeking to prove culpability and assign blame, in favor of a relentless commitment to the cold-blooded logic of theoretical construction and empirical validation, no matter where these take you.[9] This implies a strict, if provisional, ban on moral judgment and a permanent rejection of appeals to emotions which too often drive inquiry into ethnoracial inequality – as when the white author of a book on the topic feels obligated to flaunt their racial bona fides in a preface confessing their privilege and asserting their ethnic solidarity. A sociologist of class, the family, the state, modernity does not mechanically write against class, the family, the state, modernity. Why do sociologists of race feel obligated to write against race instead

---

[7] Mustafa Emirbayer and Matthew Desmond, *The Racial Order* (2015). A powerful counter to this national parochialism is Orlando Patterson, "Four Modes of Ethno-Somatic Stratification: The Experience of Blacks in Europe and the Americas" (2005).

[8] Walter F. White was the leader of the NAACP from 1929 to 1955, and the architect of its strategy of legal challenge to racial segregation. He was phenotypically white, with thin blond hair and blue eyes, and he could easily "pass" (he did so to investigate public lynchings and racial pogroms first-hand). He was "a Negro by choice," as he himself put it. On the pervasiveness of color inequality among African-, Hispanic-, and Asian-Americans, see the bold article by Ellis Monk, "The Unceasing Significance of Colorism: Skin Tone Stratification in the USA" (2021).

[9] On the seductions of the logic of the trial, see Loïc Wacquant, "For an Analytic of Racial Domination" (1997), pp. 225–7.

184   Coda: Resolving the trouble with "race"

of about race or, better, why do they so easily let the first impulse overwhelm the second, and vituperation crimp elucidation? This is not to say that social scientists should remain indifferent to ethnoracial struggles for equality and justice, far from it. It is to assert, with Max Weber, that they should participate in these struggles as citizens while making sure to dispatch their scientific duties according to specifically scientific criteria.[10] Indeed, it is when they stringently *sublimate* their social passions into rigorous theory building, robust methodological designs, and scrupulous empirical observation that sociologists best serve the historical interests of the dominated by producing cogent explications of the complex structures that keep them down.

Fourth, and correlatively, *demarcate: break with common sense*, ordinary and scholarly, and elaborate an analytic construct capacious enough to encompass the varied forms of ethnoracial domination deployed across time and space. Here are the lineaments of such an elaboration. Race is best construed as a *subtype of ethnicity*, ethnicity being defined, again following Weber, as a principle of classification and stratification *anchored by "social estimations of honor," positive or negative*. Honor may be granted or denied on a wide range of grounds, for "any cultural trait, no matter how superficial, can serve as a starting point for the familiar tendency to monopolistic closure."[11] To simplify, ethnicity runs the gamut from thin to thick, fluid to rigid, socially innocuous to socially consequential. At one end are ethnic forms avowedly based on culture, resulting from choice (identification), that are ephemeral and tend to social horizontality; at the other end ethnic forms that grow out of constraint (categorization), claim to derive from nature, and assume an enduring vertical form – the most extreme of which is the caste system.[12]

[10] Max Weber, "Science as a Vocation" (1958 [1919]). Scientific criteria include egological, textual and epistemic reflexivity (as discussed in the prologue, pp. 4–5) and thus encompass effects of "positionality."

[11] Max Weber, *Economy and Society* (1978 [1918–22]), vol. 1, pp. 388. Here I follow Weber's theory of "status group" (*Stand*) and not his theory of ethnicity, which I find less clear and useful.

[12] Gerald D. Berreman, "Race, Caste, and Other Invidious Distinctions

Coda: Resolving the trouble with "race" 185

Racialization is the historical process whereby one travels from one to the other end of the ethnic continuum, from culture to nature, identification to categorization, horizontality to verticality. Race, in turn, is *denegated ethnicity*, a thick, rigid, and consequential type of ethnicity that has this particularity that it doggedly denies being "ethnic": it purports to be rooted in the necessities of biology (or its logical analogue, culture understood as hard-wired and virtually unchanging) rather than in the vagaries of history. Most importantly, ethnicity (and thus ethnoracial division) is ultimately predicated upon *perception and discernment*, unlike other canonical principles of social vision and division which all have a self-standing material foundation independent of cognition, class (the mode of production), gender (the mode of reproduction), age (the biology of maturation and death), and nationhood (affiliation with a state). In other words, *race is a pure modality of symbolic violence*, the bending of social reality to fit a mental map of reality or, to put it more tersely still, a limiting case of the *realization of categories*, the conundrum at the heart of Pierre Bourdieu's sociology.[13]

Historicize, spatialize, forsake incrimination, and demarcate. A fifth recommendation is to *disaggregate*. The "underclass" emerged from, and traded on, the conflation of disparate social relations rooted in ethnicity, geography, the labor market, the family, and the state. It was a lumpy category that, for this reason, created empirical confusion and theoretical trouble. The lesson to draw here it is to break ethnoracial phenomena into their constituent elements, what I

---

in Social Stratification" (1972); Loïc Wacquant, "Bringing Caste Back In" (2020).

[13] The template for this analytic move is Pierre Bourdieu, "À propos de la famille comme catégorie réalisée" (1993b). An explication is Loïc Wacquant, "Symbolic Power and Group-Making: Bourdieu's Reframing of Class" (2013), pp. 276–7 and 281. A perfect illustration of the mapping of symbolic space onto social and physical space from above is the violent restructuring of a class-based into a race-based society by the Nazis, as shown by Michael Burleigh and Wolfgang Wipperman, *The Racial State: Germany 1933–1945* (1991). A mobilization seeking to realign state categories with social space from below is studied by Nancy Grey Postero, *Now We Are Citizens: Indigenous Politics in Postmulticultural Bolivia* (2007).

186 Coda: Resolving the trouble with "race"

call the *elementary forms of racial domination*: categorization (assignation to a hierarchical and naturalizing classification system, encompassing prejudice and stigma), discrimination (differential treatment based on real or putative categorical membership), segregation (differential allocation in social and physical space), ghettoization (institutional enclosure and parallelism), and violence, ranging from intimidation and assault to pogroms to ethnic cleansing and genocide (the ultimate form of ethnic domination).[14] These five elementary forms of ethnoracial rule are meshed together and articulated differently in different societies and at different times in the same society. The task of the sociology of ethnoracial domination is to dismantle such articulations on paper, thereby helping to forge better tools for possibly dismantling them in reality.

To assert that race is a subtype of ethnicity, logically as well as historically, is not to deny the brute and brutal reality of racial domination. On the contrary: it is to give ourselves the analytic means to discover under what conditions and due to what mechanisms *ordinary ethnicity gets turned into racialized (denegated) ethnicity* and the difference that naturalization makes in different arenas of social action – say, marriage, schooling, the labor market, or political membership. Clumpy terms such as "structural racism" and "systemic racism," which have diffused at blinding speed in the early 2020s (in part through the influence of think tanks and philanthropic foundations eager to rephrase old programs in the new Racespeak of the moment, not to mention academic Twitter)[15] in the tow of social movements for racial justice, may work well as political mottos to mobilize people and to give them a personal sense of moral zeal and civic benevolence; they are nonetheless poor guides for dissecting, and thence overturning, the racial order.

---

[14] An elaboration is Loïc Wacquant, "For an Analytic of Racial Domination" (1997), pp. 227–31.

[15] See, for instance, the "Glossary for Understanding the Dismantling [of] Structural Racism/Promoting Racial Equity Analysis," formulated and diffused by the Aspen Institute via its fifteen locations around the world, and the rubric "Structural Racism in America" on the web site of the Urban Institute (accessed on May 15, 2021).

Coda: Resolving the trouble with "race" *187*

Indeed, aside from its progressive valence, the resurrection of "structural racism" could turn out to be to the 2020s what the invention of the "underclass" was for the 1980s: a lumpy notion that stops analytic work just where it should begin, confuses and conflates mechanisms of ethnoracial domination (themselves racial and nonracial), and thus forms a practical obstacle to the surgical removal of operative sources of racial inequality. This is the case, for instance, with broad-brush rhetorical attacks on "structural racism in criminal justice" that amalgamate the different practices of legislating, policing, pretrial detention and conditional release, prosecution, public defense, plea negotiation and litigation, sentencing, supervising, and incarceration, each of which has layers of internal legal and administrative complexity and may or may not produce looping ethnoracial disparities.[16] "Structural racism" posits that which needs to be discovered and demonstrated. It replaces meticulous study with facile sloganeering. In so doing, it betrays its ostensive purpose: to excavate the social conditions of possibility of ethnoracial justice.

The stipulation of the concept of "race" sketched here meets the criteria that make for a solid analytic construct (as specified earlier, p. 152): it is semantically discrete, clear, and neutral; it is logically coherent, specific, and parsimonious; and it is heuristic in that it allows us to dissect empirically and bring within a single theoretical framework the varied forms assumed by ethnic ordering in history and across continents – ethnoreligious, ethnolinguistic, ethnoregional, ethnonational, and ethnoracial proper.[17] It sets for the sociology of racial

[16] A brilliant exploration of the crevasse between the slogan and the counterintuitive realities of "court reform" is Malcolm M. Feeley, *Court Reform on Trial: Why Simple Solutions Fail* (1983).

[17] A vigorous conceptual effort to unify these categories "as a single integrated family of forms" on a comparative and historical basis is Rogers Brubaker, "Ethnicity, Race, and Nationalism" (2009), and *Grounds for Difference* (2015), ch. 3. It does not go far enough: instead of subsuming race and nationalism *under ethnicity*, as biologized ethnicity and state-affiliated ethnicity, respectively, Brubaker retains them as three coequal cognitive and conative perspectives on the social world. Andreas Wimmer goes further in that direction in *Ethnic Boundary Making: Institutions, Power, Networks* (2013), esp. pp. 7–10, by developing a comparative analytic of ethnic formation

188   Coda: Resolving the trouble with "race"

domination the central task of uncovering how a system of ethnoracial *classification* (a taxonomy trading on the overt or covert correspondence between natural and social orderings) is created and inculcated, sedimented in the socialized body in the form of a racialized habitus, and "mapped" onto a system of ethnoracial *stratification* through the differential distribution of material and symbolic goods, privileges and penalties, profits and perils, across social and physical space.

The *genesis, crystallization, and recursive transmutation of classification into stratification and vice versa* constitute the core problematic suited for formulating the sociology of race as a particular modality of group-making without falling into the trap of "race-centrism."[18] A pivot here is the degree to which categorization and the correlative distribution of capitals are recognized, codified, and sponsored by the state, or supported by other paramount symbolic agencies such as the law, science, and religion as distinct from the common sense of everyday life. This problematic prompts us to determine what is generic and what is specific about race as category-to-be-realized, and to discover how it achieves (or not) the status of dominant "principle of vision and division" as a result of struggles for what Pierre Bourdieu evocatively calls "symbolic royalty."

---

in global perspective. But neither Brubaker nor Wimmer takes the next step of rolling the categories of ethnicity, race, and nationalism under a *general neo-Bourdieusian theory of group-making* (encompassing class, age, sexuality, citizenship, locality, etc.) whose very possibility and necessity they demonstrate.

[18] See the crucial article of Andreas Wimmer, "Race-Centrism: A Critique and Research Agenda" (2015).

Appendix:
The nine lives of the "underclass"

~

Surprise, surprise: the "underclass" has survived its crash of the 1990s in the American public and policy debate. It continues to be used in social science, albeit mainly as a descriptive place-holder (at the intersection of race and poverty) and in part through rote citation (many of them referring back to the debate of century's end). It also circulates widely in the news media, especially foreign, but the images of the "group" are strikingly different in the different countries.

"There's no denying that the concept is dead. I don't think any serious social scientist still uses it. That said, one of my colleagues still has an undergraduate class on the books titled 'The Urban Underclass,' although my other colleagues are quite in dismay that it's putatively on offer (even if it hasn't actually been taught in some time)." Thus wrote an anonymous reader of the manuscript commissioned by Polity Press, who also described the author of these lines as a "conceptual coroner."

The "underclass" has indeed vanished from public debate in the United States, and it has likewise disappeared from the most advanced sectors of the national social science. Its leading exponents of the 1980s and 1990s have renounced it (with the notable exception of Douglas Massey). Two recent state-of-the-art appraisals of research on poverty in America and theories of poverty cross-nationally published in *Annual*

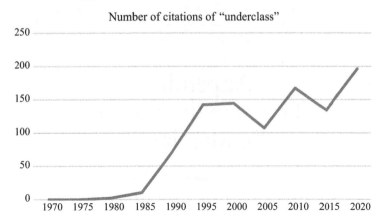

Figure 5 Mentions of "underclass" in the Social Science Citation Index, 1970–2020

Review of Sociology do not so much as mention the term, and a third review on "poverty governance" mentions it only to flag the work of Wilson.[1] According to Google's Ngram Viewer, the number of mentions of "underclass" in books rose sharply from 1977 to 1996 (to reach 3.7 times the citation peak for "culture of poverty" in 1970), before going into a steep and steady decline in this century. The fate of the concept is a settled matter.

Or is it? Like the proverbial cat, the "underclass" proves to have more than one life. Bibliometric data from the Social Science Citation Index shows that the term has indeed gone through boom and bust but it continues to be widely mentioned. Figure 5 shows that total mentions of "underclass" took off in 1987 to peak in 1996 at about 160 citations, then decreased abruptly until 2002 to 60-some citations, only to commence a slow but steady march upward until the present to return to its peak level. How many of these citations represent new work on the "underclass" as opposed to a trail of

---

[1] Matthew Desmond and Bruce Western, "Poverty in America: New Directions and Debates" (2018); David Brady, "Theories of the Causes of Poverty" (2019); Nicole P. Marwell and Shannon L. Morrissey, "Organizations and the Governance of Urban Poverty" (2020).

Appendix: The nine lives of the "underclass"

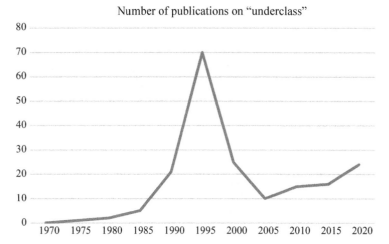

Figure 6 Publications on "underclass" in the Social Science Citation Index, 1970–2020

references to earlier publications on the topic? As depicted by figure 6, articles devoted to the "underclass" (that is, mentioning the term in the title, abstract or keywords) took off in 1987 to peak in 1993 with 68, then decreased abruptly until 2002 to a dozen, only to continue in the 15–25 range afterwards.

The notion has also endured across disciplines: in the 2010s, one-quarter of the articles on the "underclass" came from sociology, another quarter from urban studies and ethnic studies, with the rest sprinkled among anthropology, political science, criminology, and education (each with 7%). Scholars in the United Kingdom rivaled their American colleagues as the most prolific producers of "underclass" articles with 31% and 37% respectively, ahead of Australia (9%) and Canada (6%), with China closing the march at 5%. Dissertations on the "underclass" likewise show a pattern of precipitous rise and fall followed by endurance: their number jumped from 3 in the 1970s to 55 in the 1980s to 171 in the 1990s, before dropping to 147 in the 2000s and a surprisingly solid 117 in the 2010s.

Although it no longer makes headlines in the United States as it frequently did in the 1990s, the "underclass" has maintained a stubborn presence in national newspapers, especially

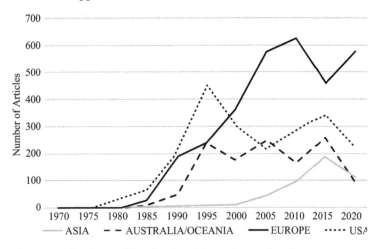

Figure 7 Mentions of "underclass" in major national newspapers, 1970–2020 (source: Lexis-Nexis)

in foreign countries (see figure 7). American newspapers continue to deploy the term at a fairly high clip (the *New York Times* did so 27 times and the *Washington Post* 28 times this past year), matched by their Australian counterparts after 2000. English-language newspapers in Asia picked up the notion this century: in Hong-Kong and China, the "underclass," composed of lower-class migrants, is feared to be growing, permanent, suppressed, and invisible.[2] Most spectacular is the sharp spike in uses by European newspapers, especially in the United Kingdom, where it regained front-page status in public debate in reaction to the 2011 London riots, which the UK Minister of Justice publicly attributed to a "feral underclass."[3]

---

[2] Jane H. Johnson and Alan Partington, "'Underclass' in the English-Language Press: Who Are They, How Do They Behave, and Who Is to Blame for Them?" (2017), p. 310.

[3] Imogen Tyler, "The Riots of the Underclass? Stigmatisation, Mediation and the Government of Poverty and Disadvantage in Neoliberal Britain" (2013); Paul Michael Garrett, "'Castaway Categories': Examining the Re-emergence of the 'Underclass' in the UK" (2019). Following the riots, John Welshman's *Underclass: A History of the Excluded Since 1880*, first published in 2006 by Continuum, was

Appendix: The nine lives of the "underclass"   *193*

The comparative iconography of the "underclass" reveals what the cultural bourgeoisie of each country (academics, politicians, and journalists) sees as the most pressing menace to social integration, moral order, and political stability in the metropolis. In the United States, the teenage welfare mother and the jobless streetcorner man prone to crime are the two figureheads of the category against a backdrop of inner-city dilapidation and danger. In the United Kingdom, the "underclass" is incarnated by a dysfunctional and parasitic white family residing in the infamous "sink estates" and "welfare ghettos" of the metropolitan periphery. In China, the threat comes from the "floating population" of young male migrants streaming by the tens of millions from the countryside into the megacity to power its factories and populate its poor districts, but who are excluded from education, welfare, and housing due to their undocumented residential status.

The wide *epistemic lag* observed between leaders and followers in social science has been reinforced by the gradual *epistemic decomposition* of the "underclass": the notion has grown more incoherent semantically and logically as it has diffused, losing all specificity both intensively (as regards its core attributes) and extensively (as regards the cases it covers).[4] In the 2010s, it variously referred to the black or immigrant poor in the inner city, the long-term unemployed, the downwardly mobile or immobile fractions of the working class, the residents of stigmatized housing estates or "slums," workers in the informal economy, undocumented foreign migrants and internal migrants from rural areas, beggars and the homeless, servants and domestics, "troubled families" defined by cultural and moral deficiencies, children in foster care, youths prone to pillage and rioting, street criminals and gang members, a generic subordinate category not getting its

---

republished in 2013 by Bloomsbury Academic in an updated edition. In this book, revealingly, "underclass" is used as an umbrella term encompassing "the residuum," the "problem family," the "culture of poverty," the "cycle of deprivation," the "troubled family," the "underclass" properly so-called in its US and UK variants, and the "excluded."

[4] Giovanni Sartori, "Concept Misformation in Comparative Politics" (1970).

194   Appendix: The nine lives of the "underclass"

rightful due (of income, housing, education, civil rights, and lately vaccines), distressed and dangerous neighborhoods, a discourse of denigration or depoliticization, and more. This partial list suggests that *the word has survived and even thrived, but the concept has died.*

Acknowledgments

~

It would take another book to properly express my gratitude to all the teachers, students, and colleagues who have shaped this study in ways big and small, oftentimes unbeknownst to them, over the past several decades by shaping how I think about urban marginality and social epistemology – an odd couple if there ever was one. Two people deserve special mention for their role as mentors and friends: Pierre Bourdieu steadfastly nourished my taste for epistemic reflexivity, initially acquired as a high-school reader of Gaston Bachelard and Marc Bloch (I have not forgotten the cryptic sentence written on the board by my philosophy teacher then: "*les faits sont faits*"); Bill Wilson shared with me his passion for knowledge of the ghetto and his commitment to social justice for its residents. The present book would not have been conceivable without their intellectual guidance and personal support. A special place and its people deserve mention: the Berkeley Department of Sociology, where the craft is valued and bold intellectual endeavors encouraged.

Among the people who generously took from their precious time to share their reactions, suggestions, doubts, and criticisms of this manuscript with me, I would like to acknowledge Javier Auyero, Sara Brothers, Rogers Brubaker, Jenae Carpenter, Matt Desmond, Jason Ferguson, Marion Fourcade, Chris Herring, Cathy Hu, Ellis Monk, Chris Muller,

196   Acknowledgments

Orlando Patterson, Khoi Quach, Victor Lund Shammas, David Showalter, Alan Sica, Andreas Wimmer, Bill Wilson (yes, again), and Michael Zanger-Tischler. I am thankful also to Eli Martinez for his patient and inspired assistance with the cover. The three anonymous readers for Polity Press gave me a shot in the arm just when I needed one (in addition to my Covid-19 vaccine). John Thompson has proven to be as steadfast and patient as one can hope an editor to be.

I also want to thank Raphaël G., Fabrice R., and Sara S., and my family in France and the United States for their unflagging love and support over the past five years, with special hugs for Mumusse, Little Leo for the small joys of the Big-Big-Field, Sophie pour sa présence et son affection de tous les instants et Megan pour être la lumière de ma vie malgré tout.

References

~

Abercrombie, Nicholas, and John Urry. 1983. *Capital, Labour, and the Middle Classes*. London: Routledge.

Abrahams, Roger D. 1970. *Down in the Jungle: Negro Narrative Folklore from the Streets of Philadelphia*, 2nd ed. New York: Aldine de Gruyter.

Adler, Jeffrey S. 1994. "The Dynamite, Wreckage, and Scum in our Cities: The Social Construction of Deviance in Industrial America." *Justice Quarterly* 11, no. 1: 33–49.

Alesina, Alberto, and Edward L. Glaeser. 2004. *Fighting Poverty in the US and Europe: A World of Difference*. New York: Oxford University Press.

Andersen, John. 1995. "The Underclass Debate: A Spreading Disease?" Pp. 147–82 in *Social Integration and Marginalisation*. Edited by Jørgen Elm Larsen and John Andersen. Copenhagen: Samfundslitteratur.

Anderson, David C. 1995. *Crime and the Politics of Hysteria: How the Willie Horton Story Changed American Justice*. New York: Crown.

Anderson, Elijah. 1990. *Streetwise: Race, Class, and Change in an Urban Community*. Chicago, IL: University of Chicago Press.

Anderson, Elijah. 1999. *Code of the Street: Decency, Violence, and the Moral Life of the Inner City*. New York: Norton.

Andersson, David E., Åke E. Andersson, and Charlotta Mellander (eds.). 2011. *Handbook of Creative Cities*. London: Edward Elgar Publishing.

Aponte, Robert. 1990. "Definitions of the Underclass: A Critical

Analysis." Pp. 117–37 in *Sociology in America*. Edited by Martha White Riley. Newbury Park, CA: Sage.

Armacost, Michael H. "Preface." Pp. vii–viii in *The New Paternalism*. Edited by Lawrence M. Mead. Washington, DC: The Brookings Institution.

Auletta, Ken. 1982. *The Underclass*. New York: Vintage (2nd rev. ed., 1999).

Avenel, Cyprien. 1997. "La question de l'*underclass* des deux côtés de l'Atlantique." *Sociologie du travail* 97: 211–34.

Bachelard, Gaston. 1934. *Le Nouvel esprit scientifique*. Paris: Presses Universitaires de France.

Bachelard, Gaston. 1938. *La Formation de l'esprit scientifique. Contribution à une psychanalyse de la connaissance objective*. Paris: Vrin.

Bagguley, Paul, and Kirk Mann. 1992. "'Idle Thieving Bastards'? Scholarly Representations of the 'Underclass'." *Work, Employment & Society* 6: 113–26.

Beauregard, Robert A. 1993. *Voices of Decline: The Postwar Fate of US Cities*. Cambridge, MA: Blackwell.

Beckett, Katherine. 1999. *Making Crime Pay: Law and Order in Contemporary American Politics*. New York: Oxford University Press.

Bell, Daniel. 1960. *The End of Ideology: On the Exhaustion of Political Ideas*. Glencoe, IL: Free Press.

Bell, Derrick. 1993. *Faces at the Bottom of the Well: The Permanence of Racism*. New York: Basic Books.

Berger, Dan. 2014. *Captive Nation: Black Prison Organizing in the Civil Rights Era*. Chapel Hill, NC: University of North Carolina Press.

Berreman, Gerald D. 1972. "Race, Caste, and Other Invidious Distinctions in Social Stratification." *Race* 23, no 4: 385–414.

Black, Timothy, and Sky Keyes. 2020. *It's A Setup: Fathering from the Social and Economic Margins*. New York: Oxford University Press.

Blumer, Herbert. 1954. "What is Wrong with Social Theory?" *American Sociological Review* 19, no. 1: 3–10.

Bonilla-Silva, Eduardo. 2019. "Feeling Race: Theorizing the Racial Economy of Emotions." *American Sociological Review* 84, no. 1: 1–25.

Bourdieu, Pierre. 1977. *Algérie 1960. Structures économiques et structures temporelles*. Paris: Minuit. (English: *Algeria 1960*. Cambridge: Cambridge University Press, 1979.)

Bourdieu, Pierre. 1979. *La Distinction. Critique sociale du juge-*

References

ment. Paris: Minuit. (English: *Distinction: A Critique of the Judgment of Taste.* Cambridge, MA: Harvard University Press.)

Bourdieu, Pierre. 1980a. "L'identité et la représentation. Éléments pour une réflexion critique sur l'idée de région." *Actes de la recherche en sciences sociales* 35: 63–72.

Bourdieu, Pierre. 1980b. "Le mort saisit le vif: les relations entre l'histoire réifiée et l'histoire incorporée." *Actes de la recherche en sciences sociales* 32–33: 3–14.

Bourdieu, Pierre. 1984. *Homo Academicus.* Paris: Minuit. (English: *Homo Academicus.* Cambridge, UK: Polity Press, 1988.)

Bourdieu, Pierre. 1985 [1984]. "The Social Space and the Genesis of Groups." *Theory & Society* 14, no. 6: 723–44.

Bourdieu, Pierre. 1987. "What Makes a Social Class? On the Theoretical and Practical Existence of Groups." *Berkeley Journal of Sociology* 32: 1–17.

Bourdieu, Pierre. 1989. *La Noblesse d'État. Grandes écoles et esprit de corps.* Paris: Minuit. (English: *The State Nobility: Elite Schools in the Field of Power.* Cambridge: Polity Press, 1996.)

Bourdieu, Pierre. 1990. "The Scholastic Point of View." *Cultural Anthropology* 5, no. 4: 380–91.

Bourdieu, Pierre. 1991. "The Peculiar History of Scientific Reason." *Sociological Forum* 6, no. 1: 3–26.

Bourdieu, Pierre. 1993a. "Esprits d'État. Genèse et structure du champ bureaucratique." *Actes de la recherche en sciences sociales* 96, no. 1: 49–62. (English: "Rethinking the State: Genesis and Structure of the Bureaucratic Field." *Sociological Theory* 12, no 1, 1994, pp. 1–18).

Bourdieu, Pierre. 1993b. "À propos de la famille comme catégorie réalisée." *Actes de la recherche en sciences sociales* 100: 32–6.

Bourdieu, Pierre. 1993c. *Fields of Cultural Production.* New York: Columbia University Press.

Bourdieu, Pierre. 1996. "Champ politique, champ des sciences sociales, champ journalistique." *Les Cahiers de Recherche du GRS*, no 15. (English: "The Political Field, the Social Field, and the Journalistic Field." Pp. 29–30 in *Bourdieu and the Journalistic Field.* Edited by Rodney Benson and Erik Neveu. Cambridge: Polity, 2005.)

Bourdieu, Pierre. 2000. *Langage et pouvoir symbolique.* Paris: Seuil/Points. (English: *Language and Symbolic Power.* Cambridge, MA: Harvard University Press, 1990.)

Bourdieu, Pierre. 2001. *Science de la science et réflexivité.* Paris: Raisons d'agir Éditions. (English: *Science of Science and Reflexivity.* Cambridge: Polity Press, 2004.)

Bourdieu, Pierre. 2003. "Participant Objectivation: The Huxley

Medal Lecture." *Journal of the Royal Anthropological Institute* 9, no. 2: 281–94.

Bourdieu, Pierre. 2011. "Champ du pouvoir et division du travail de domination." *Actes de la recherche en sciences sociales* 190: 126–39.

Bourdieu, Pierre. 2012. *Sur l'État. Cours du Collège de France 1989–1992*. Paris: Seuil/Raisons d'agir Éditions.

Bourdieu, Pierre. 2015. *Sociologie générale. Cours du Collège de France 1981–1983*, vol. 1. Paris: Seuil/Raisons d'agir Éditions.

Bourdieu, Pierre, and Loïc Wacquant. 1992. *An Invitation to Reflexive Sociology*. Chicago, IL: University of Chicago Press.

Bourdieu, Pierre, and Loïc Wacquant. 1993. "From Ruling Class to Field of Power." *Theory, Culture & Society* 10, no. 3: 19–44.

Bourdieu, Pierre, and Loïc Wacquant. 1999 [1998]. "On the Cunning of Imperialist Reason." *Theory, Culture & Society* 16, no. 1: 41–58.

Bourdieu, Pierre, Jean-Claude Chamboredon, and Jean-Claude Passeron. 1968, 1973. *Le Métier de sociologue. Préalables épistémologiques*. Paris: Mouton, 2nd ed. (English: *The Craft of Sociology: Epistemological Preliminaries*. New York: De Gruyter, 1991.)

Bourgois, Philippe. 1995. *In Search of Respect: Selling Crack in El Barrio*. New York: Cambridge University Press.

Boyer, Paul S. 1978. *Urban Masses and Moral Order in America, 1820–1920*. Cambridge, MA: Harvard University Press.

Brady, David. 2009. *Rich Democracies, Poor People: How Politics Explain Poverty*. New York: Oxford University Press.

Brady, David. 2019. "Theories of the Causes of Poverty." *Annual Review of Sociology* 45: 155–75.

Brubaker, Rogers. 2004. *Ethnicity Without Groups*. Cambridge, MA: Harvard University Press.

Brubaker, Rogers. 2005. "The 'Diaspora' Diaspora." *Ethnic & Racial Studies* 28, no. 1: 1–19.

Brubaker, Rogers. 2009. "Ethnicity, Race, and Nationalism." *Annual Review of Sociology* 35: 21–42.

Brubaker, Rogers. 2015. *Grounds for Difference*. Cambridge, MA: Harvard University Press.

Bryant, Christopher G.A. 1985. *Positivism in Social Theory and Research*. New York: Macmillan.

Burayidi, Michael A., Adriana Allen, John Twigg, and Christine Wamsler (eds.). 2019. *The Routledge Handbook of Urban Resilience*. New York: Routledge.

Burke, Kenneth. 1966. *Language as Symbolic Action*. Berkeley, CA: University of California Press.

References

Burke, Kenneth. 1968. "Dramatism." Pp. 447–8 in *The International Encyclopedia of the Social Sciences*. Edited by David L. Sills and Robert K. Merton. London: Macmillan.

Burleigh, Michael, and Wolfgang Wipperman. 1991. *The Racial State: Germany 1933–1945*. Cambridge: Cambridge University Press.

Burns, Sarah. 2012. *The Central Park Five: The Untold Story behind One of New York City's Most Infamous Crimes*. New York: Vintage.

Bussard, Robert L. 1987. "The 'Dangerous Class' of Marx and Engels: The Rise of the Idea of the Lumpenproletariat." *History of European Ideas* 8, no. 6: 675–92.

Canguilhem, Georges. 1952. *La Connaissance de la vie*. Paris: Vrin.

Canguilhem, Georges. 1955. *La Formation du concept de réflexe aux XVIIe et XVIIIe siècles*. Paris: Vrin.

Canguilhem, Georges. 1981. *Idéologie et rationalité dans l'histoire des sciences de la vie. Nouvelles études d'histoire et de philosophie des sciences*. Paris: Vrin.

Castel, Robert. 1978. "La 'guerre à la pauvreté' et le statut de l'indigence dans une société d'abondance." *Actes de la recherche en sciences sociales* 19: 47–60.

Castel, Robert. 1995. *Les Métamorphoses de la question sociale. Une chronique du salariat*. Paris: Fayard.

Castel, Robert. 2007. "Au-delà du salariat ou en deçà de l'emploi? L'institutionnalisation du précariat?" Pp. 416–33 in *Repenser la solidarité. L'apport des sciences sociale*. Edited by Serge Paugam. Paris: Presses Universitaires de France.

Castel, Robert, and Klaus Dörre (eds.). 2009. *Prekarität, Abstieg, Ausgrenzung: Die soziale Frage am Beginn des 21. Jahrhunderts*. Frankfurt: Campus Verlag.

Castells, Manuel. 2015. *Networks of Outrage and Hope: Social Movements in the Internet Age*. Cambridge: Polity Press.

Chevalier, Louis. 1958. *Classes laborieuses et classes dangereuses à Paris pendant la première moitié du XIXe siècle*. Paris: Librairie Générale Française (new ed. Plon, 1985).

Chicago Commission on Race Relations. 1923. *The Negro in Chicago: A Study of Race Relations and a Race Riot*. Chicago, IL: University of Chicago Press.

Chicago Tribune (Staff of the). 1986. *The American Millstone: An Examination of the Nation's Permanent Underclass*. Chicago, IL: Contemporary Books.

Cingolani, Patrick. 2006. *La Précarité*. Paris: Presses Universitaires de France.

202 References

Clark, Kenneth B. 1965. *Dark Ghetto: Dilemmas of Social Power*. New York: Harper & Row.

Clark, Kenneth B. 1980. "The Black Plight, Race or Class?" *New York Times Magazine*, October 5.

Clear, Todd R. 2009. *Imprisoning Communities: How Mass Incarceration Makes Disadvantaged Neighborhoods Worse*. New York: Oxford University Press.

Cleaver, Eldridge. 1968. *Soul on Ice*. New York: Dell.

Cohen, Stanley. 1972. *Folk Devils and Moral Panics: The Creation of the Mods and Rockers*. Oxford: Basic Blackwell (3rd ed. 1987).

Collier, David, and Robert Adcock. 1999. "Democracy and Dichotomies: A Pragmatic Approach to Choices about Concepts." *Annual Review of Political Science* 2: 537–65.

Collier, David, and James E. Mahon Jr. 1993. "Conceptual 'Stretching' Revisited: Adapting Categories in Comparative Analysis." *American Political Science Review* 87, no. 4: 845–55.

Comfort, Megan L. 2007. "Punishment Beyond the Legal Offender." *Annual Review of Law and Social Science* 3: 271–96.

Condliffe Lagemann, Ellen. 1992. *The Politics of Knowledge: The Carnegie Corporation, Philanthropy, and Public Policy*. Chicago, IL: University of Chicago Press.

Conley, Dalton. 2000. *Being Black, Living in the Red: Race, Wealth, and Social Policy in America*. Berkeley, CA: University of California Press (new ed. 2010).

Conn, Steven. 2013. *Americans Against the City: Anti-Urbanism in the Twentieth Century*. New York: Oxford University Press.

Contreras, Randol. 2012. *The Stickup Kids: Race, Drugs, Violence, and the American Dream*. Berkeley, CA: University of California Press.

Crane, Stephen G. 1990. "The Trial of Bernhard Goetz." *Cornell Law Forum* 16, no. 3: 2–6.

Daly, Mary, and Hilary Silver. 2008. "Social Exclusion and Social Capital: A Comparison and Critique." *Theory & Society* 37, no. 6: 537–66.

Dangschat, Jens S. 1994. "Concentration of Poverty in the Landscapes of 'Boomtown' Hamburg: The Creation of a New Urban Underclass?" *Urban Studies* 31, no. 7: 1133–47.

Dash, Leon. 1989. *When Children Want Children: The Urban Crisis of Teenage Childbearing*. New York: William Morrow.

Davis, F. James. 1990. *Who Is Black? One Nation's Definition*. University Park, PA: Penn State University Press.

Davis, Peter. 1995. *If You Came This Way: A Journey Through the Lives of the Underclass*. New York: John Wiley & Son.

Deckard, Faith M., and Javier Auyero. 2022. "Poor People's

References

Survival Strategies: Two Decades of Research in the Americas." *Annual Review of Sociology* 48: in press.

De La Cadena, Marisol. 2000. *Indigenous Mestizos: The Politics of Race and Culture in Cuzco, Peru, 1919–1991.* Durham, NC: Duke University Press.

De León, Jason. 2015. *The Land of Open Graves: Living and Dying on the Migrant Trail.* Berkeley, CA: University of California Press.

Deparle, Jason. 1990. "What to Call the Poorest Poor?" *New York Times*, August 26.

Desmond, Matthew. 2016. *Evicted: Poverty and Profit in the American City.* New York: Penguin Random.

Desmond, Matthew. 2018. "Heavy is the House: Rent Burden among the American Urban Poor." *International Journal of Urban and Regional Research* 42, no. 1: 160–70.

Desmond, Matthew, and Tracy Shollenberger. 2015. "Forced Displacement from Rental Housing: Prevalence and Neighborhood Consequences." *Demography* 52, no. 5: 1751–72.

Desmond, Matthew, and Bruce Western. 2018. "Poverty in America: New Directions and Debates." *Annual Review of Sociology* 44: 305–18.

Devine, Joel A., and James D. Wright. 1993. *The Greatest of Evils: Urban Poverty and the American Underclass.* Hawthorne, NY: Aldine de Gruyter.

Dikötter, Frank. 1992. *The Discourse of Race in Modern China.* New York: Oxford University Press.

Dikötter, Frank (ed.). 1997. *The Construction of Racial Identities in China and Japan: Historical and Contemporary Perspectives.* Honolulu, HA: University of Hawaii Press.

Douglas, Mary. 1966. *Purity and Danger: An Analysis of Concepts of Pollution and Taboo.* London: Routledge.

Doussard, Marc. 2013. *Degraded Work: The Struggle at the Bottom of the Labor Market.* Minneapolis, MN: University of Minnesota Press.

Drake, St. Clair, and Horace R. Cayton. 1945. *Black Metropolis: A Study of Negro Life in a Northern City.* Chicago, IL: University of Chicago Press (exp. ed. 1993).

Du Bois, W.E.B. 1978. *On Sociology and the Black Community.* Edited by Dan S. Green and Edwin D. Driver. Chicago, IL: University of Chicago Press.

Duncan, Cynthia M. 1999. *Worlds Apart: Why Poverty Persists in Rural America.* Foreword by Robert Coles. New Haven, CT: Yale University Press (exp. ed. 2014).

Durkheim, Émile. 2017 [1895]. *Les Règles de la méthode sociologique.* Paris: Flammarion.

References

Duster, Troy. 1987. "Crime, Youth Unemployment, and the Black Urban Underclass." *Crime & Delinquency* 33, no. 2: 300–16.

Duus, Peter. 1998. *The Abacus and the Sword: The Japanese Penetration of Korea, 1895–1910*. Berkeley, CA: University of California Press.

Edin, Kathryn, and Laura Lein. 1997. *Making Ends Meet: How Single Mothers Survive Welfare and Low-Wage Work*. New York: Russell Sage Foundation.

Edsall, Thomas B. 1990. "'Underclass' Term Falls from Favor: Leading Poverty Researcher May Abandon Politically Charged Word." *The Washington Post*, August 13.

Edsall, Thomas Byrne, and Mary D. Edsall. 1991. *Chain Reaction: The Impact of Race, Rights, and Taxes on American Politics*. New York: Norton.

Elias, Norbert. 1998. "Group Charisma and Group Disgrace" (1964). Pp. 104–12 in *The Norbert Elias Reader*. Edited by Johan Goudsblom and Stephen Mennell. Malden, MA: Blackwell.

Emirbayer, Mustafa, and Matthew Desmond. 2015. *The Racial Order*. Chicago, IL: University of Chicago Press.

Engels, Friedrich. 1993 [1845]. *The Condition of the Working Class in England*. New York: Oxford University Press.

Esping-Andersen, Gøsta. 1990. *The Three Worlds of Welfare Capitalism*. Princeton, NJ: Princeton University Press.

Fassin, Didier. 1996. "Exclusion, 'underclass', 'marginalidad': Figures contemporaines de la pauvreté urbaine en France, aux États-Unis et en Amérique latine." *Revue française de sociologie* 37, no. 1: 37–75.

Feeley, Malcolm M. 1983. *Court Reform on Trial: Why Simple Solutions Fail*. New York: Basic Books.

Ferme, Mariane C. 2018. *Out of War: Violence, Trauma, and the Political Imagination in Sierra Leone*. Berkeley, CA: University of California Press.

Fisher, Donald. 1983. "The Role of Philanthropic Foundations in the Reproduction and Production of Hegemony: Rockefeller Foundations and the Social Sciences." *Sociology* 17, no. 2: 206–33.

Fishman, Robert. 1988. *Bourgeois Utopias: The Rise and Fall of Suburbia*. New York: Basic Books.

Fletcher, George P. 1990. *A Crime of Self-Defense: Bernhard Goetz and the Law On Trial*. Chicago, IL: University of Chicago Press.

Florida, Richard. 2002. *The Rise of the Creative Class: And How It's Transforming Work, Leisure, Community and Everyday Life*. New York: Basic Books.

Florida, Richard. 2003. "Cities and the Creative Class." *City & Community* 2, no. 1: 3–19.

References

Florida, Richard. 2012. *The New Urban Crisis: How our Cities are Increasing Inequality, Deepening Segregation, and Failing the Middle Class – And What we Can Do about It.* New York: Basic Books.

Fogelson, Robert M. 1967. "White on Black: A Critique of the McCone Commission Report on the Los Angeles Riots." *Political Science Quarterly* 82, no. 3: 337–67.

Fogelson, Robert M. 2007. *Bourgeois Nightmares: Suburbia, 1870–1930.* New Haven, CT: Yale University Press.

Foster, Carly Hayden. 2008. "The Welfare Queen: Race, Gender, Class, and Public Opinion." *Race, Gender & Class* 15, nos. 3–4: 162–79.

Fraser, Nancy, and Linda Gordon. 1994. "A Genealogy of Dependency: Tracing a Keyword of the US Welfare State." *Signs: Journal of Women in Culture and Society* 19, no. 2: 309–36.

Fredrickson, George M. 2002. *Racism: A Short History.* Princeton, NJ: Princeton University Press.

Fried, Morris L. 1983. "Review of Ken Auletta, *The Underclass.*" *Contemporary Sociology* 12, no. 4: 460–1.

Galbraith, John Kenneth. 1958. *The Affluent Society.* New York: Houghton Mifflin.

Gans, Herbert J. 1990. "Deconstructing the Underclass: The Term's Danger as a Planning Concept." *Journal of the American Planning Association* 56, no 3: 271–7.

Gans, Herbert J. 1991. *People, Plans, and Policies: Essays on Poverty, Racism, and Other National Urban Problems.* New York: Columbia University Press.

Gans, Herbert J. 1994. "Positive Functions of the Undeserving Poor: Uses of the Underclass in America." *Politics & Society* 22, no. 3: 269–83.

Gans, Herbert J. 1995. *The War Against the Poor: The Underclass and Anti-Poverty Policy.* New York: Basic Books.

Gans, Herbert J. 1996. "From 'Underclass' to 'Undercaste': Some Observations about the Future of the Post-Industrial Economy and its Major Victims." Pp. 141–52 in *Urban Poverty and the Underclass: A Reader.* Edited by Enzo Mingione. Oxford: Blackwell.

Garrett, Paul Michael. 2019. "'Castaway Categories': Examining the Re-emergence of the 'Underclass' in the UK." *Journal of Progressive Human Services* 30, no. 1: 25–45.

Gephart, Martha A., 1989. "Neighborhoods and Communities in Concentrated Poverty." *Items* 43, no. 4: 84–92.

Gephart, Martha A. and Robert W. Pearson. 1988. "Contemporary Research on the Urban Underclass: A Selected Review of the

Research that Underlies a New Council Program." *Items* 42, no. 1–2: 1–10.

Geremek, Bronislaw. 1978. *La Potence ou la pitié. L'Europe et les pauvres du Moyen Âge à nos jours.* Paris: Gallimard.

Gerring, John. 1999. "What Makes a Concept Good? A Criterial Framework for Understanding Concept Formation in the Social Sciences." *Polity* 31, no. 3: 357–93.

Giddens, Anthony. 1973. *The Class Structure of the Advanced Societies.* London: Hutchinson.

Gilbert, Alan. 2007. "The Return of the Slum: Does Language Matter?" *International Journal of Urban and Regional Research* 31, no. 4: 697–713.

Gilens, Martin. 2009. *Why Americans Hate Welfare: Race, Media, and the Politics of Antipoverty Policy.* Chicago, IL: University of Chicago Press.

Gilens, Martin. 2012. *Affluence and Influence: Economic Inequality and Political Power in America.* Princeton, NJ: Princeton University Press.

Glasgow, Douglas. 1980. *The Black Underclass: Poverty, Unemployment, and Entrapment of Ghetto Youth.* New York: Vintage.

Glazer, Nathan, and Daniel Patrick Moynihan. 1963. *Beyond the Melting Pot: The Negroes, Puerto Ricans, Jews, Italians and Irish of New York City.* Cambridge, MA: MIT Press.

Go, Julian. 2018. "Postcolonial Possibilities for the Sociology of Race." *Sociology of Race and Ethnicity* 4, no. 4: 439–51.

Go, Julian. 2021. "Three Tensions in the Theory of Racial Capitalism." *Sociological Theory* 39, no 1: 38–47.

Goertz, Gary. 2020. *Social Science Concepts and Measurements.* Princeton, NJ: Princeton University Press.

Goetz, Edward G. 2003. *Clearing the Way: Deconcentrating the Poor in Urban America.* Washington, DC: Urban Institute Press.

Gooding-Williams, Robert (ed.). 2013. *Reading Rodney King, Reading Urban Uprising.* New York: Routledge.

Gould-Wartofsky, Michael A. 2015. *The Occupiers: The Making of the 99 Percent Movement.* New York: Oxford University Press.

Graeber, David. 2013. *The Democracy Project: A History, a Crisis, a Movement.* New York: Random House.

Grossman, James R. 1989. *Land of Hope: Chicago, Black Southerners, and the Great Migration.* Chicago, IL: University of Chicago Press.

Guillory, Monique, and Richard C. Green (eds.). 1998. *Soul: Black Power, Politics, and Pleasure.* New York: NYU Press.

References 207

Gurr, Ted Robert, and Desmond S. King. 1987. *The State and the City*. Chicago, IL: University of Chicago Press.

Gutting, Gary (ed.). 2008. *Continental Philosophy of Science*. Oxford: Basil Blackwell.

Hacker, Andrew. 1982. "The Lower Depths." *New York Review of Books*, August 12.

Hagedorn, John M. 1988. *People and Folks: Gangs, Crime, and the Underclass in a Rustbelt City*. Chicago, IL: Lake View Press.

Hall, Bruce S. 2011. *A History of Race in Muslim West Africa, 1600–1960*. Cambridge: Cambridge University Press.

Hall, Peter. 2014. *Cities of Tomorrow: An Intellectual History of Urban Planning and Design Since 1880*, 4th ed. Malden, MA: Wiley Blackwell.

Hancock, Ange-Marie. 2004. *The Politics of Disgust: The Public Identity of the Welfare Queen*. New York: NYU Press.

Hannaford, Ivan. 1996. *Race: The History of an Idea in the West*. Baltimore, MD: Johns Hopkins University Press.

Hannerz, Ulf. 1968. "The Rhetoric of Soul: Identification in Negro Society." *Race* 9, no 4: 453–65.

Hannerz, Ulf. 1969. *Soulside: Inquiries into Ghetto Culture and Community*. New York: Columbia University Press.

Hannerz, Ulf. 2004. "Afterword: Soulside Revisited." Pp. 211–20 in *Soulside: Inquiries into Ghetto Culture and Community*. Chicago, IL: University of Chicago Press.

Harrington, Brooke. 2017. *Capital without Borders: Wealth Managers and the One Percent*. Cambridge, MA: Harvard University Press.

Harrington, Michael. 1962. *The Other America: Poverty in the United States*. New York: Scribner.

Hatuka, Tali, Issachar Rosen-Zvi, Michael Birnhack, Eran Toch, and Hadas Zur. 2018. "The Political Premises of Contemporary Urban Concepts: The Global City, the Sustainable City, the Resilient City, the Creative City, and the Smart City." *Planning Theory & Practice* 19, no. 2: 160–79.

Häußermann, Hartmut. 1997. "Armut in den Großstädten – eine neue städtische Unterklasse?" *Leviathan* 25, no. 1: 12–27.

Haveman, Robert H. 1987. *Poverty Policy and Poverty Research: The Great Society and the Social Sciences*. Madison, WI: University of Wisconsin Press.

Hays, Sharon. 2004. *Flat Broke with Children: Women in the Age of Welfare Reform*. New York: Oxford University Press.

Heisler, Barbara Schmitter. 1991. "A Comparative Perspective on the Underclass: Questions of Urban Poverty, Race, and Citizenship." *Theory & Society* 19, no 4: 455–84.

208 References

Henderson, Vivian. 1975. "Race, Economics, and Public Policy." *Crisis* 82: 50–5.

Herpin, Nicolas. 1993. "L'*urban underclass*' chez les sociologues américains: exclusion sociale et pauvreté." *Revue française de sociologie* 34, no. 4: 421–39.

Herring, Chris. 2019. "Concentrated Poverty." Pp. 1–10 in *The Wiley Blackwell Encyclopedia of Urban and Regional Studies.* Edited by Anthony M. Orum. Malden, MA: Wiley Blackwell.

Himmelfarb, Gertrude. 1983. *The Idea of Poverty: England in the Early Industrial Age.* New York: Knopf.

Hirsch, Arnold R. 1983. *Making the Second Ghetto: Race and Housing in Chicago 1940–1960.* New York: Cambridge University Press (new exp. ed. University of Chicago Press, 1998).

Hirschman, Albert O. 1970. *Exit, Voice, and Loyalty: Responses to Decline in Firms, Organizations, and States.* Cambridge, MA: Harvard University Press.

Hirschman, Albert O. 1991. *The Rhetoric of Reaction: Perversity, Futility, Jeopardy.* Cambridge, MA: Harvard University Press.

Horton, John. 1967. "Time and Cool People." *Trans-Action* 4, no. 5: 5–12.

Hovden, Jan Fredrik. 2008. *Profane and Sacred: A Study of the Norwegian Journalistic Field.* Bergen: University of Bergen Press.

Huysmans, Jef. 2008. "The Jargon of Exception – On Schmitt, Agamben and the Absence of Political Society." *International Political Sociology* 2, no. 2: 165–83.

Hyra, Derek S. 2008. *The New Urban Renewal: The Economic Transformation of Harlem and Bronzeville.* Chicago, IL: University of Chicago Press.

Iceland, John, and Erik Hernandez. 2017. "Understanding Trends in Concentrated Poverty: 1980–2014." *Social Science Research* 62: 75–95.

Innis, Leslie, and Joe R. Feagin. 1989. "The Black Underclass Ideology in Race Relations Analysis." *Social Justice* 16: 12–34.

Irwin, John. 1985. *The Jail: Managing the Underclass.* Berkeley, CA: University of California Press.

Jackson, Kenneth T. 1987. *Crabgrass Frontier: The Suburbanization of the United States.* New York: Oxford University Press.

Jackson, Walter A. 1990. *Gunnar Myrdal and America's Conscience: Social Engineering and Racial Liberalism, 1938–1987.* Chapel Hill, NC: University of North Carolina Press (new ed. 2014).

Jacobs, James B. 2015. *The Eternal Criminal Record.* Cambridge, MA: Harvard University Press.

Jargowsky, Paul A. 2013. *Concentration of Poverty in the New*

Millennium. Rutgers, NJ: The Century Foundation and Rutgers Centre for Urban Research and Education.

Jargowsky, Paul A., and Mary-Jo Bane. 1990. "Ghetto Poverty: Basic Questions." Pp. 16–67 in *Inner-City Poverty in the United States*. Edited by Laurence E. Lynn and Michael G.H. McGeary. Washington, DC: National Academies Press.

Jargowsky, Paul A., and Rebecca Yang. 2006. "The 'Underclass' Revisited: A Social Problem in Decline." *Journal of Urban Affairs* 28, no. 1: 55–70.

Jencks, Christopher. 1991. "Is the American Underclass Growing?" Pp. 28–100 in *The Urban Underclass*. Edited by Christopher Jencks and Paul E. Peterson. Washington, DC: The Brookings Institution.

Jencks, Christopher. 1992. *Rethinking Social Policy: Race, Poverty, and the Underclass*. Cambridge, MA: Harvard University Press.

Jencks, Christopher, and Paul E. Peterson (eds.). 1991. *The Urban Underclass*. Washington, DC: The Brookings Institution.

Jencks, Christopher, Lawrence M. Mead, and Isabel Sawhill. 1989. "GAO Features: The Issue of Underclass." *GAO Journal* 5: 15–22.

Johnson, Jane H., and Alan Partington. 2017. "'Underclass' in the English-Language Press: Who Are They, How Do They Behave, and Who Is to Blame for Them?" Pp. 293–318 in *Studies in Corpus-Based Sociolinguistics*. Edited by Eric Friginal. New York: Routledge.

Johnson, Matthew (ed.). 2016. *Precariat: Labour, Work and Politics*. London: Routledge.

Joint Economic Committee. 1989. *The Underclass, Hearing Before the Joint Economic Committee of the 101st Congress of the United States, 25 May 1989*. Washington, DC: US Government Printing Office.

Jones, Gareth Stedman. 1971. *Outcast London: A Study in the Relationship between Classes in Victorian Society*. New York: Pantheon.

Jones, Jacqueline. 1992. *The Dispossessed: America's Underclasses from the Civil War to the Present*. New York: Basic Books.

Jones, Nikki. 2010. *Between Good and Ghetto: African American Girls and Inner-City Violence*. New Brunswick, NJ: Rutgers University Press.

Kahlenberg, Richard D. (ed.). 2010. *Affirmative Action for the Rich: Legacy Preferences in College Admissions*. Washington, DC: Century Foundation Press.

Kalifa, Dominique. 2013. *Les Bas-fonds. Histoire d'un imaginaire*. Paris: Seuil. (English: *Vice, Crime, and Poverty: How the Western*

Imagination Invented the Underworld. New York: Columbia University Press, 2019.)

Kalleberg, Arne L. 2011. *Good Jobs, Bad Jobs: The Rise of Polarized and Precarious Employment Systems in the United States, 1970s to 2000s*. New York: Russell Sage Foundation.

Kantor, Harvey, and Barbara Brenzel. 1993. "Urban Education and the 'Truly Disadvantaged': The Historical Roots of the Contemporary Crisis, 1945–1990." Pp. 366–402 in *The "Underclass" Debate: Views from History*. Edited by Michael B. Katz. Princeton, NJ: Princeton University Press.

Kasarda, John D. 1992. *Urban Underclass Database: An Overview and Machine-Readable File Documentation*. New York: Social Science Research Council.

Katz, Michael B. 1989. *The Undeserving Poor: From the War on Poverty to the War on Welfare*. New York: Random House.

Katz, Michael B. (eds.) 1993a. *The "Underclass" Debate: Views from History*. Princeton, NJ: Princeton University Press.

Katz, Michael B. 1993b. "The Urban Underclass as a Metaphor of Social Transformation." Pp. 3–23 in *The "Underclass" Debate: Views from History*. Edited by Michael B. Katz. Princeton, NJ: Princeton University Press.

Katz, Michael B. 1996. *In the Shadow of the Poorhouse: A Social History of Welfare in America*. New York: Basic Books.

Katz, Michael B. 1997. *Improving Poor People: The Welfare State, the "Underclass," and Urban Schools as History*. Princeton, NJ: Princeton University Press.

Katz, Michael B. 2012. "From Underclass to Entrepreneur: New Technologies of Poverty Work in Urban America." Pp. 101–50 in *Why Don't American Cities Burn?* Philadelphia, PA: University of Pennsylvania Press.

Keil, Charles. 1966. *Urban Blues*. Chicago, IL: University of Chicago Press.

Keister, Lisa A. 2014. "The One Percent." *Annual Review of Sociology* 40: 347–67.

Kelso, William A. 1994. *Poverty and the Underclass: Changing Perceptions of the Poor in America*. New York: NYU Press.

Kennedy, Randall. 2008. *Nigger: The Strange Career of a Troublesome Word*. New York: Vintage.

Kerner Commission. 1989 [1968]. *The Kerner Report: The 1968 Report of the National Advisory Commission on Civil Disorders*. New York: Pantheon.

Killewald, Alexandra, Fabian T. Pfeffer, and Jared N. Schachner. 2017. "Wealth Inequality and Accumulation." *Annual Review of Sociology* 43: 379–404.

References

Kloosterman, Robert C. 1990. "The Making of the Dutch Underclass? A Labour Market View." Paper presented at the Workshop on Social Policy and the Underclass, University of Amsterdam, the Netherlands.

Kornblum, William. 1984. "Lumping the Poor: What is the Underclass?" *Dissent* 31, no. 3: 295–302.

Koselleck, Reinhart. 1982. "*Begriffsgeschichte* and Social History." *Economy & Society* 11, no. 4: 409–27.

Koselleck, Reinhart. 2002. *The Practice of Conceptual History: Timing History, Spacing Concepts.* Stanford, CA: Stanford University Press.

Koselleck, Reinhart. 2004. "The Historical-Political Semantics of Asymmetric Counterconcepts." Pp. 155–91 in *Futures Past: On the Semantics of Historical Time.* New York: Columbia University Press.

Koselleck, Reinhart, Javiér Fernández Sebastián, and Juan Francisco Fuentes. 2006. "Conceptual History, Memory, and Identity: An Interview with Reinhart Koselleck." *Contributions to the History of Concepts* 2: 99–127.

Kronauer, Martin. 1998. "Armut, Ausgrenzung, Unterklasse." Pp. 126–46 in *Großstadt: Soziologische Stichworte.* Edited by Hartmut Häußermann. Wiesbaden: VSA Verlag.

Labbens, Jean. 1969. *Le Quart-monde. La condition sous-prolétarienne.* Paris: Éditions Science et Service.

Labbens, Jean. 1978. *Sociologie de la pauvreté. Le tiers-monde et le quart-monde.* Paris: Gallimard.

Lagrée Jean-Charles. 1995. "Exclusion sociale ou formation d'une *underclass*?" Pp. 297–325 in *Trajectoires sociales et inégalités. Recherches sur les conditions de vie.* Edited by Frank Bouchoyer. Paris: MIRE, INSEE, ERES.

Lawson, Bill E. (ed.). 1992. *The Underclass Question.* Preface by William Julius Wilson. Philadelphia, PA: Temple University Press.

Lees, Andrew. 1985. *Cities Perceived: Urban Society in European and American Thought, 1820–1840.* New York: Columbia University Press.

Lemann, Nicholas. 1986. "The Origins of the Underclass." *Atlantic Monthly,* June: 31–55; July: 54–68.

Levin, Josh. 2019. *The Queen: The Forgotten Life behind an American Myth.* Boston, MA: Little, Brown.

Levy, Frank. 1977. *How Big Is the American Underclass?* Working paper. Washington, DC: Urban Institute.

Levy, Peter B. 2018. *The Great Uprising: Race Riots in Urban America during the 1960s.* New York: Cambridge University Press.

References

Lewis, Bernard. 1990. *Race and Slavery in the Middle East: An Historical Enquiry.* Oxford: Oxford University Press.

Lewis, Oscar. 1959. *Five Families: Mexican Case Studies in the Culture of Poverty.* New York: Basic Books.

Lewis, Oscar. 1966a. *La Vida: A Puerto Rican Family in the Culture of Poverty, San Juan and New York.* New York: Random House.

Lewis, Oscar. 1966b. "The Culture of Poverty." *Scientific American* 215, no. 4: 19–25.

Lie, John, 2009. *Multiethnic Japan.* Cambridge, MA: Harvard University Press.

Lis, Catharina, and Hugo Soly. 1979. *Poverty and Capitalism in Pre-industrial Europe.* Brighton: Harvester Press.

Litwack, Leon F. 1999. *Trouble in Mind: Black Southerners in the Age of Jim Crow.* New York: Vintage.

Logan, John R., and Harvey L. Molotch. 2007 [1987]. *Urban Fortunes: The Political Economy of Place.* Berkeley, CA: University of California Press.

Loury, Glenn. 1998. "An American Tragedy: The Legacy of Slavery Lingers in our Cities' Ghettos." *The Brookings Review*, Spring: 36–40.

Loveman, Mara. 2014. *National Colors: Racial Classification and the State in Latin America.* New York: Oxford University Press.

Luker, Kristin. 1996. *Dubious Conceptions: The Politics of Teenage Pregnancy.* Cambridge, MA: Harvard University Press.

Lukes, Steven. 1973. *Émile Durkheim, his Life and Work: A Historical and Critical Study.* Stanford, CA: Stanford University Press.

Lybarger, Jeremy. 2019. "The Price You Pay: On the Life and Times of the Woman Known as the Welfare Queen." *The Nation*, July 19.

Lynn, Laurence E., and Michael G.H. McGeary (eds.). 1990. *Inner-City Poverty in the United States.* Washington, DC: National Academies Press.

Magnet, Myron. 1993. *The Dream and the Nightmare: The Sixties, Legacy to the Underclass.* New York: William Morrow.

Marks, Carole. 1991. "The Urban Underclass." *Annual Review of Sociology* 17: 445–66.

Martin, Bill, and Iván Szélényi. 1988. "Three Waves of New Class Theory." *Theory & Society* 17: 645–67.

Marwell, Nicole P., and Shannon L. Morrissey. 2020. "Organizations and the Governance of Urban Poverty." *Annual Review of Sociology* 46: 233–50.

Marx, Karl. 2020 [1859]. *A Contribution to the Critique of Political Economy.* New York: Vintage.

References

Massey, Douglas S. 1993. "Latinos, Poverty, and the Underclass: A New Agenda for Research." *Hispanic Journal of Behavioral Sciences* 15, no. 4: 449–75.

Massey, Douglas S. 2006. "Race, Class, and Markets: Social Policy in the 21st Century." Pp. 117–32 in *Poverty and Inequality*. Edited by David B. Grusky and Ravi Kanbur. Stanford, CA: Stanford University Press.

Massey, Douglas S. 2007. *Categorically Unequal: The American Stratification System*. New York: Russell Sage Foundation.

Massey, Douglas, and Nancy A. Denton. 1993. *American Apartheid: Segregation and the Making of the Underclass*. Cambridge, MA: Harvard University Press.

Matza, David. 1966. "The Disreputable Poor." Pp. 310–39 in *Social Structure and Mobility in Economic Development*. Edited by Neil J. Smelser and Seymour Martin Lipset. New Brunswick, NJ: Transaction.

McCraw, Benjamin W. 2018. "Appeal to the People." Pp. 112–14 in *Bad Arguments: 100 of the Most Important Fallacies in Western Philosophy*. Edited by Robert Arp, Steven Barbone, and Michael Bruce. New York: John Wiley & Sons.

McDonald, John F. 2004. "The Deconcentration of Poverty in Chicago: 1990–2000." *Urban Studies* 41, no. 11: 2119–37.

Mead, Lawrence M. 1986. *Beyond Entitlement: The Obligations of Citizenship*. New York: Free Press.

Mead, Lawrence M. 1992. *The New Politics of Poverty: The Nonworking Poor in America*. New York: Basic Books.

Mead, Lawrence M. (ed.) 1997. *The New Paternalism: Supervisory Approaches to Poverty*. Washington, DC: The Brookings Institution.

Mears, Ashley. 2020. *Very Important People: Status and Beauty in the Global Party Circuit*. Princeton, NJ: Princeton University Press.

Medvetz, Thomas. 2012. *Think Tanks in America*. Chicago, IL: University of Chicago Press.

Merton, Robert K. 1984. "Socio-Economic Duration: A Case Study of Concept Formation in Sociology." Pp. 262–83 in *Conflict and Consensus: A Festschrift in Honor of Lewis A. Coser*. Edited by Walter W. Powell and Richard Robbins. New York: Free Press.

Merton, Robert K., and Elinor Barber. 2004. *The Travels and Adventures of Serendipity: A Study in Sociological Semantics and the Sociology of Science*. Princeton, NJ: Princeton University Press.

Milkman, Ruth. 2017. "A New Political Generation: Millennials and the Post-2008 Wave of Protest." *American Sociological Review* 82, no. 1: 1–31.

References

Milkman, Ruth. 2020. *Immigrant Labor and the New Precariat.* Cambridge: Polity Press.

Miller, Reuben Jonathan. 2021. *Halfway Home: Race, Punishment, and the Afterlife of Mass Incarceration.* Boston, MA: Little, Brown.

Mincy, Ronald B. 1989. "Paradoxes in Black Economic Progress: Incomes, Families, and the Underclass." *The Journal of Negro Education* 58, no. 3: 255–69.

Mincy, Ronald B. 1991. "Underclass Variations by Race and Place: Have Large Cities Darkened Our Picture of the Underclass?" Research Paper. Washington, DC: Urban Institute.

Mincy, Ronald B. 1994. "The Underclass: Concept, Controversy and Evidence." Pp. 109–46 in *Poverty and Public Policy: What Do We Know? What Should We Do?* Edited by Sheldon H. Danziger, Gary D. Sandefur, and Daniel H. Weinberg. Cambridge, MA: Harvard University Press.

Mincy, Ronald B., Isabel V. Sawhill, and Douglas A. Wolf. 1990. "The Underclass: Definition and Measurement." *Science* 248, no. 4954: 450–3.

Mingione, Enzo (ed.). 1995. *Urban Poverty and the Underclass: A Reader.* Cambridge, MA: Basil Blackwell.

Monk Jr., Ellis. 2021. "The Unceasing Significance of Colorism: Skin Tone Stratification in the United States." *Daedalus* 150, no. 2: 76–90.

Monkkonen, Erik H. 1984. *Walking to Work: Tramps in America, 1790–1935.* Lincoln, NE: University of Nebraska Press.

Moore, Joan, and Raquel Pinderhughes (eds.). 1993. *In the Barrio: Latinos and the Underclass Debate.* New York: Russell Sage Foundation.

Moore, Robert. 2014. "Rediscovering the Underclass." Pp. 301–25 in *Developments in Sociology.* Edited by Robert Burgess and Anne Murcott. London: Routledge.

Morris, Lydia D. 1993. "Is There a British Underclass?" *International Journal of Urban and Regional Research* 17, no. 3: 404–12.

Morris, Lydia. 1994. *Dangerous Classes: The Underclass and Social Citizenship.* London: Routledge.

Morris, Michael. 1989. "From the Culture of Poverty to the Underclass: An Analysis of a Shift in Public Language." *The American Sociologist* 20, no. 2: 123–33.

Moynihan, Daniel Patrick. 1965. *The Negro Family: The Case for National Action.* Washington, DC: Office of Policy Planning and Research, US Department of Labor.

Muhammad, Khalil Gibran. 2010. *The Condemnation of Blackness:*

Race, Crime, and the Making of Modern Urban America. Cambridge, MA: Harvard University Press.

Munck, Ronaldo. 2013. "The Precariat: A View from the South." *Third World Quarterly* 34, no. 5: 747–62.

Murray, Charles. 1984. *Losing Ground: American Social Policy, 1950–1980*. New York: Basic Books.

Murray, Charles. 1993a. "The Coming White Underclass." *Wall Street Journal*, October 29.

Murray, Charles. 1993b. "The Emerging White Underclass and How to Save It." *Philadelphia Inquirer*, November 15.

Murray, Charles. 1993c. *The Coming White Underclass*. Washington, DC: American Enterprise Institute.

Murray, Charles. 1999. *The Underclass Revisited*. Washington, DC: The AEI Press.

Musterd, Sako. 1994. "A Rising European Underclass?" *Built Environment* 20, no. 3: 185–92.

Myers, Dowell, and Cathy Yang Liu. 2005. "The Emerging Dominance of Immigrants in the US Housing Market 1970–2000." *Urban Policy and Research* 23, no. 3: 347–66.

Myrdal, Gunnar. 1944. *An American Dilemma: The Negro Problem and Modern Democracy*, 2 vols. New York: Harper.

Myrdal, Gunnar. 1963. *Challenge to Affluence*. New York: Random House.

Myrdal, Gunnar. 1973. "Twisted Terminology and Biased Ideas." Pp. 158–66 in *Against the Stream: Critical Essays on Economics*. New York: Pantheon.

Myrdal, Gunnar. 2005. *The Essential Gunnar Myrdal*. Edited by Örjan Appelqvist and Stellan Andersson. New York: New Press.

Nadasen, Premilla. 2004. *Welfare Warriors: The Welfare Rights Movement in the United States*. New York: Routledge.

Neckerman, Kathryn M. 1993. "The Emergence of 'Underclass' Family Patterns, 1900–1940." Pp. 194–219 in *The "Underclass" Debate: Views from History*. Edited by Michael B. Katz. Princeton, NJ: Princeton University Press.

Newman, Katherine S. 1988. *Falling from Grace: Downward Mobility in the Age of Affluence*. New York: Vintage.

O'Connor, Alice. 2000. "Poverty Research and Policy for the Post-Welfare Era." *Annual Review of Sociology* 26: 547–62.

O'Connor, Alice. 2001. *Poverty Knowledge: Social Science, Social Policy, and the Poor in Twentieth-Century US History*. Princeton, NJ: Princeton University Press.

O'Connor, Alice. 2007. *Social Science for What? Philanthropy and the Social Question in a World Turned Rightside Up*. New York: Russell Sage Foundation.

216 References

Oliver, Melvin L., and Thomas M. Shapiro. 2006. *Black Wealth, White Wealth: A New Perspective on Racial Inequality*. New York: Routledge.

Olsen, Niklas. 2012. *History in the Plural: An Introduction to the Work of Reinhart Koselleck*. New York: Berghahn Books.

Pagden, Anthony. 2015. *The Burdens of Empire: 1539 to the Present*. Cambridge: Cambridge University Press.

Page, Benjamin I., and James R. Simmons. 2002. *What Government Can Do: Dealing with Poverty and Inequality*. Chicago, IL: University of Chicago Press.

Page, Benjamin I., Jason Seawright, and Matthew J. Lacombe. 2018. *Billionaires and Stealth Politics*. Chicago, IL: University of Chicago Press.

Pager, Devah. 2007. *Marked: Race, Crime, and Finding Work in an Era of Mass Incarceration*. Chicago, IL: University of Chicago Press.

Paik, Leslie. 2021. *Trapped in a Maze: How Social Control Institutions Drive Family Poverty and Inequality*. Berkeley, CA: University of California Press.

Pandey, Gyanendra. 2013. *A History of Prejudice: Race, Caste, and Difference in India and the United States*. New York: Cambridge University Press.

Park, Robert E., Ernest W. Burgess, and Roderick D. McKenzie. 1923. *The City*. Chicago, IL: University of Chicago Press.

Patterson, James. 2000. *America's Struggle Against Poverty in the Twentieth Century*, 4th ed. Cambridge, MA: Harvard University Press.

Patterson, James T. 2010. *Freedom Is Not Enough: The Moynihan Report and America's Struggle over Black Family Life – From LBJ to Obama*. New York: Basic Books.

Patterson, Orlando. 2005. "Four Modes of Ethno-Somatic Stratification: The Experience of Blacks in Europe and the Americas." Pp. 67–122 in *Ethnicity, Social Mobility, and Public Policy: Comparing the USA and UK*. Edited by Glenn C. Loury, Tariq Modood, and Steven M. Teles. Cambridge: Cambridge University Press.

Patterson, Orlando. 2019. "The Denial of Slavery in Contemporary American Sociology." *Theory & Society* 48, no. 6: 903–14.

Pattillo, Mary. 2007. *Black on the Block: The Politics of Race and Class in the City*. Chicago, IL: University of Chicago Press.

Paugam, Serge (ed.). 1996. *L'Exclusion. L'état des savoirs*. Paris: La Découverte.

Paugam, Serge. 2000. *Le Salarié de la précarité*. Paris: Presses Universitaires de France.

References

Paugam, Serge, Bruno Cousin, Camila Giorgetti, and Jules Naudet. 2017. *Ce que les riches pensent des pauvres*. Paris: Seuil.

Pearson, Robert W. 1989. "Economy, Culture, Public Policy, and the Urban Underclass." *Items* 43, no. 1–2: 23–9.

Pearson, Robert W. 1991. "Social Statistics and an American Urban Underclass: Improving the Knowledge Base for Social Policy in the 1990s." *Journal of the American Statistical Association* 86, no. 414: 504–12.

Peck, Jamie. 2005. "Struggling with the Creative Class." *International Journal of Urban and Regional Research* 29, no. 4: 740–70.

Perrin, Évelyne. 2004. *Chômeurs et précaires au coeur de la question sociale*. Paris: La Dispute.

Phillips, Kevin. 2003. *Wealth and Democracy: A Political History of the American Rich*. New York: Crown.

Phillips, Kristin. 2018. *An Ethnography of Hunger: Politics, Subsistence, and the Unpredictable Grace of the Sun*. Bloomington, IN: Indiana University Press.

Philpott, Thomas Lee. 1978. *The Slum and the Ghetto: Neighborhood Deterioration and Middle-Class Reform*. New York: Oxford University Press.

Pickering, Kathleen Ann, Mark H. Harvey, and David Mushinsky. 2006. *Welfare Reform in Persistent Rural Poverty: Dreams, Disenchantments, and Diversity*. University Park, PA: Pennsylvania State University Press.

Pierson, Paul. 1994. *Dismantling the Welfare State? Reagan, Thatcher and the Politics of Retrenchment*. Cambridge: Cambridge University Press.

Pimpare, Stephen. 2004. *The New Victorians: Poverty, Politics, and Propaganda in Two Gilded Ages*. New York: New Press.

Pinçon, Michel, and Monique Pinçon-Charlot. 2011. *Le Président des riches*. Paris: La Découverte.

Pinkney, Alphonso. 1986. *The Myth of Black Progress*. New York: Cambridge University Press.

Piven, Frances Fox, and Richard A. Cloward. 1977. *Poor People's Movements: Why they Succeed, How they Fail*. New York: Vintage.

Piven, Frances Fox, Richard A. Cloward, and Fred Block. 1987. *The Mean Season: The Attack on the Welfare State*. New York: Pantheon.

Pontusson, Jonas. 2005. *Inequality and Prosperity: Social Europe vs. Liberal America*. Ithaca, NY: Cornell University Press.

Postero, Nancy Grey. 2007. *Now We Are Citizens: Indigenous Politics in Postmulticultural Bolivia*. Stanford, CA: Stanford University Press.

References

Proctor, Robert N., and Londa Schiebinger (eds.). 2008. *Agnotology: The Making and Unmaking of Ignorance*. Stanford, CA: Stanford University Press.

Purser, Gretchen, and Brian Hennigan. 2018. "Disciples and Dreamers: Job Readiness and the Making of the US Working Class." *Dialectical Anthropology* 42, no. 2: 149–61.

Quadagno, Jill S. 1994. *The Color of Welfare: How Racism Undermined the War on Poverty*. New York: Oxford University Press.

Rainwater, Lee. 1970. *Behind Ghetto Walls: Black Family Life in a Federal Slum*. New York: Aldine.

Rainwater, Lee, and William L. Yancey (eds.). 1967. *The Moynihan Report and the Politics of Controversy*. New Brunswick, NJ: Transaction.

Ralph, Michael, and Maya Singhal. 2019. "Racial Capitalism." *Theory & Society* 48, no. 6: 851–81.

Raymond, Chris. 1989. "Scholars Examining the Plight of the Urban Poor Broaden Scope of Research on the 'Underclass'." *Chronicle of Higher Education*, November 29.

Raymond, Chris. 1990. "American Underclass Grew from 1970 to 1980, Study Indicates." *The Chronicle of Higher Education*, May 9.

Reed, Adolph L., Jr. 1992. "The 'Underclass' as Myth and Symbol: The Poverty of Discourse about Poverty." *Radical America* 24: 21–40.

Reese, Ellen. 2005. *Backlash Against Welfare Mothers: Past and Present*. Berkeley, CA: University of California Press.

Rex, John. 1988. *The Ghetto and the Underclass: Essays on Race and Social Policy*. Aldershot: Avebury.

Rex, John, and Sally Tomlinson. 1979. *Colonial Immigrants in a British City*. London: Routledge and Kegan Paul.

Rheinberger, Hans-Jörg. 2010 [2007]. *On Historicizing Epistemology: An Essay*. Stanford, CA: Stanford University Press.

Ricketts, Erol R. 1992. "The Underclass: Causes and Responses." Pp. 216–35 in *The Metropolis in Black and White: Place, Power and Polarization*. Edited by George C. Galster and Edward W. Hill. New Brunswick, NJ: Rutgers Center for Urban Policy Research.

Ricketts, Erol R., and Ronald B. Mincy. 1990. "Growth of the Underclass: 1970–80." *The Journal of Human Resources* 25, no. 1: 137–45.

Ricketts, Erol R., and Isabel V. Sawhill. 1988. "Defining and Measuring the Underclass." *Journal of Policy Analysis and Management* 7, no 2: 316–25.

References

Rieder, Jonathan. 1985. *Canarsie: The Jews and Italians of Brooklyn Against Liberalism*. Cambridge, MA: Harvard University Press.

Rockefeller Foundation. 1992. *Annual Report 1992*. New York: Rockefeller Foundation.

Rodman, Hyman. 1977. "Culture of Poverty: The Rise and Fall of a Concept." *The Sociological Review* 25, no. 4: 867–76.

Roelandt, Theo, and Justus Veenman. 1992. "An Emerging Ethnic Underclass in the Netherlands? Some Empirical Evidence." *New Community* 19, no. 1: 129–41.

Roelofs, Joan. 2003. *Foundations and Public Policy: The Mask of Pluralism*. Albany, NY: SUNY Press.

Room, Graham (ed.). 1995. *Beyond the Threshold: The Measurement and Analysis of Social Exclusion*. Bristol: Policy Press.

Room, Graham, Roger Lawson, and Frank Laczko. 1989. "'New Poverty' in the European Community." *Policy & Politics* 17, no. 2: 165–76.

Rose, Tricia. 1994. *Black Noise: Rap Music and Black Culture in Contemporary America*. Middletown, CT: Wesleyan University Press.

Rowbottom, Jacob. 2010. *Democracy Distorted: Wealth, Influence and Democratic Politics*. Cambridge: Cambridge University Press.

Royce, Edward. 2018. *Poverty and Power: The Problem of Structural Inequality*. Lanham, MD: Rowman and Littlefield.

Rubin, Lillian B. 1986. *Quiet Rage: Bernie Goetz in a Time of Madness*. Berkeley, CA: University of California Press.

Rusche, Georg, and Otto Kirchheimer. 2003 [1939]. *Punishment and Social Structure*. New Brunswick, NJ: Transaction Books.

Russell, George. 1977. "The American Underclass: Destitute and Desperate in the Land of Plenty." *Time Magazine*, August 20: 14–27.

Ryan, William. 1971. *Blaming the Victim*. New York: Pantheon.

Sampson, Robert J. 2012. *Great American City: Chicago and the Enduring Neighborhood Effect*. Chicago, IL: University of Chicago Press.

Sampson, Robert J. 2019. "Neighbourhood Effects and Beyond: Explaining the Paradoxes of Inequality in the Changing American Metropolis." *Urban Studies* 56, no. 1: 3–32.

Sampson, Robert J., Jeffrey D. Morenoff, and Thomas Gannon-Rowley. 2002. "Assessing 'Neighborhood Effects': Social Processes and New Directions in Research." *Annual Review of Sociology* 28: 443–78.

Sánchez-Jankowski, Martín. 1991. *Islands in the Street: Gangs in Urban American Society*. Berkeley, CA: University of California Press.

220 References

Sandefur, Gary D. 1989. "American Indian Reservations: The First Underclass Areas?" *Focus* 12, no. 1: 37–41.

Sartori, Giovanni. 1970. "Concept Misformation in Comparative Politics." *American Political Science Review* 64, no. 4: 1033–53.

Sartori, Giovanni (ed.). 1984. *Social Science Concepts: A Systematic Analysis*. Beverly Hills, CA: Sage.

Sawhill, Isabel V. 1988. "What About America's Underclass?" *Challenge* 31, no. 3: 27–36.

Sawhill, Isabel. 2003. "The Behavioral Aspects of Poverty." Brookings Institution, available at: https://www.brookings.edu/articles/the-behavioral-aspects-of-poverty/.

Scheve, Kenneth, and David Stasavage. 2017. "Wealth Inequality and Democracy." *Annual Review of Political Science* 20: 451–68.

Seim, David L. 2013. *Rockefeller Philanthropy and Modern Social Science*. London: Pickering and Chatto.

Shapiro, Thomas M. 2004. *The Hidden Cost of Being African American: How Wealth Perpetuates Inequality*. New York: Oxford University Press.

Sherman, Rachel. 2017. *Uneasy Street: The Anxieties of Affluence*. Princeton, NJ: Princeton University Press.

Shin, Gi-Wook. 2006. *Ethnic Nationalism in Korea: Genealogy, Politics, and Legacy*. Stanford, CA: Stanford University Press.

Showalter, David. 2020. "Steps Toward a Theory of Place Effects on Drug Use: Risk, Marginality, and Opportunity in Small and Remote California Towns." *International Journal of Drug Policy* 85: 102–19.

Silver, Christopher. 1985. "Neighborhood Planning in Historical Perspective." *Journal of the American Planning Association* 51, no. 2: 161–74.

Simon, Jonathan. 1993. *Poor Discipline: Parole and the Social Control of the Underclass, 1890–1990*. Chicago, IL: University of Chicago Press.

Slater, Tom. 2018. "The Invention of the 'Sink Estate': Consequential Categorisation and the UK Housing Crisis." *The Sociological Review* 66, no. 4: 877–97.

Slater, Tom. 2021. *Shaking Up the City: Ignorance, Inequality and the Urban Question*. Berkeley, CA: University of California Press.

Sloop, John. 2001. *The Cultural Prison: Discourse, Prisoners, and Punishment*. Tuscaloosa, AL: University of Alabama Press.

Small, Mario Luis. 2004. *Villa Victoria: The Transformation of Social Capital in a Boston Barrio*. Chicago, IL: University of Chicago Press.

Small, Mario Luis, and Katherine Newman. 2001. "Urban Poverty After *The Truly Disadvantaged*: The Rediscovery of the Family, the Neighborhood, and Culture." *Annual Review of Sociology* 27: 23–45.

Smucker, Jonathan. 2017. *Hegemony How-To: A Roadmap for Radicals*. Chico, CA: AK Press.

Social Science Research Council. 1988. *A Proposal for the Establishment of a Program of Research on the Urban Underclass*. New York: SSRC.

Spear, Allan H. 1967. *Black Chicago: The Making of a Negro Ghetto, 1890–1920*. Chicago, IL: University of Chicago Press.

Stallybrass, Peter. 1990. "Marx and Heterogeneity: Thinking the Lumpenproletariat." *Representations* 31: 69–95.

Standing, Guy. 2011. *The Precariat: The New Dangerous Class*. London: Bloomsbury Academic.

Standing, Guy. 2014. *A Precariat Charter: From Denizens to Citizens*. London: Bloomsbury.

Steinmetz, George. 2014. "The Sociology of Empires, Colonies, and Postcolonialism." *Annual Review of Sociology* 40: 77–103.

Sugrue, Thomas J. 2008. *Sweet Land of Liberty: The Forgotten Struggle for Civil Rights in the North*. New York: Random House.

Swedberg, Richard. 2014. *The Art of Social Theory*. Princeton, NJ: Princeton University Press.

Swedberg, Richard. 2020. "On the Use of Definitions in Sociology." *European Journal of Social Theory* 23, no. 3: 431–45.

Tarkowska, Elżbieta. 1999. "In Search of an Underclass in Poland." *Polish Sociological Review* no. 125: 3–16.

Taylor, Keeanga-Yamahtta. 2016. *From #BlackLivesMatter to Black Liberation*. Chicago, IL: Haymarket Books.

Taylor, Keeanga-Yamahtta. 2019. *Race for Profit: How Banks and the Real Estate Industry Undermined Black Homeownership*. Chapel Hill, NC: University of North Carolina Press.

Taylor, Jonathan B., and Joseph P. Kalt. 2005. *American Indians on Reservations: A Databook of Socioeconomic Change between the 1990 and 2000 Censuses*. Cambridge, MA: Harvard Project on American Indian Economic Development, Malcolm Wiener Center for Social Policy.

Teaford, Jon C. 1990. *The Rough Road to Renaissance: Urban Revitalization in America, 1940–1985*. Baltimore, MD: Johns Hopkins University Press.

Telles, Edward. 2014. *Pigmentocracies: Ethnicity, Race, and Color in Latin America*. Chapel Hill, NC: University of North Carolina Press.

Teltsch, Kathleen. 1989. "Charity to Focus on Underclass." *New York Times*, January 22.

Teschke, Benno Gerhard. 2011. "Fatal Attraction: A Critique of Carl

References

Schmitt's International Political and Legal Theory." *International Theory* 3: 179–227.

Thelen, Kathleen. 2019. "The American Precariat: US Capitalism in Comparative Perspective." *Perspectives on Politics* 17, no. 1: 5–27.

Therborn, Gorän. 2014. *The Killing Fields of Inequality*. Cambridge: Polity Press.

Thompson, Heather Ann. 2016. *Blood in the Water: The Attica Prison Uprising of 1971 and Its Legacy*. New York: Vintage.

Tonry, Michael. 1995. *Malign Neglect: Race, Crime and Punishment in America*. New York: Oxford University Press.

Tonry, Michael (ed.). 1998. *Youth Violence*. Chicago, IL: University of Chicago Press.

Topalov, Christian. 1993 [1991]. "The City as *Terra Incognita*: Charles Booth's Poverty Survey and the People of London, 1886–1891." *Planning Perspective* 8, no. 4: 395–425.

Trotter, Joe William, Jr. 1985. *Black Milwaukee: The Making of an Industrial Proletariat, 1915–45*. Chicago, IL: University of Chicago Press.

Trounstine, Jessica. 2018. *Segregation by Design: Local Politics and Inequality in American Cities*. New York: Cambridge University Press.

Tuttle, William M. 1970. *Race Riot: Chicago in the Red Summer of 1919*. Urbana, IL: University of Illinois Press.

Tyler, Imogen. 2013. "The Riots of the Underclass? Stigmatisation, Mediation and the Government of Poverty and Disadvantage in Neoliberal Britain." *Sociological Research Online* 18, no. 4: 25–35.

Useem, Bert, and Peter Kimball. 1991. *States of Siege: US Prison Riots, 1971–1986*. New York: Oxford University Press.

Vale, Lawrence J. 2013. *Purging the Poorest: Public Housing and the Design Politics of Twice-Cleared Communities*. Chicago, IL: University of Chicago Press.

Vale, Lawrence J. 2014. "The Politics of Resilient Cities: Whose Resilience and Whose City?" *Building Research & Information* 42, no. 2: 191–201.

Valentine, Charles A. 1968. *Culture and Poverty*. Chicago, IL: University of Chicago Press.

Van Deburg, William L. 1992. *New Day in Babylon: The Black Power Movement and American Culture, 1965–1975*. Chicago, IL: University of Chicago Press.

Van Parijs, Philippe, and Yannick Vanderborght. 2017. *Basic Income: A Radical Proposal for a Free Society and a Sane Economy*. Cambridge, MA: Harvard University Press.

References

Venkatesh, Sudhir Alladi. 2000. *American Project: The Rise and Fall of a Modern Ghetto*. Cambridge, MA: Harvard University Press.

Vergara, Camilo José. 1995. *The New American Ghetto*. New Brunswick, NJ: Rutgers University Press.

Visher, Christy A., and Jeremy Travis. 2003. "Transitions from Prison to Community: Understanding Individual Pathways." *Annual Review of Sociology* 29: 89–113.

Wacquant, Loïc. 1997. "For an Analytic of Racial Domination." *Political Power & Social Theory* 11, no. 1: 221–34.

Wacquant, Loïc. 2001. "Deadly Symbiosis: When Ghetto and Prison Meet and Mesh." *Punishment & Society* 3, no. 1: 95–133.

Wacquant, Loïc. 2002. "Scrutinizing the Street: Poverty, Morality, and the Pitfalls of Urban Ethnography." *American Journal of Sociology* 107, no 6: 1468–532.

Wacquant, Loïc. 2004 [2000]. *Body and Soul: Notebooks of an Apprentice Boxer*. New York: Oxford University Press, exp. anniversary ed. 2022.

Wacquant, Loïc. 2005. "Race as Civic Felony." *International Social Science Journal* 57, no. 183: 127–42.

Wacquant, Loïc. 2008. *Urban Outcasts: A Comparative Sociology of Advanced Marginality*. Cambridge: Polity Press.

Wacquant, Loïc. 2009a. "The Body, the Ghetto and the Penal State." *Qualitative Sociology* 32, no. 1: 101–29.

Wacquant, Loïc. 2009b. *Punishing the Poor: The Neoliberal Government of Social Insecurity*. Durham, NC: Duke University Press.

Wacquant, Loïc. 2009c. *Prisons of Poverty*. Minneapolis, MN: University of Minnesota Press.

Wacquant, Loïc. 2010. "Designing Urban Seclusion in the 21st Century." *Perspecta: The Yale Architectural Journal* 43: 165–78.

Wacquant, Loïc. 2011. "The Wedding of Workfare and Prisonfare Revisited." *Social Justice* 38, nos 1–2: 203–21.

Wacquant, Loïc. 2012a. "A Janus-Faced Institution of Ethnoracial Closure: A Sociological Specification of the Ghetto." Pp. 1–31 in *The Ghetto: Contemporary Global Issues and Controversies*. Edited by Ray Hutchison and Bruce Haynes. Boulder, CO: Westview Press.

Wacquant, Loïc. 2012b. "Three Steps to a Historical Anthropology of Actually Existing Neoliberalism." *Social Anthropology* 20, no. 1: 66–79.

Wacquant, Loïc. 2013. "Symbolic Power and Group-Making: On Pierre Bourdieu's Reframing of Class." *Journal of Classical Sociology* 13, no. 2: 274–91.

224 References

Wacquant, Loïc. 2014. "Marginality, Ethnicity and Penality in the Neo-liberal City: An Analytic Cartography." *Ethnic & Racial Studies* 37, no 10: 1687–711.

Wacquant, Loïc. 2020. "Bringing Caste Back In." Unpublished paper, Department of Sociology, University of California, Berkeley.

Wacquant, Loïc. 2022. *The Zone: Making Do in the Hyperghetto*. Cambridge: Polity Press.

Wagatsuma, Hiroshi, and George DeVos. 2021 [1966]. *Japan's Invisible Race: Caste in Culture and Personality*. Berkeley, CA: University of California Press.

Wagley, Charles. 1965 [1958]. "On the Concept of Social Race in the Americas." Pp. 531–45 in *Contemporary Cultures and Societies in Latin America*. Edited by Dwight B. Heath and Richard N. Adams. New York: Random House.

Wakefield, Sara, and Christopher Wildeman. 2013. *Children of the Prison Boom: Mass Incarceration and the Future of American Inequality*. New York: Oxford University Press.

Waldinger, Roger, and Michael I. Lichter. 2003. *How the Other Half Works: Immigration and the Social Organization of Labor*. Berkeley, CA: University of California Press.

Ward, David. 1989. *Poverty, Ethnicity, and the American City, 1840–1925: Changing Conceptions of the Slum and the Ghetto*. Cambridge: Cambridge University Press.

Weaver, R. Kent. 2000. *Ending Welfare As We Know It*. Washington, DC: The Brookings Institution.

Weber, Max. 1947 [1904]. "'Objectivity' in Social Science and Social Policy." Pp. 50–112 in *The Methodology of the Social Sciences*. New York: Free Press.

Weber, Max. 1947. *The Methodology of the Social Sciences*. New York: Free Press.

Weber, Max. 1958 [1919]. "Science as a Vocation." *Daedalus* 87, no. 1: 111–34.

Weber, Max. 1978 [1918–22]. *Economy and Society*, 2 vols. Berkeley, CA: University of California Press.

Welshman, John. 2006. *Underclass: A History of the Excluded Since 1880*. London: Continuum, 2nd ed. 2013. London: Bloomsbury Academic.

West, Cornell. 1993. *Keeping Faith: Philosophy and Race in America*. New York: Routledge.

Westergaard, John. 1992. "About and Beyond the 'Underclass': Some Notes on Influences of Social Climate on British Sociology Today." *Sociology* 26, no. 4: 575–87.

Western, Bruce. 2006. *Punishment and Inequality in America*. New York: Russell Sage Foundation.

References   225

Whelan, Christopher T. 1996. "Marginalization, Deprivation, and Fatalism in the Republic of Ireland: Class and Underclass Perspectives." *European Sociological Review* 12, no. 1: 33–51.

White, Morton Gabriel, and Lucia White. 1962. *The Intellectual Versus the City: From Thomas Jefferson to Frank Lloyd Wright.* Cambridge, MA: Harvard University Press.

Wilentz, Sean. 2008. *The Age of Reagan: A History, 1974–2008.* New York: HarperCollins.

Williams, Lee E. 2008. *Anatomy of Four Race Riots: Racial Conflict in Knoxville, Elaine (Arkansas), Tulsa, and Chicago, 1919–1921.* Jackson, MI: University Press of Mississippi.

Wilson, James Q. 1992. "Redefining Equality: The Liberalism of Mickey Kaus." *Public Interest*, no. 109: 101–8.

Wilson, William Julius. 1978. *The Declining Significance of Race: Blacks and American Institutions.* Chicago, IL: University of Chicago Press, 2nd exp. ed., 1980.

Wilson, William Julius. 1987. *The Truly Disadvantaged: The Inner City, the Underclass and Public Policy.* Chicago, IL: University of Chicago Press.

Wilson, William Julius. 1988. "The American Underclass: Inner-City Ghettos and the Norms of Citizenship." The Godkin Lecture, John F. Kennedy School of Government, Harvard University, April 26 (transcript of the lecture as delivered).

Wilson, William Julius. 1991a. "Studying Inner-City Social Dislocations: The Challenge of Public Agenda Research: 1990 Presidential Address." *American Sociological Review* 56, no 1: 1–14.

Wilson, William Julius. 1991b. "Public Policy Research and 'The Truly Disadvantaged'." Pp. 460–81 in *The Urban Underclass.* Edited by Christopher Jencks and Paul E. Peterson. Washington, DC: The Brookings Institution.

Wilson, William Julius (ed.). 1993a. *The Ghetto Underclass: Social Science Perspectives.* Newbury Park, CA: Sage.

Wilson, William Julius (ed.). 1993b. *Sociology and the Public Agenda.* Newbury Park, CA: Sage.

Wilson, William Julius. 1996. *When Work Disappears: The World of the New Urban Poor.* New York: Knopf.

Wilson, William Julius. 1999. *The Bridge over the Racial Divide: Rising Inequality and Coalition Politics.* Berkeley, CA: University of California Press.

Wilson, William Julius. 2006. "Social Theory and the Concept Underclass." Pp. 103–16 in *Poverty and Inequality.* Edited by David B. Grusky and Ravi Kanbur. Stanford, CA: Stanford University Press.

226 References

Wilson, William Julius. 2009. *More than Just Race: Being Black and Poor in the Inner City*. New York: Norton.

Wilson, William Julius. 2012. "Reflections on Responses to *The Truly Disadvantaged*." Pp. 251–309 in *The Truly Disadvantaged*, 2nd exp. edn. Chicago, IL: University of Chicago Press.

Wimmer, Andreas. 2013. *Ethnic Boundary Making: Institutions, Power, Networks*. New York: Oxford University Press.

Wimmer, Andreas. 2015. "Race-Centrism: A Critique and Research Agenda." *Ethnic & Racial Studies* 38, no. 13: 2186–205.

Winant, Howard. 2001. *The World is a Ghetto: Race and Democracy Since World War II*. New York: Basic Books.

Winkler, Karen J. 1990. "Researcher's Examination of California's Poor Latin Population Prompts Debate over the Traditional Definitions of the Underclass." *Chronicle of Higher Education*, October 10.

Wittgenstein, Ludwig. 1977. *Culture and Value*. Cambridge: Basil Blackwell.

Wittgenstein, Ludwig. 2009 [1953]. *Philosophical Investigations*. Malden, MA: Blackwell.

Woodall, Ann M. 2005. *What Price the Poor? William Booth, Karl Marx and the London Residuum*. London: Ashgate.

Wright, Erik Olin. 1994. *Interrogating Inequality: Essays on Class Analysis, Socialism, and Marxism*. London: Verso.

Wright, Erik Olin (ed.). 2005. *Approaches to Class Analysis*. Cambridge: Cambridge University Press.

Wright, Erik Olin. 2016. "Is the Precariat a Class?" *Global Labour Journal* 7, no. 2: 123–35.

Young Jr., Alford A. 2011. *The Minds of Marginalized Black Men: Making Sense of Mobility, Opportunity, and Future Life Chances*. Princeton, NJ: Princeton University Press.

Young, Cristobal. 2017. *The Myth of Millionaire Tax Flight: How Place Still Matters for the Rich*. Stanford, CA: Stanford University Press.

Zacka, Bernardo. 2017. *When the State Meets the Street: Public Service and Moral Agency*. Cambridge, MA: Harvard University Press.

Zucman, Gabriel. 2019. "Global Wealth Inequality." *Annual Review of Economics* 11: 109–38.

Index

~

Page numbers in *italics* refer to a box in the text.
Page numbers in **bold** refer to a figure.

accusation, public 2, 34
activism 110, *158*, 174
  black 24, 135, 182
Addams, Jane 18, 19–20
advanced marginality *see*
  marginality
affluence 42, 67, *157–9*
African Americans 130
  and class 119, 125
  and inequality 69, 98, 149
  and race 58–9, 79, 183
  and stereotyping 136, *137*
  and subordination/seclusion
    69, 124–5
  see also black people; ethnicity;
    race
Agamben, Georgio 172, 173
American Bible Society *17*
American Political Science
  Association *162–3*
analysis, tool v. object of 2, 15,
  34
Andersen, John 62
Anderson, Elijah 57–8

Anglo-Saxons 18
*Annals of the American Academy
  of Social and Political
  Science* 60
Annual Review of Sociology 60,
  189–90
Anti-Saloon League *20*
antisocial activity *see* behavior,
  antisocial
anti-statist reaction 79
anti-urbanism 15–26, 133, 182
anxiety 18, 25
applied rationalism 3
  see also historical epistemology
argumentum ad populum 64
Asia/Asians 74, 183n8, 192
assemblage (Deleuze) 172
asymmetric counter-concept
  (Koselleck) 4, 147
Atlantic Monthly 79, *114*
Attica penitentiary 135
Auletta, Ken 29n1, 44–7, 49, 65,
  77, 81, *90*, *114*, 115, 128
Australia 191, 192

Index

autonomy, intellectual/scientific 130n18, 177

Bachelard, Gaston 5, 141, 151, 168
backlash 37, 48, 79–80
Bandura, Albert 100
bandwagons 64–5, 172
bare life (Agamben) 172, 173
behavior, antisocial 23–4, 36, 50, 78–93, 97
  and class inequality 79, 87, 88–9
  and conservative politics 80, 88–9
  and criminal justice 134, 137, 148
  and criminality 36, 42, 78–9, 90, 91–2, 136–7
  and educational opportunities 81–2, 87, 90
  and employment opportunities/ unemployment 81–2, 83, 87–8, 90, 91, 163
  and hyperghettos 78, 83
  and journalism 78–9, 84–5
  and morality 80–1, 85–7, 93
  and neighborhoods 83, 85–7, 91, 100–1, 120
  and poverty 46, 85, 87, 88–9, 90, 91, 123
  and race 58–9, 79, 87, 107, 128–9, 136–7, 148
  and Sawhill, Isabel 82–4, 86–8, 90
  and single-parent families 81–2, 87, 88, 90
  and state responsibility/policy 80, 88–9, 115, 148
  and think tanks 50, 80, 82, 84
  and welfare dependency 81–2, 88, 90, 91
behavior concept 49, 54–9, 75, 115, 124
  and think tanks 96, 114, 148

and Wilson 100–1, 107, 144
Behind Ghetto Walls (Lee) 71, 72
Bell, Daniel 67
Bhabha, Homi K. 172
black culture 26n53, 120–1
Black Lives Matter movement 182
black people 58–9, 64, 69, 79, 98, 119, 125, 130, 149, 150, 183
  and anti-urbanism 16, 23–6
  and class 25, 42, 97, 104, 125, 149–50
  and criminality 23–4, 80, 90, 135, 137, 170
  employment opportunities/ unemployment 43, 64, 163
  men 14, 24, 37, 38, 43, 57, 64, 163
  and poverty 64, 98, 150
  precariat/precarity, black 112–13, 130, 148, 163
  and segregation 125, 149–50
  and stereotyping 136, 137
  and subordination/seclusion 69, 124–5
  and welfare dependency 135, 137
  see also African Americans; ethnicity; race
Black Power activism 23–4
Black Scholar journal 60
black scholars 58–9, 82, 131
blackness 16, 26n53, 116, 135–6, 144, 165, 182
Blackwell, Basil 63
Booth, Charles 17, 50, 127
Bourdieu, Pierre 1, 5–6, 8, 14, 96, 113, 116, 132, 144, 151, 159, 185, 188
classification struggles 35, 129, 144–5, 188
  and concepts/categories 151, 185

Index

cultural fields theory 1, 5–6, 113–16
and reflexivity 3, 5, 132
Bourgois, Philippe 155
boxing 14
Brace, Charles Loring 56
Bronzeville 11, 21, 33
Brookings Institution 13, 60, 84, 86, 139, 148
Brubaker, Rogers 150, 174, 187n17
Burakumin people 181, 183
bureaucratic field 5, 150, 153, 157
Bush administration/Bush, George 79, *136*

Canada 191
Canguilhem, Georges 3, 5, 8, 151
capital 5, 87, 89, 145, 149, 153, 157, *163, 165*
symbolic 53, 89, *163*
capitalism 10, 39, 125, 174, 177, 178
and class inequality 94, 104, 176–7
and precarity 127, *164–5*, 168–9
capitalism, racial 174
car-window sociology (Du Bois) 13, *127–8*
caste 3, 7, 14, 23, 26, 30, 35, 40, 48, 58, 63, 101, 103, 118, 120, 125, 133, 140, *165*
and educational opportunities 69, 125
and race 153, 181, 184
see also class; inequality, class
Castel, Robert *162*
categoreme, social 185
categories, analytic and folk 131, 172, 174, 178, 180
categories, dispossessed and

dishonored 8, 81, 134, 145, *162*
categories, scientific 131, 145, 178
categories of perception 9, 147, 184, 185
categorization 9, 26, 184, 185–6, 188
Cato Institute 48
causal chain 98, **99**, 102
census data 116, 117, 118
Centaur state, neoliberal 134, *164, 170*
charisma, group 146
see also honor
Chevalier, Louis 10
Chicago 9–10, 11–12, 23, 170
Chicago school of sociology 18, 100–1
Chicago Tribune 78–9, *114*, *137*
children
and educational opportunities 87, 90, 125
and poverty 69, 72, 85, 105
China 191, 192, 193
Christianity, Evangelical 16
Christopher Columbus complex 129
Chronicle of Higher Education 60
Cingolani, Patrick *162*
circular causation/circles, vicious 69, 70, 83, 124
citations of "underclass" 190–1
cities, creative 175, 176–7
cities, dangerous 34
cities, sites of dissolution 16
cities, wicked 16
Civil Rights Movement 23, 135
civil rights organizations *115–16*
Civilian Conservation Corps 22
Clark, Kenneth B. 36, *96*
class 125, 133, 171
and housing 125, 149
and poverty 88, 140, 150

230 Index

class (*cont.*)
  and precariat/precarity 163–4,
    165–6, 171
    and middle-classes 99,
      112–13, 146–7, *163*
    and working class *164, 166,*
      167n10, 168–9
    and race 40, 74, 94, 96, 104,
      140, 149–50
    and middle-class 23, 112–13
    see also inequality; middle-
      class; precariat;
      "underclass"; upper class/
      elites; working class
class reaction 79
class structure 39, 70, 87, *91,*
    130, 149–50, 153, 158,
    181
    and race 94, 96
classification 34, 67, 188
  classification struggles
    (Bourdieu) 35, 129,
    144–5, 188
  principle of 40, 144, 181, 184,
    188
  and stratification 8, 93, 181,
    188
    and race 181, 184, 188
Clinton administration 110, *137*
colonialism 182
Committee on the Urban
    Underclass (SSCR) 61,
    109, 110, 117
common sense 13, 81, 85–6,
    117
  and science 145, 152, 158,
    180, 181, 184
  see also doxa
communal ghetto 2, 11, *165*
community development
    corporations 50
community leadership/mentoring
    57, 58
community liaison 110
Community Planning and Action
    Program (CPAP) 110

competence, economic 56
complicity 116, 180
concentration effects/
    concentration of poverty
    99–100, 101–2, 118, 126,
    154
concepts 2, 150–68, 172–8
  analytic concepts 132, 151–2
  behavioral concept (Sawhill,
    Mead, Mincy, Ricketts)
    82, 84, 93, 107, 115, 142
  Bourdieu 151, 185
  circulation of 7, 9, 35, 47, 63,
    106, 131, 143, 145–6,
    151, 178, 189
  concept formation x, 9, 150,
    177–8
  conceptual history
    (*Begriffsgeschichte*) 1,
    3–6, 35, 47, 140
  conceptual speculative bubbles
    129, 172, 173–5
  counter-concepts 4, 19, 147
  folk concepts 121, 145,
    151–2, 174
  and heuristics 152, 153–4
  hybrid constructs 145, 151
  and journalism 175, 189–92
  and logics 152, 153
  moral concept *114*
  neo-ecological concept
    (Wilson) 118, 143,
    148–50
  neo-Weberian concept 73, 75,
    93, 143–4
  of poverty 103, 155–6
  proto-concepts 2, 47
  and race 153, 187–8
  relational concept 6, 40, 88
  sensitizing concept 172
  specular concept 7, 120
  and state responsibility 103,
    148–50
  structural concept (Myrdal) 3,
    54–5, 67–71, 75, 93, *114,*
    147

Index

of "underclass" 47, 63, 93–105, 153–6, 161, 189–92
see also behavior concept; heuristics; logics; semantics
conservatism 93, 176
and antisocial behavior 80, 88–9
neo-conservatism 3, 88, 97, 109
construction/reconstruction 5, 9, 59
containment, racial/punitive 21, 25
Corcoran, Mary 52
cosmopolitanism 175
courts 43, 127, 157, *161*, 171
criminal justice 41, *138*
and antisocial behavior 134, 148
and gender 148, 187
and neighborhoods 104, 169–70
and poverty 50, 169–70
and race 77, 187
see also penal state; punishment
criminality
and antisocial behavior 78–9, 90, *91*–2
and class inequality 70, 76, 102
and educational opportunities 138, 170
and gender 80, 133–4, 135, 138, 170
and hyperghettos 80, 104, 169–79
images of the "underclass"/ stereotyping 134, *137*, 138, 193
and race 23–4, 76, 90, 135, *137*, *138*, 170
and black people 23–4, 80, 90, 135, *137*, 170

and single parenthood 138, 170
and state responsibility/policy 78–80, *137*
drop in crime 110, 112
and social policy reform 110–11, 112
teenage criminals 134, 138
and violence 10, 23–4
and welfare dependency 47, 138
crisis 25, 42, 48
urban crisis 24, 26
cultural production 1, 5–6, 113–16, 131
cultural production theory (Bourdieu) 1, 5–6, 113–16
culture of poverty 35, 39, 47, 59, 71, 99–100, 175, 190
Lewis 39–40
see also ghetto, culture; subculture, "underclass" as
culture of segregation 102
culture of survival 76
culture of wealth *159*
culture, black 120–1
Current Population Survey 116

Dalit people 183
danger 34, 113, 123, 124, 128, 193, 194
dangerous class 17, 31, 34, 44, 56, 109, 118, 130, 132, 163, 168
Danziger, Sheldon 81, 108
data revolution 116
decentralists 21–2
deindustrialization 12, 25, 35, 98, **99**, *162*, 168
Deleuze, Gilles 172
delinquency 17, 21, 23, 34, 36, 42, *90*
demarcation 69, 123, 151, 184
demographics 18, 83, 100, 169

232 Index

demonization 2, 79, 93, 116,
136, 144
Deparle, Jason 108
Department of Labor, US 41
deproletarianization 125, 130,
164
Desmond, Matthew and Western,
Bruce 156
Devine, Joel A. and Wright,
James D. 92
diaspora 174
dignity, social 69
disaggregation 161, 185
discipline 38, 87n50, 88, 123,
134
symbolic 2
see also prisonfare; workfare
discrimination 9, 37, 74, 77, 94,
97, 101, 104, 145n6, 163,
183
disgrace, group 146
see also stigma
dishonor 2, 81, 134, 145, 162,
182
disorganization 1, 37, 38, 79,
131, 155
dispossession 2, 3n6, 60, 123,
145, 147, 156
and class inequality 40, 76,
158, 162, 164
and race 10, 76, 81, 98, 153,
157n31
see also marginality; poverty;
precariat
distribution, politics of 158
domination 79–80, 157, 158,
177
domination, racial/ethnoracial 9,
10, 23, 73, 94, 101, 183,
184–8
doxa 8, 53, 120
Drake, St Clair and Cayton,
Horace R. 11
dramatism (Burke) 54n2
dramatization 43, 68
drug addiction 23, 34, 36, 41,

42, 43, 45, 47, 57, 65, 90,
105, 148, 170
drug economy/trafficking 54, 57,
90, 129
Du Bois, W.E.B. 13, 128
Dukakis, Michael 137
Durkheim, Émile 131, 151n18,
152, 153, 178
Duster, Troy 77–8

ecology see neo-ecology
economy 81, 93, 94, 95–101
and class inequality 72–5, 79,
95–6, 97
economic structure 66, 67–78
and education and employment
opportunities 70, 97,
99–100, 112, 147
and ghetto/neighborhoods
96–7, 98, 99–101, 112
and local institutions 98, 99
and race 73–4, 94, 95–7
and United Kingdom 72–3,
74–5
and welfare dependency 58,
97, 98
Edin, Kathryn and Lein, Laura
155
Edsall, Thomas 108
education, higher 68–9, 70
education, secondary 10, 86,
164
educational opportunities 70,
103–4, 164
and antisocial behavior 81–2,
87, 90
and caste 69, 125
and children 87, 90, 125
and class inequality 68–9, 76,
87, 102, 125
and criminality 138, 170
Elias, Norbert 146
emotion 140, 146, 183
collective 26, 139, 153
and race 152, 153, 183–4
see also fear

Index

empiricism 7–8, 50, 64, 117,
153–4, 156, 184
and Wilson 103, 161
employment opportunities/
unemployment
and antisocial behavior 81–2,
83, 87–8, *90*, *91*, *163*
and class inequality 67–71, 74,
75, 76, 87–8, *163*
and economy 70, 97, 99–100,
112, 147
and insecurity/precarity
162–4, 168–9
and migrants 87, 169
nonwork/"underclass" image
47, 56, *92*, 193
and race 43, 64, 76, 77–8,
105, *163*
reasons for unemployment
57–8, 68–9, 100–1
scarecrow "groups" ii, 81, *90*,
91
training programs/educational
opportunities 41, 43,
45–6, 58, 103–4
Engels, Friedrich 10
environmentalist approach 18,
19–20
envy 42
epistemic lag and decomposition
193
epistemic opportunity cost
168–71
epistemic reflexivity *5*, 8, 195
epistemic trap 166
epistemological obstacles *5*, 178,
187
epistemological vigilance 1, 9,
132
epistemology, historical *5*, 8n8,
151
epistemology, social 122–32
error x, 1, 141
Eta people 181
ethnicity 8, 37n9, 73, 104–5,
119, 144, *163*, 179,

180–1, 183, 184–5
see also caste; group-making;
race
ethnography 1, 8, 39, 54, 57,
77, 173
Eurocentrism 181
Europe 30, 73
European Commission 62
European influences 17, 19
eviction rates 169
exclusion 62, 122, 145
racial 76, 125, *163*
exploitation 153n21, 157, *165*,
174
extra-scientific agencies 130

fabrication, collective/symbolic
3, 35n4, 53, 114, 144
fallacy, logical 64, 131
families, black 37–8
families, dysfunctional white 193
families, single-parent 10, 37–8,
47, 87, 88
families, white middle-class 38
fear 15–26, 29, 120
and middle-classes 112–13,
120
and race 26, 112–13, 136,
140, 182
see also emotions
feminism 131, *164*
fields
bureaucratic field *5*, 145, 157
circulation across fields 35, 59,
63, 131
field of cultural production 1,
3, *5*, 59, 113, 114–16,
131
field of power *5*, 103
field triad of social science,
journalism, and policy-
politics-philanthropy 1, 6,
35, 59, 78, 106, 114, **115**,
116, 140, 143
intersection of fields 114, **115**,
116n21

Index

fields (*cont.*)
  journalistic field 5, 47, 64, 114, **115**, 129
  political field 80, 110
  scientific field 5, 9, 59, 130, 145
financial support 40–2, 48, 49–52, 59, 60, 109, *115*
Florida, Richard 176–7
Focus journal 60
folk concepts 121, 132, 145, 151–2, 174
folk devil (Cohen) 1, 106–21, 131, 136
Ford Foundation 41–2, 43, 50, 52, 60, *114*, 130
Fordism 2, 125, 127, *164*, *165*
Fortune Magazine 79

Galbraith, John Kenneth 67
gangs 80, 134, 146, 193
Gans, Herbert J. 41, 61–2, 107, *115*
Garden Cities 22
gender
  femininity 123, 133–4, 135
    and single parenthood 133, 134, 138
    and teenage pregnancy 10, 47, 54, 133, 134
    and welfare dependency 43, 64, 133, 134, 135
  masculinity 34n2, 123, 133–4
    and criminal justice 148, 187
    and criminality 80, 135, 138, 170
  see also criminal justice; criminality; families, single-parent; parenthood, single; pregnancy, teenage; welfare dependency
genealogy 3, 5, 33–52, *162*
General Accounting Office, US 84
gentrification 149, 177

Gerring, John 177–8
ghetto 12, 36, 140, 171
  and anti-urbanism 21, 23, 25
  communal 2, 11, *165*
  crash/implosion 25, 81, 104, 105, 123, 140, *165*, 171
  culture 99–100
  and economy 96–7, 98, 99–101
  "ghetto poor" 107, 108, 161
  and local institutions 98, 99
  and race 21, 96–7
    black people 80–1, 98, 150
  see also hyperghetto; neighborhoods
Giddens, Anthony 72–3, 95, 144
Gilded Age 18
Glasgow, Douglas 75–6, 78
Global South *165*
Go, Julian 174
Goetz, Bernhard "Bernie" *137–9*
Goffman, Erving 77
Goldmark, Peter 49–50
Google Scholar 101
Great Black Migration 22–3
greenbelt towns 22
Grossman, James 11
groupism *166*
groupness 166
groups 120–1, 124, 129, 144, 146, 161, 189
  see also classification struggles; fabrication
groups, scarecrow *90–3*
guns *138*

habitus 8, 153, *163*, 188
Hacker, Andrew 44
Harlem blackout riots 7
Harrington, Michael 71, 72
Hempel, Carl 153
Henderson, Vivian 95
Heritage Foundation 48
heteronomy 7, 130, 144
heuristics 152, 153–4, 187
Hinin people 181

Index

Hirsch, Arnold 11–12
Hirschman, Albert *166*
Hispanics 64, 69, 104
historical epistemology
(Bachelard, Canguilhem)
5, 8n8, 151
historicization 15–26, 125, 132,
166, 180–1, 185
history, conceptual
(*Begriffsgeschichte*) 1,
3–6, 35, 47, 140
homelessness *45*, *90*, 112, 147
Hong Kong 192
honor 184
dishonor 81, 134–5, 145,
182
see also disgrace, group; stigma
Horton, William *136*, *137*
housing 12, 22, 38, 74, 101,
103, 138, 150, 169
and class 125, 149
and race 149–50, *163*
Housing Act 22
housing policy 101, 103, 104
housing, public 104, 149
housing, rented 149, 169
Howard, Ebenezer 22
Hurston, Zora Neale 179
hybridity (Bhabha) 172
hygiene, social 20
hyperghetto 14, 59, 120, *164*
and antisocial behavior 78, 83
and class 125, 171
and criminality 80, 104,
169–79
and marginality 99, 124–5,
150, 171
and poverty 89, 98, 99, 119,
150
and race 33, 57, 80, 98,
99–100, 104–5, 119, 150,
171
and state responsibility/policy
134, 148, 164
see also communal ghetto,
ghetto; neighborhoods

idleness 120
illegitimacy 21, 36, 37, 43, 56n8,
146, 168
Illinois Department of
Corrections 170
incarceration 34, 43, 77–8, 104,
111, 134, 157, 170, 187
see also penal state; prisonfare
income 43, 46, 72, 78, 85, 86,
89, 92, 95, 102, 116, 118,
124, 147, *158*, 168
indicators 4, 55, 117–18
individual behavior 88, 93, 97
individual responsibility 48, 50,
57, 148
industrialization 10–11, 118,
126
inequality, class 67–76, 87–90
and antisocial behavior 79, 87,
88–9
and capitalism 94, 104, 176–7
and criminality 70, 76, 102
and dispossession 40, 76, *158*
and economy 72–5, 79
and educational opportunities
68–9, 76, 87, 102, 125
and employment opportunities/
unemployment 67–71, 74,
75, 76, 87–8, *163*
and migrants 73–4, 87
and poverty 87, 102, 123
and race 69, 73–4, 76, 101–2,
104–5, 130, 149
rising and falling rates of 47,
49, *158*
and single-parent families 87,
88, 102
and social class 76, 79, 89–90,
149, 177
and state responsibility/policy
75, 77–8, 88–90, 130, 136
United Kingdom 72–3, 74–5
and welfare dependency 76,
88, 102
and Wilson 101–2, 104–5,
144

236 Index

inequality, economic 98, 147, 157–9
inequality, racial 95–6, 123, 183–4, 187
inequality, urban 25, 144, 158–60
inequality, wealth 158
insecurity/instability, social 7n7, 89, 146–7, 162–4, 168–9
Institute for Research on Poverty (IRP) 48, 60, 84, 115
institutions, local 98, 99, 127, 155, 157
International Journal of Urban and Regional Research 60
intersectionality 177, 182
Irwin, John 76–7
isolation, social 2, 56, 69, 91, 92, 99–100, 126–7, 155, 161

Jackson, Walter A. 71
Japan 181
Jargowsky, Paul A. and Bane, Mary-Jo 127–8
Jefferson, Thomas 15
Jencks, Christopher 61, 84–5, 92, 157, 172
job networks 100
Joint Center for Political and Economic Studies 52, 84
Joint Economic Committee of the 101st Congress 53–9
Jones, Gareth Stedman 10–11
Jones, Jacqueline 61, 115
journalism 35, 44–7, 60–1, 111–12
    and antisocial behavior 78–9, 84–5
    and concept of "underclass" 175, 189–92
    and images of the "underclass" 136–9, 145–6
    and race 96, 114, 136
    and sensationalism 79, 107, 114, 126, 145–6

United Kingdom 191, 192
use of "underclass" as a term 106, 107, 108
see also fields, journalistic field

Kasarda, John 117
Katz, Michael B. 61, 115, 158
Kennedy, Edward 44
Kerner Report 24
Keynesianism 71, 147, 164
keyword 4, 10, 38, 47, 78, 131, 140
King, Rodney 26
knowledge 1, 5, 110
    knowledge production 9, 130
    poverty knowledge 48, 80, 130
Koselleck, Reinhart 1, 3–4, 6, 35, 47, 140, 147

labor, casualization, destabilization and degradation of 130, 163, 164–5, 168–9
    see also precariat
labor, unskilled manual 97–8, 164
Lawson, Bill E. 61
Lemann, Nicolas 114
lemming effect 8, 64–5, 172–3, 174
Levy, Frank 72
Levy, Peter 23
Lewis, Oscar 35, 39–40, 71
liberalism 39, 41, 48–9, 82, 96–7, 136
Local Initiatives Support Corporation 50
logic of the trial 183
logics 152, 153
    see also concept formation; fallacy
London riots 192
Los Angeles riots 26, 110
Loury, Glenn 93
love, tough 88

Index

Lumpenproletariat 11, 44n32, 118, *164*
lumping 34, 152, 153
lumpy notions 9, *165*, 185, 186, 187

Maclean, John 67
mainstream 18, 50, 76, 78, 87, 91, 92, 97, 99, 112–13, 146, 157–8
Manhattan Institute 48, 112
Manpower Development Research Corporation (MDRC) 41, *114*
marginality 122–32, 144, 145–6, 147
  advanced 93, 113, 132, *165*, *166*
  and hyperghettos 99, 124–5, 150, 171
  hypermarginality 134, 153, 165, 170, 171
  and morality 123, 126
  and race 37, 38
  and state responsibility/policy 133, 136
market capacity 7n7, 73, 75, 80
Marks, Carole 31
marriageability 98
Marx/Marxism 31, 67, 80, 94, 178
Massey, Douglas 64, 102, 189
  and Denton 61, 101, *115*, 149
matriarchy 37–8, 47
Mead, Lawrence 55–6, 84–5, 128–9, 148
meaning 131, 143, 144, 145
measurement *see* empiricism; operationalization; positivism
men, black 14, 24, 37, 38, 57
  and unemployment 43, 64, 163
Merton, Robert K. 2, 150n18
middle-class
  attitudes to "underclass" 11,
  18, 89–90, 122–3, 145–6, 193
  and fear 112–13, 120
  leaving cities 19, 22, 23, 125
  black middle-class people 25, 42, 97, 125
  image of 86, 92
  and race 23, 112–13
  segregation from poor people 126, 161
  white middle-class people 23, 38, 146–7
migrants 77–8, 97, 193
  and anti-urbanism 16, 22–3
  and class inequality 73–4, 87
  and employment opportunities 87, 169
  and housing 169
Mill, John Stuart 27
Mincy, Ronald 54–5, 82, *115*
Mincy, Ronald, Sawhill, Isabel, and Wolf, A. 85–6
mobility, social and economic 69, 76, 103, 146–7
Montaigne, Michel de 27
moral concept *114*
moral judgment 153, 183–4
moralism 19, 49, 85, 123n2
morality 34, 85
  and antisocial behavior 80–1, 85–7, 93
  and anti-urbanism 18, 19–20
  and marginality 123, 126
Moynihan, Daniel Patrick 35, 36–8
Muhammad, Khalil 116
Mumford, Lewis 21–2
Murray, Charles 92, 97, 112–13, 123, *129*
Myrdal, Gunnar 35, 42, 94, 141
  structural concept 3, 54–5, 67–71, 75, 93, *114*, 147
mystery of "underclass" 21, 50, 58, 59
myth 33–52, 76, 147

238 Index

naming 53, 143–50, 151, *166*
National Association for the
    Advancement of Colored
    People 44–6
National Research Council 85
National Welfare Rights
    Organization 135
Native Americans 104–5, 127
naturalization 63, 176, 186
neighborhood effects 111,
    149n13, 154
neighborhood hierarchy 103
neighborhood renewal 50
neighborhoods 110
    and behavior 83, 85–7, *91*,
        100–1, 120, 126
    and concentration effects 99,
        101–2, 126
    and criminal justice system
        104, 169–70
    and economy 96–7, 98,
        99–101, 112
    and neo-ecology 66, 93–105,
        148–9
    and race 104–5, 169
    and state responsibility/policy
        101–4, 148–50
    stigmatization of 120, 134,
        163, 193
    and Wilson 93–105, 149n13
    see also ghetto; hyperghetto;
        social isolation;
        underclass, neighborhood
neo-conservatism 3, 88, 97, 109
neo-ecology 93–105
    concept 118, 148–50
    and neighborhoods 66,
        93–105, 148–9
    and Wilson 3, 99–100, 115,
        118
neoliberalism 130, 134, *164–5*,
    170, 175–6
    see also Centaur state
neo-Weberian class theory 72–3,
    75, 95, 143–4
New Deal 22

"new poor" 31, 108
New Republic magazine 111
New York City blackout riots
    42–3, 133
New York Times 108, 138, 192
Newman, Katherine 146–7
Newsweek 79
Ngram Viewer 190
nonwork 55, 56
North Lawndale, Chicago 170

O'Connor, Alice 12, 48, 49
offenders, young 134
officialization 53, 59, 120,
    131n19, 150
ontology 151, *166*
operationalization 54, 83, 85–6
Oxford English Dictionary 67

Panel Study of Income Dynamic,
    University of Michigan
    72, 116
parasites, social 47
parenthood, single
    and antisocial behavior 81–2,
        90
    and criminality 138, 170
    and economic change 97,
        98–9
    and gender 133, 134, 138
    and segregation 102, 125
    and "underclass" image 92,
        123, 193
    and welfare dependency 43,
        47, 64, 123
parochialism 144, 156, 181
paternalism 56, 148, *165*, 170
pathology, tangle of 35, 36–9,
    40, 47, 96
patriarchy 34n2, 37, 38
Patterson, James 112
Patterson, Orlando 133
Paugam, Serge *162*
pauperism 17, 49, 118, 135
penal policy 80, 104, 134, 165,
    169–70

Index 239

prisonfare 79, 119, 134, 136, 148, *163*
penal state/prison 11, *90*
  and race 77–8, 134, 136, *163–4*, 169–70
Perrin, Évelyne *162*
Personal Responsibility And Work Opportunity Act 148
Peterson, Paul *32*, 51
petitio principii 131
philanthropic foundations 80
  influences on knowledge *114*, 130
  and research funding 40–2, 48, 49–52, 59, 60, 109, *115*
  training programs 41, 43, 45–7
  see also Ford Foundation, Rockefeller Foundation
philosophers, black 61
place, politics of 103, 154
place, stigma of 12, 30, 120, *163, 165*
place/location *see* neighborhoods
police 39, 57, 74, 76, 129, 170, 171
policy institutes 13, 48, 49, 72, 80, 82, 119
  see also think tanks
policy, public 53–65, 70
  see also economy; housing policy; penal state/prison; prisonfare; social policy; state responsibility/policy; welfare state; workfare
political representation 69
poor relief 11
population statistics 72, 83, 105
positivism 8n8, 54, 117
postindustrialism 3, 35, 69, 93, 125, 147, *162, 165*
poverty 11, 116–21
  and antisocial behavior 46, 85, 87, 88–9, *90, 91*, 123

as a cause of the development of the "underclass" 85, 86–7
  and children 69, 72, 85, 105
  and class 88, 140, 150
  and class inequality 87, 98, 102, 123, 147, *157–9*
  concepts of 103, 155–6
  and criminal justice 50, 169–70
  deserving and undeserving poor 33, 49, 58, 123, 126
  destitution 39, 68, 140
  and hyperghettos 89, 98, 99, 119, 150
  and images of "underclass" 92
  and local institutions 127, 155, 157
  and race 64, 87, 98, 119, 120–1, 123, 149–50
  and racialization 38, 123, 140
  and scholarship 116–18, *157–9*
  and state responsibility/policy 88–9, 103
poverty, concentration of 10, 118, 126
poverty, culture of 35, 39–40, 47, 71, 99–100
  Lewis 39–40, 71
  see also ghetto culture; subculture, "underclass" as
poverty data revolution 116–17
poverty knowledge 48, 80, 130
poverty line 72, 105, 116, 154
poverty, rates of 72, 118
poverty research industry 12, 48, 116, 119–20
poverty, rural 55, 127–8
"Poverty, the Underclass, and Public Policy" Research and Training Program 52

240 Index

power 5–6, 23, 156–7, *158*, 171
  symbolic power 1, 5, 63, 120, 129, 144
  see also field of power
Precari nati collective *162*
precariat/precarity 7, *162–6*
  black 2, 7, 38, 99, 101, 112–13, 130, 148, *163*
  and capitalism 127, *164–5*, 168–9
  and class *165–6*, 171
    and middle-classes 99, 112–13, 146–7, *163*
    and working class *164*, *166*, *167n10*, 168–9
  and employment opportunities/unemployment 38, *162*, *163*, *164*, 168–9
  global *165*
  and race 112–13, 130, 148, *163*
preconstructed object 130
pregnancy, teenage 10, 47, 54, 133, 134
prejudice, sociopolitical 130
presentism 133
prison riots 135
prisonfare 79, 119, 134, 136, 148, *163*
problematic 5, 8, 9, 13, 48, 59, 62, 111, 117, 129–30, 168, 175
Progressive Era 19–22
proletariat 17, *162*, *165–6*
  deproletarianization 125, 130, *164*
  subproletariat 31, 104, 161
  see also precariat
promiscuity, epistemic 9
prostitution *90*, 113
proto-concepts 2, 47
Public Advocacy Inc. 84
Public Enemy rap group 26
public goods 21, 89, 103, 130, 177

punishment 79, 104, 136, 148, 170
  see also incarceration; penal policy; penal state/prison
purification 113
Puritanism 19, 69

Quality Housing and Work Responsibility Act 149
quantification 55, 118, 126

rabble 77, 118
race 8–9, 34, 70, *95*, 179–88
  and antisocial behavior 58–9, 79, 87, 107, 128–9, 148
  and anti-urbanism 16, 21, 22–6
  black people 58–9, 79, 182–3
    and criminality 23–4, 90, 135, 170
  and caste 153, 181, 184
  as civic felony 182
  and class 40, 74, 94, 96, 104, 140, 149–50
    and middle-class 23, 112–13
  and class inequality 69, 73–4, 76, *95–6*, 97, 101–2, 104–5, 130, 149
  and colonial domain 182
  and concepts 153, 187–8
  and constructivism/essentialism 181
  and criminal justice 77, 187
  and criminality 76, 135, *138*
    and black people 23–4, 90, 135, 170
  as denegated ethnicity 8, 184, 186
  and discipline 119, 163
  and discrimination 97, 101, 183
  and dishonor 134–5, 182
  and dispossession 10, 76, 153
  and East/West 181
  and economy 73–4, 94, *95–7*
  and emotion 152, 153, 183–4

Index

and employment opportunities/
unemployment 43, 64,
76, 77–8, 105, *163*
and ethnicity 104–5, 119, *163*,
180–1, 183, 184–5
and fear 26, 112–13, 136,
140, 182
and ghettos 21, 96–7
and hyperghettos 33, 57,
80, 98, 99–100, 104–5,
119, 150, 171
and housing 149–50, *163*
and journalism 96, *114*, 136
and marginality 37, 38
and naturalization 186
and neighborhoods 104–5,
169
and penal state/prison 77–8,
134, 136, *163–4*, 169–70
and poverty 64, 87, 119,
120–1, 149–50
and racialization 38, 123,
140
and precariat/precarity
112–13, 130, 148, *163*
and racial exclusion 76, 125,
163
and racism duet 181
as realized category 188
as sin of the West 180
as a social problem 55, 58,
102n83
and state responsibility/policy
130, 136
and stigmatization 34, 39
and stratification 181, 184,
188
as symbolic violence 8, 185
and violence 23–4, 185
and welfare dependency 43,
64, 76, 97, 135, *137*
and workfare 119, 136, *163*
race-centrism 188
racial capitalism 174
racial domination 9, 94, 101,
183, 184–8

elementary forms of 9, 185–6
racial exclusion 76, 125, *163*
racial reaction 79
racial stereotyping 64, 107,
136–7
racialization 44, 49, 113, 114,
123, 133, 135, *137*, 185
and folk devils 106–21, 131
and poverty 38, 123, 140
and Wilson 94, 96
racism 9, 98, 175, 181, 186–7
Radical America journal 61
Rainwater, Lee 71, 72
reaction 79–80
Reader's Digest 79
Reagan, Ronald/Reagan
administration 48, 79,
136, *137*
"Red Summer" riots 21
Reed, Adolph 61
reflexive sociology 3–6
reflexivity, egological 4, 5
reflexivity, epistemic 5, 8, 195
reflexivity, reformist 132
reflexivity, textual 4–5
reform, urban 16, 18–22
relational concept 6, 40, 70n9,
88, 93
rental sector 149, 169
research 59–60, 82–3, 126–7,
136, 175, 189–91
and philanthropic foundations
and think tanks 49, 54–5,
114–15, 130
research funding 13, 40–2, 48,
49–52, 59, 60, 109–10,
115
see also Ford Foundation,
Rockefeller Foundation,
Russell Sage Foundation,
Social Science Research
Council
Research Committee on the
Urban Underclass (SSRC)
61, 109, 110
reservation 105, 127

Index

Resettlement Administration 22
residuum 17, 118, 193n3
resilience, urban 175–7
Rex, John 73–4, 144
rhetoric 5, 40, 122, 175, 187
Ricketts, Erol 82, 83–4, 90, *115*
rights, social and economic 74,
102–3
Riis, Jacob 18
riots 7, 21, 23–6, 135, 171
Los Angeles 26, 110
New York City 42–3, 133
United Kingdom 74, 76, 192
see also fear; reaction; trauma
Rockefeller Foundation 49–51,
84, 86, 176
and SSRC *115*, 117
funding by 13, 52, 60,
109–10
Rodney King riots, Los Angeles
110
role models 18, 50, 57, 100
"Roma pride" march 145n6
Roosevelt, Franklin D. 22
rural living 22, 55, 127–8
Russell Sage Foundation 64, 81,
130
Ryan, William 40

Sampson, Robert J. 161
Sánchez-Jankowski, Martín 155
Sartori, Giovanni 173
Sawhill, Isabel 82, 83–9, 90, *115*
scarecrow "groups" *90–3*
Schmitt, Carl 4, 172–3
scholarship, American 60–2,
63–5, 75, 76–8, 101
scholarship, black 131
scholarship, British 72–3
scholarship, European 62–3
Science journal 85–6
segregation 26, 61, 101–2, 124,
125, 126, 149–50, 161,
171, 183n8
see also ghetto
self-efficacy 100

self-perpetuation 36, 39, 69, 79,
102
self-respect 69
semantics 4, 66, 78, 119, 120,
131, 173–5
and concept of "underclass"
13, 47, 119, 124, 152–3,
193–4
sensationalism 79, 107, 114,
126, 145–6
services, public 150
settlement house movement 18,
20
sexual deviancy 19, 34, 80, 113
sexuality 80, 188n17
siege, sense of 113
see also fear; trauma
skills 91, 103, 124
Slater, Tom 175–6
slum 18, 21, 22, 69, 103, 126,
193
social control 3n6, 16, 20, 76,
148, 171
social movements 175, 186
social policy 48, 78, 79–80, 148,
165
changes in 87, 89–90, 110–12
link to penal policy 25, 80,
164, 165, 170
see also welfare; workfare
social problem 49, 148n12
"underclass" as 53, 55, 59
wealth as 102n93, *158*
social relationships 34, 57, 58,
153, 155, 185
Social Science Citation Index
190–1
Social Science Research Council
(SSRC) 51–2, 61, 109–10,
115, 117
and Rockefeller Foundation
115, 117
funding of 13, 52, 60,
109–10
social space 8, 89, 103, 144,
153, 166

Index

soul 120–1
Spear, Allan 11
Standing, Guy *162*, *165*
state responsibility/policy *115*
  and antisocial behavior 80,
    88–9, *115*, 148
  and concepts 103, 148–50,
    188
  and criminality 78–80, *137*
  drop in crime 110, 112
  and social policy reform
    110–11, 112
  and housing policy 101, 103,
    104
  and hyperghettos 134, 148,
    164, 171
  and inequality 75, 77–8,
    88–90, 102–3, 130, 136,
    160n7
  and marginality 133, 136
  and neighborhoods 101–4,
    148–50
  and poverty 88–9, 103
  and race 130, 136
  social and economic rights 74,
    102–3
  see also policy, public
states of exception (Schmitt)
  172–3
stereotyping 123
  racial 64, 107, *136–7*
  of "underclass" image 134,
    137, 138, 193
stigma 34, 39, 91, *91*
stigmatization, territorial 120,
  134, 163, 193
stigmatization, triple 30, 120,
  165
stratification 8, 39, 93, 149–50,
  153, 181
  and race 181, 184, 188
structural concept 3, 54–5,
  67–71, 75, 93, *114*, 147
structural racism 9, 175, 186–7
structuralism 88, 156
structure, economic 66, 67–78

struggle 5, 103, 110, 143n1, 184
  and classification (Bourdieu)
    35, 129, 144–5, 188
subculture, "underclass" as 39,
  56, 79, 99
submerged tenth 118
subordination 32, 69, 94, 104,
  157
suburbanism 19, 22, 23
"subway vigilante" case *137–9*
surveys, social 126–7
Sviridoff, Mitchell 41, *114*
symbolic inversion 145
symbolic power 1, *5*, 63, 120,
  129, 185n13
symbolic violence 8, 185

"tangle of pathology" 33, 35,
  36–9, 40, 47, *96*
tautology 124, 177
taxation 22, 79, 103
Taylor, Linda ("welfare queen")
  136, *137*
technological advancements
  68–9, 94, *164*
terminology *see* concepts;
  meaning; semantics
think tanks 8, 35, 48, 63, 80, 82,
  84, 106, 114, *115*, 119,
  130, 145, 186
  and antisocial behavior 80, 84
  and behavior concept *96*, *114*,
    148
  and research 49, 54–5,
    114–15, 130
  see also policy institutes
threat 11, 17, 78, 120, 122–3,
  134
  and criminality 24, 80, 163
  and race 2, 23, 24, 33, 42, 70,
    80
thugs, male 123, 138
Time Magazine 30, 42, 43–4,
  60, *114*
timing of conceptual development
  47

244   Index

training programs 41, 43, 45–7
transport, public 104
trauma 23, 26, 123, 133
turnkey problematics 129–30,
  172, 175

"underclass"
  behavioral conception of 3,
    44, 46, 48, 49, 54–5, 57,
    62, 66–7, 75, 79–93, 107,
    115, 148
    see also Mead; Mincy;
    Ricketts; Sawhill
  Bermuda triangle of 3
  circulation of conceptions of
    7, 35, 63, 101, *115*
  concept of 47, 63, 93–105,
    106, 153–6, 161
  journalism *136–9*, 189–92
  definitions 2, 29–32, 33–5,
    81–3, 92, 109
  ecological conception of 3, 59,
    93–101, 161
    see also Massey and Denton;
    Wilson
  ethnic composition of 34, 70,
    94, 104–5, 128, *129*
  fear of 30, 81, 135
  and images of the
    "underclass"
    criminality 92, 134, *137*,
      138, 193
    employment opportunities/
      unemployment 47, 56,
      92, 193
    journalism *136–9*, 145–6
    single parenthood 92, 123,
      193
    stereotyping 134, *137*, 138,
      193
    welfare dependency 138,
      193
  importation of (in Western
    Europe) 42, 62–3
  mystery of "underclass" 21,
    58, 59

neighborhood 50, 54, 83, 85,
  92, 112
  as official social problem 53–9
  origins of 67–8
  policy implications of 147–50
  population statistics 72, 83,
    105
  structural conception of 3, 47,
    54, 67–78, 88, 94–5, 119,
    147
  as subculture 39, 56, 79, 99
  as terministic screen 2, 161
  as tool/object of analysis 2, 15,
    34
  use of "underclass" as a term
    67–8, 106–8, 118–21,
    161, 189–94
    "ghetto poor" as a new term
      107, 108, 161
    meaning 131, 143, 144,
      145
    naming 53, 143–50, 151
    semantics 13, 47, 119, 124,
      152–3, 193–4
    and turnkey problematics
      129–30, 172, 175
  see also behavior, antisocial;
    class; concepts;
    ghetto; hyperghetto;
    inequality, class;
    journalism; marginality;
    neighborhoods;
    philanthropic foundations;
    policy institute; precariat;
    race; state responsibility/
    policy; think tanks
Underclass Database 117
Underclass Project 82, *114–15*
underklass and *överklass* 68
underworld 11, 118, 146n7
undeserving poor 33, 49, 76,
  107, 109, 120, 123, 135,
  158
unemployment *see* employment
  opportunities/
  unemployment

Index

United Kingdom 72–3, 74–5, 191, 192, 193
University of Michigan 52, 72, 116
upper class/elites 16, 72, 122, 123, 130, 146, 176–7
Urban Geography journal 60
Urban Institute 48, 49, 52, 82–4, 107
urban planning 20, 22
urban reform 16, 18, 20
urban renewal 22, 103
urbanization 10–11, 22, 23, 118, 124–5, 126
"us" and "them" 112–13
US News and World Report 79

Vera Institute of Justice 41
victim blaming 40
victimization 134, *137–9*
vigilante 137–8
violence 10, 23–4, *45*, 134, 185
violence, symbolic 8, 185
Violent Crime Control and Law Enforcement Act 148

Wagner, Richard *32*
Wall Street Journal 61
Walter White paradox 183
War on Poverty 43, 47, 116
Washington Post 108, 192
Watts riots 76
wealth 102n83, *158–9*
Weber, Max/Weberianism 9, 80, *163*, 178, 179, 184
  neo-Weberian class theory 72–3, 75, 95, 143–4
welfare dependency 10, *45*, 48, *163–4*
  and antisocial behavior 81–2, 88, *90, 91*
  and class inequality 76, 88, 102
  and criminality 47, 138
  and economy 58, 97, 98
  and gender 43, 64, 133, 134, 135

and images of "underclass" 138, 193
and race 43, 64, 76, 97, 135, *137*
and single parenthood 43, 47, 64, 123
"welfare queen" *136–7*
Welfare Reform Bill 133
welfare state 74, 79, 110–12, 133, 134, 136, *137*, *164–5*
West, Cornell 121
West Indians 74
white people
  families 38, 193
  and race 26, 123, 133, *137–9*
  white middle-class 23, 38, 146–7
  white "underclass" 128–9, 135, 193
white trauma 26, 123, 133
Wilson, James Q. 65
Wilson, William Julius 131n19
  class inequality 101–2, 104–5, 144
  concepts *114*, 190
    behavior concept 100–1, 107, 144
    neo-ecology concept 3, 99–100, 115, 118
  empiricism 103, 161
  "ghetto poor" as a new term 107, 108, 161
  influence on author 10, 11–12, 14–15
  neighborhoods 93–105, 149n13
  racialization 94, 96
  use of "underclass" as a term 106–7, 161
  works
    Bridge over the Racial Divide 131n19
    Declining Significance of Race 10, 93, 95, 104, *114*, 144

246   Index

Wilson, William Julius (*cont.*)
    works (*cont.*)
      "Responses to *The Truly*
        Disadvantaged" 161
      Truly Disadvantaged 38–9,
        60, *68*, *91*, *93*, *96*, 101,
        104
      When Work Disappears
        108
Wimmer, Andreas 187n17
Wittgenstein, Ludwig 143
work ethic 14, 57, 69, 78
workfare 25, 43, 79, 119, 134,
    148, 150, *163*
    and race 119, 136, *163*

    see also welfare dependency;
      welfare state
working class 3, 10, 16, 19, 35,
    57, 69, 72n17, 73–4, 79,
    100n75, 123, 125, 147,
    162, 182, 193
    and precariat/precarity *164*,
      166, *167n10*, 168–9
Wright, Erik 153n21

young people 23–4, 36, 97,
    133–4
    teenage criminals 134, 138
    thugs 123, 138
    see also pregnancy, teenage